Lecture Notes of the Institute for Computer Sciences, Social Informatics and Telecommunications Engineering 267

More information about this series at http://www.springer.com/series/8197

Joao Carlos Ferreira · Ana Lúcia Martins ·
Vitor Monteiro (Eds.)

Intelligent Transport Systems, From Research and Development to the Market Uptake

Second EAI International Conference, INTSYS 2018
Guimarães, Portugal, November 21–23, 2018
Proceedings

 Springer

Editors
Joao Carlos Ferreira (iD)
ISCTE-IUL
Lisbon, Portugal

Ana Lúcia Martins (iD)
ISCTE-IUL
Lisbon, Portugal

Vitor Monteiro (iD)
University of Minho
Guimaraes, Portugal

ISSN 1867-8211   ISSN 1867-822X   (electronic)
Lecture Notes of the Institute for Computer Sciences, Social Informatics
and Telecommunications Engineering
ISBN 978-3-030-14756-3   ISBN 978-3-030-14757-0   (eBook)
https://doi.org/10.1007/978-3-030-14757-0

Library of Congress Control Number: 2019932914

This Springer imprint is published by the registered company Springer Nature Switzerland AG
The registered company address is: Gewerbestrasse 11, 6330 Cham, Switzerland

Preface

We are delighted to introduce the proceedings of the second edition of the International Conference on Intelligent Transport Systems (INTSYS 2018) organized by European Alliance for Innovation (EAI), which was held in Guimarães, Portugal. This conference brought together researchers, developers, and practitioners from around the world who are leveraging and developing intelligent transportation systems (ITS) to increase efficiency, safety, mobility, and tackle Europe's growing emission and congestion problems. The theme of INTSYS 2018 was "Intelligent Transport Systems (ITS) and Logistics," allowing participants to discuss relevant topics connecting these two subjects.

The technical program of INTSYS 2018 consisted of 11 full papers in oral presentation sessions at the main conference tracks selected from 16 submissions. All papers were subject to a peer-review blinded process with a minimum of three reviewers per paper and an average of 3.5 reviews per paper. It was a great pleasure to work with the excellent organizing team of the EAI, which was essential for the success of the INTSYS 2018 conference. In particular, we would like to express our gratitude to Kristina Lappyova and Marek Kaleta for all the support they provided in all areas. We would like also to express our gratitude to all the members of the Technical Program Committee, who helped in the peer-review process of the technical papers, which allowed us to have a high-quality technical program. We would like to thank the extensive list of external reviewers from several areas of expertise and from numerous countries around the world.

We strongly believe that the INTSYS conference provides a good forum for researchers, developers, and practitioners to discuss science and technology aspects that are relevant to ITS. We expect that the future INTSYS conference will be as successful and stimulating as indicated by the contributions presented in this volume.

February 2019

Joao Carlos Ferreira
Ana Lúcia Martins
Vitor Monteiro

Conference Organization

Steering Committee

Imrich Chlamtac   Bruno Kessler Professor, University of Trento, Italy

Organizing Committee

General Chair

Joao Carlos Ferreira   Instituto Universitário de Lisboa (ISCTE-IUL), Portugal

General Co-chair

Ana Lúcia Martins   Instituto Universitário de Lisboa (ISCTE-IUL), Portugal

TPC Chair and Co-chairs

Ana de Almeida   Instituto Universitário de Lisboa (ISCTE-IUL), Portugal
Paulo Novais   University of Minho, Portugal

Sponsorship and Exhibit Chair

Alexander Kocian   Pisa University, Italy

Local Chair

Vitor Monteiro   University of Minho, Portugal

Workshops Chair

Jose Aguilar Madeira   IST, Portugal

Publicity and Social Media Chair

Sara Eloy   Instituto Universitário de Lisboa (ISCTE-IUL), Portugal

Publications Chair

Sophia Kalakou   Instituto Universitário de Lisboa (ISCTE-IUL), Portugal

Web Chair

Frederica Gonçalves   Madeira University, Portugal

Posters and PhD Track Chair

Ana Madureira   ISEP, Portugal

Panels Chair

Alberto Silva   IST, Portugal

Demos Chair

Stefano Chessa   Pisa University, Italy

Tutorials Chair

Porfirio Filipe   ISEL, Portugal

Conference Managers

Kristina Lappyova   EAI, Slovakia
Marek Kaleta   EAI, Slovakia

Technical Program Committee

Alberto Fernandez   European GNSS Agency
  Wyttenbach
Alberto Silva   IST, Portugal
Ana de Almeida   Instituto Universitário de Lisboa (ISCTE-IUL), Portugal
Ana Martins   Instituto Universitário de Lisboa (ISCTE-IUL), Portugal
Dagmar Caganova   Slovak University of Technology in Bratislava, Slovakia
Ghadir Pourhashem   Slovak University of Technology in Bratislava, Slovakia
Giuseppe Lugano   University of Žilina, Slovakia
Joao C. Ferreira   Instituto Universitário de Lisboa (ISCTE-IUL), Portugal
Lorna Uden   Staffordshire University, UK
Lubos Buzna   University of Zilina, Slovakia
Marek Kvet   University of Žilina, Slovakia
Michal Kohani   University of Žilina, Slovakia
Michal Kvet   University of Žilina, Slovakia
Miroslav Svitek   Czech Technical University in Prague, Czech Republic
Peter Brida   University of Žilina, Slovakia
Peter Holečko   University of Žilina, Slovakia
Peter Jankovic   University of Zilina, Slovakia
Peter Pocta   University of Žilina, Slovakia
Porfirio Filipe   ISEL, Portugal
Sara Eloy   Instituto Universitário de Lisboa (ISCTE-IUL), Portugal
Sophia Kalakou   Instituto Universitário de Lisboa (ISCTE-IUL), Portugal
Tatiana Kováčiková   University of Žilina, Slovakia
Veronika Sramova   University of Žilina, Slovakia
Vitor Monteiro   University of Minho, Portugal

Contents

Parking and Collaborative Approaches

A Blockchain and Gamification Approach for Smart Parking   3
    João Carlos Ferreira, Ana Lúcia Martins, Frederica Gonçalves,
    and Rui Maia

A Low-Cost Smart Parking Solution for Smart Cities Based on Open
Software and Hardware   15
    Carlos Serrão and Nuno Garrido

Collaborative Gamified Approach for Transportation   26
    Ana Lúcia Martins, João Carlos Ferreira, and Rui Maia

Case Studies and Simulation

Improving Fleet Solution – A Case Study   41
    Ana Lúcia Martins, Ana Catarina Nunes, Rita Pereira,
    and João Carlos Ferreira

Challenges in Object Detection Under Rainy Weather Conditions   53
    Sinan Hasirlioglu and Andreas Riener

Simulation and Testing of a Platooning Cooperative
Longitudinal Controller   66
    Vadym Hapanchak, António Costa, Joaquim Macedo, Alexandre Santos,
    Bruno Dias, M. João Nicolau, Bruno Ribeiro, Fábio Gonçalves,
    Oscar Gama, and Paulo Araújo

ROM-P: Route Optimization Management of Producer Mobility
in Information-Centric Networking   81
    Low Xian Wee, Zhiwei Yan, Yong Jin Park, Yu-Beng Leau, Kashif Nisar,
    and Ag Asri Ag Ibrahim

Mobility and Planning

Smart Mobility: A Mobile Approach   95
    Ricardo Faria, Lina Brito, Karolina Baras, and José Silva

Prediction of Journey Destination for Travelers of Urban Public Transport:
A Comparison Model Study 113
    Vera Costa, Tânia Fontes, José Luís Borges, and Teresa Galvão Dias

X   Contents

With Whom Transport Operators Should Partner? An Urban Mobility
and Services Geolocation Data Analysis. 133
   Marta Campos Ferreira, Teresa Galvão Dias, and João Falcão e Cunha

Intermodal Routing Model for Sustainable Transport Through
Multi-objective Optimization 144
   Cecília Vale and Isabel M. Ribeiro

Future 5V

A Low Latency SCAN-Flip Polar Decoder for 5G Vehicular
Communication. 157
   Yu Wang, Lirui Chen, Shikai Qiu, Li Huang, and Zuocheng Xing

Author Index 171

Parking and Collaborative Approaches

A Blockchain and Gamification Approach for Smart Parking

João Carlos Ferreira[1,3,5(✉)], Ana Lúcia Martins[1,2],
Frederica Gonçalves[4], and Rui Maia[5]

[1] Instituto Universitário de Lisboa (ISCTE-IUL), Lisbon, Portugal
jcafa@iscte-iul.pt
[2] Business Research Centre (BRU-IUL), Lisbon, Portugal
[3] Information Sciences, Technologies and Architecture Research Center
(ISTAR-IUL), Lisbon, Portugal
[4] Madeira-ITI, University of Madeira, Funchal, Portugal
[5] Inov Inesc Inovação - Instituto de Novas Tecnologias and Instituto Superior
Tecnico, Lisbon, Portugal

Abstract. City parking is increasingly complex and available parking spaces
are scarce. Being able to identify a space to park their cars can lead many drivers
to drive around the intended parking area several times, increasing traffic density
and pollution. In this research we propose a collaborative blockchain solution
with gamification for parking. Users collaborate to report free spaces and receive
free parking minutes for their service to the community. In parallel, this
approach can be used to collect beacon information from the parked vehicles
and create a low-cost collaborative approach for managing a parking control
process platform Blockchain that can handle this distributed process and the
gamification platform increases users' participation.

Keywords: Blockchain · Collaborative · Gamification · Parking

1 Introduction

Parking is one of the major concerns in the cities due to the reduced availability of
space and the time-consuming process for finding a parking place. Several studies show
that in the majority of cities about one-third of traffic is generated by drivers on the
search for a parking space, which corresponds to average times of 10 min [1]. Drivers
cover, on average, a distance of 4.5 km to find a parking place [1], which corresponds
to an average of 1.3 kg of CO_2 per month, or about 100 km per month, and to an
additional estimated cost of about 10€ per month. In the Lisbon region (Portugal's
capital), for example, the average number of vehicles per day is of 250 to 300 thousand
[2]; if one considers that the demand for parking spaces affects part of this number of
vehicles, an estimate of 100 thousand vehicles could be removed from the roads. In this
scenario, it can also be estimated 1 M€ per month of additional expenses and additional
production of 130 tons of CO_2 that could be avoided. Considering only the example of
Lisbon, the annual distance traveled in search of parking place (4.5 km-day × 230
days annual work × 100 000 cars) would allow to take about 2800 rounds to the planet

J. C. Ferreira et al. (Eds.): INTSYS 2018, LNICST 267, pp. 3–14, 2019.
https://doi.org/10.1007/978-3-030-14757-0_1

and represents about 36 000 h of work lost. In the city, inner zones parking spots are difficult to find. It is often that trucks looking for cargo unloading spots find that those spots have been used by another driver (not involving logistics). This scenario stresses the need for solutions to identify if a parking spot is free and, consequently, guide the driver to those places. One such conventional system in closed environments (an example of parking spaces at malls) has sensors at each parking spot with a light that indicates if it is available or not. The same approach can be applied to street parking, and this data can be transferred to a driver's App, but the cost of this solution is prohibitive and involves high maintenance cost. For example, Avenida Liberdade, in Lisbon, has around 1.1 km and a solution with parking sensors was implemented with an investment value of 80 K€ with the associated annual maintenance cost of 10 K€. The proposal in this research aims at avoiding these costs (investment and maintenance) and is based on a collaborative approach to detect if parking spaces are occupied, along with a gamification incentive.

2   State of the Art

2.1   Sensors

Many parking systems have been proposed in recent years. These work based on installed sensors that collect information about each individual parking spot. These sensors detect the presence of a vehicle or other objects. They can range from a simple ultrasonic sensor that detects a vehicle based on a threshold distance or RFID chips that are activated based on distance to complex optical sensors. These sensors can be divided into two main categories: intrusive and non-intrusive sensors [3]. Intrusive sensors are sensors that are typically installed in holes on the road surface, including active infrared sensors, inductive loops, magnetometers, magneto-resistive sensors, pneumatic road tubes, piezoelectric cables, and weigh-in-motion sensors. The main problem of these sensors is the installation and maintenance cost. Non-intrusive sensors, by their nature, do not have the installation problem and encompasses microwave radar, passive acoustic array sensors, passive infrared sensor, RFID, ultrasonic, BLE beacons and video image processing. Non-intrusive sensors can be easily installed and maintained and do not affect the surface involved in the process.

Active infrared sensors detect vehicles based on infrared energy. These can detect the amount of energy reflected, and most of the installation effort is based on multiple beams that can measure the vehicle position, speed and class [3, 4]. The main working problem is its sensitivity to weather conditions (examples are fog or snow).

The Inductive Loop Detectors are used mainly for getting accurate occupancy measurements based on wire loops with frequencies ranging from 10 to 50 kHz. This frequency oscillation changes with vehicle presence, and it is one of the most used sensors to detect the presence of a vehicle in a spot. The main issues are the installation and maintenance costs and the fact that these sensors are sensitive to water, especially if the pavement is cracked.

Fluxgate magnetometers work by detecting a perturbation in a magnetic field and have as main advantage being insensitive to weather condition such as snow, rain, and fog. They are also more accurate and less susceptible to traffic stress than loop detectors. Among the disadvantages of using fluxgate magnetometers are the small detection zones in some models that require that multiple units are needed for full lane detection as well as the close proximity required for accurate detection [3, 5].

Magnetometer Induction or search coil magnetometer identifies the presence of a vehicle in a spot by measuring the change in the magnetic flux lines caused by the moving vehicle according to Faraday's Law of induction [3, 6]. Some models can be installed without the need for pavement changes and have the advantage of being insensitive to weather conditions.

The magnetoresistive sensor is in general light and small, allowing versatile installation, low cost and are able to work in all temperature registers in earth surface [7]. They work by simply being energized with constant current [6].

Piezoelectric sensors are created from a material that is able to convert kinetic energy into electrical energy when subjected to vibration or mechanical impact, so it can detect when the vehicle is on and can detect speed and vehicle distance axle. For parking situations, it has the disadvantage of the need to use multiple detectors to detect a vehicle presence in a parking spot.

There is also a diversity of others sensors like: Pneumatic road tube, Weight-in-Motion (WIM) sensors, Microwave radar, Passive infrared sensors, RFID and Ultrasonic sensors.

There is also the possibility of using CCTV systems with the drawback of some incident position of the working system. This approach works well in closed environments, but on streets there is the problem of the sunlight reflecting at the beginning and end of the day. They are based on advanced digital signal processing (DSP) that transforms video cameras into intelligent counting sensors. Its stand-alone design enables it to detect and count vehicles utilizing video received from an IP and/or analog video cameras. The software even stabilizes the video image by removing the camera and vibration effects. Advanced background algorithms then ignore any nuisance images, such as shadows or lighting changes uncertain limits. Once an object is detected, a filter is applied to avoid counting nonvehicle items, such as humans and luggage, or vehicles not moving in the desired direction.

Sensors implanted, in general, are expensive to deploy and maintain (e.g., [8] cost USD$500 per system for each parking space, and [9] cost USD$400 per system for each car). These sensors may underperform in extreme weather conditions. Using mobile phones is cheaper, more convenient, and more flexible.

There is a new type of sensor devices that opens several business opportunities in healthcare, sports, beacons, security, monitor and home entertainment industries, the Bluetooth Low Energy (BLE) sensors. A BLE sensor is a wireless personal area network technology that once compared to the Classic Bluetooth is intended to provide much-reduced power consumption and cost while maintaining a similar communication range. Bluetooth is a low-cost, short-range wireless technology with small footprint, small power consumption, reasonable throughput and hence suitable for various small, battery-driven devices like mobile phones, PDAs, cameras, laptops, etc. Also in this context, there are beacons with around 3-5 cm, a small hardware radio device that broadcasts data over Bluetooth Low Energy (BLE). BLE operates a spectrum band (2402-2480 MHz), divided in 40x2 MHz physical channels and uses GFSK variation, attaining a data rate up to 1 Mbps. Typical ranges of the radio signal are up to 20 or 100 m (60–300 ft.), and it is easy to fit it in many applications and contexts. Beacons offer the versatility of being placed anywhere - indoors or outdoors position. The challenge arises when beacons are deployed in environments that are disposed to weather conditions such as rain or humidity. Also, beacons can be managed centrally without the need of going physically to where they are located.

Additionally, it is very easy to interact BLEs with mobile devices sensors, like GPS, Accelerometer, and gyroscope creating a continuous monitoring process since users carry mobile devices all the time. This generates massive data (big data).

2.2 Parking Solutions

Most of the parking solutions implement the concept of reservation and the evaluation of available places based on the information in video cameras or sensors, to detect the occupation of the parking place. From the diversity of existing systems many are in the sense of allowing the reservation of place and the consequent elimination of search for a parking space in the private car park. For example, the Reservation of places with recourse to short message services (SMS) [10], or the New "Smart Parking" System Based on Resource Allocation and Reservations. [11], which implements the concept of seat reservation with the problem of another driver taking the reserved seat because he arrived first. This mechanism can in itself be a barrier to the dissemination of the system, since depending on the parking regulations and operational models of the management companies, the concept of reservations in street places is difficult to implement or simply impracticable. Hence there is the need for a concept that is not dependent on the concept of the reserve, but which optimizes the search for a vacant place. Other examples are: An Intelligent Parking Guidance and Information System by using the image processing technique. [12] and Intelligent Parking Management System Based on Image Processing. [13], which, based on video image processing, allow us to determine whether the place is vacant or not. Another example is the Automatic Parking Management System and Parking Fee Collection Based on Number Plate Recognition [14]. This solution is more management oriented and not so operational, therefore not giving the necessary support to the end user and, consequently, self-limiting the dissemination of the concept.

2.3 Collaborative Approach - Gamification

Mobile devices allow accurate tracking of world-related information and (physical) activities of citizens by taking advantage of people willing to collaborate toward a continuous data harvesting process called crowdsensing. According to [15]: "While crowdsourcing aims to leverage collective intelligence to solve complex problems by splitting them into smaller tasks executed by the crowd, crowdsensing splits the responsibility of harvesting information (typically urban monitoring) to the crowd". In other words, crowdsensing is the process where people or their mobile devices act as sensors and actuators to continuously harvest data and take actions upon the results [15]. It is a challenging task since several socio-technical issues may occur, such as the quantification of the sensing density. The users' participation and cooperation are essential in crowdsourcing [16], but users' participation consumes their resources such as battery and computing capacity [17]. This problem leads to an inevitable fact that many users might be reluctant to participate, which is a major obstacle to mobile crowdsourcing [13]. To avoid this, an incentive mechanism is needed to ensure users' participation.

Geo-referencing is available through GPS on mobile devices, and the mobile app only receives the beacon signal. Rinne et al. [18] presented the pros and cons of mobile crowdsensing. As observed, parking can be made smart, then it can be gamified. Some gaming thoughts and techniques can be added to make this parking process more exciting and safe. To gamify the parking process, the concept is introduced for providing points to drivers. The greater the number of points the more will be the chances of winning. This gamified version of parking can create a process of virtual learning to the drivers who have just started their driving duty.

3 Proposed Approach to Control Parking Process

The present proposal intends to work with the problem of the management of places in open spaces using probabilistic calculation on data history, and the collaboration of the users, which allows to determine in which places have a higher probability of being empty. The use of probabilities allows dealing with the uncertainty associated with this process through past data analysis (data history), which allows reducing uncertainty using Artificial Intelligence (AI) algorithms. This uncertainty will also be incorporated into the route optimization algorithms, allowing to indicate optimal paths to find the desired parking place function of the probability functions associated with the location. For example, it is possible that the optimal path is not related to the higher probability of a vacant place, but rather the route of maximizing the different probabilities. From the research done by the authors of this idea, it is innovative and has not yet been implemented in any solution of this type. Figure 1 shows the developed approach for mobile device application. It is possible to control parking spots based on the use of BLE beacons in vehicles. These beacons transmit an identification signal that can be captured by mobile devices, which can add a GPS position and be transmitted to a central system.

The current proposal is distinguished by the involvement of users, by analyzing the data history to determine the probability of empty space, by combining the concept of carpooling and by not implying the installation of any infrastructure, which increases complexity and makes any solution more expensive.

We implemented in a test environment a Steemit (www.steemit.com) that allows the account the distributed user inputs about free parking places and associated points (free parking minutes) in a gamified approach. Each street we define a number of inputs needed for system work proper, when a number of inputs are bellow we point increased and when are above points decrease. The platform allows this flexible configuration, and in a big implementation scenario (not available yet) we can explore the power of this approach.

To incentive users' participation, a reward mechanism based on free parking is introduced. First-time drivers should register and request for a beacon. Being part of this network allows them to have reduced parking fees. In order to monitor parking activity, our proposal is the installation of a beacon in each vehicle (it costs around 3€, with a battery lifetime span of 2 years). These requirements should be reinforced by law and maintenance should be the responsibility of the owner of the vehicle. This works like an electronic plate number that allows vehicle identification. To avoid the creation of infrastructure and networking, our approach is innovative as it uses citizens and their mobile devices. In this model, users get rewards for each different beacon picked and transmitted to the central parking application. This reward could be free parking time (for instance, 5 min parking for each transmission) and the reward could be increased if an infraction is identified. This process is performed centrally, where the beacon ID is used to check if the vehicle-parking place was previously paid for or not. This is performed by an App (in the case of Lisbon the e-parking App from EMEL (epark.emel.pt)). This ad hoc transmission checks the beacon ID and verifies if it is paid for. Infraction data can be immediately sent to the nearest parking agent who can then issue an infraction ticket, or the central system can send the invoice directly to the vehicle's owner. Figure 1 shows the overall working idea for the main system with beacon signals captured by mobile devices and position is added and transmitted to a central server. This information is used to check if the parking spot is reserved or not. To avoid errors, because users can receive beacons from a moving vehicle in front of the parking place, the system waits for a second notification from a different user before proceeding with the identification of a violation.

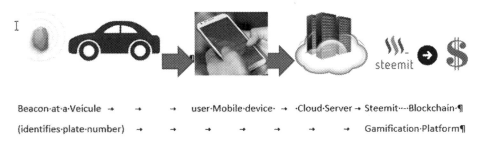

Beacon·at·a·Veícule →   →   →   user·Mobile·device· →   ·Cloud·Server → Steemit····Blockchain·¶

(identifies·plate·number) →   →   →   →   →   →   → Gamification·Platform¶

Fig. 1. Overview of proposed approach to creating a parking monitoring facility without investment costs using an ad hoc network of user mobile device collaborative process.

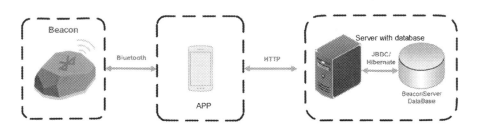

Fig. 2. Beacon signal transmission process using users mobile device collaborative approach

In terms of communication, Fig. 2 illustrates the process, with a local Bluetooth communication with a range of 20–30 m between vehicle beacon and mobile user device and a HTTP connection from the mobile device to the central server.

4 Identification of Free Parking Slots Based on User Input

We developed an interface to allow an easy report on the number of free parking places in a street or to alert that the booked parking place will be free within x minutes. This collaborative process only requires power from users' mobile devices and consumes network communication, but since we are transmitting data in usual communication packages, this communication process does not have any impact on prices. This collaborative reporting can be performed by: (1) drivers in a car using NLP (Natural Language Processing), where the application asks about the number of identified available places the driver saw. The application is calibrated to understand numbers in different languages (we tested in English and Portuguese); (2) Pedestrians, who give feedback about a number of places available on the street. Geo-referencing is available through GPS on mobile devices. Under these conditions, the user needs only to introduce an estimation of the number of free places he remembers on that street. Figure 3 shows the automatic voice recognition process implemented.

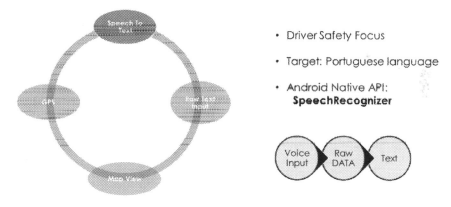

Fig. 3. Users inputs of free space using a voice to text recognize the system

These two crowdsensing approaches are complementary, and users are incentivized to participate by the reward mechanisms introduced. Every input performed that match average performed in a pre-defined window time (this is to avoid spam inputs without any sense) gives free parking minutes in a city.

For drivers, it is possible to integrate mobile devices into the vehicle's infotainment systems, it is possible to create an easy interface for drivers to give feedback about empty parking places while driving.

We tested several approaches regarding the reward. We tested using a population of 90 information providers (60 drivers and 30 pedestrians) in a three months test.

In a first scenario, every input gave 5 min of free parking in a green zone (low-cost parking area). During the test period, we had an average of 43 notifications per day (monthly notification divided by the working days). This rewards gave around 3.6 h of free parking in a green zone per day;

In a second scenario, every input gave 1 min of free parking in a green zone. During the test period, we had an average of 9 notifications per day. This reward gave around 9 min of free parking in a green zone. This meant we should increase the reward.

In the third and last scenario, every input gave 10 min of free parking in the green zone. During the test period, we had an average of 58 notifications per day. Perhaps this is too much.

As a model, the system depends on the numbers of users versus the number of notifications received. Lisbon has about half a million people living, a surface of 100 thousand km^2 and around 1500 streets [19].

To be able to work in peak times (9am to 6pm), the system needs notifications with a periodicity of 5 min; we need around 108 notifications per street. In the remaining hours of the day: (1) 6pm to 12am and 6am to 9am, we need notifications with a periodicity of about 10 min, which gives 90 notifications per street; and (2) the remaining time, from 12am to 6am, only hour to hour notifications are required. This gives the need for 200 notifications per day per street, which is about 300 thousand per day. Estimating a goal of 50 notifications per user per day, the system needs 6000 users. Figure 4 illustrates this process.

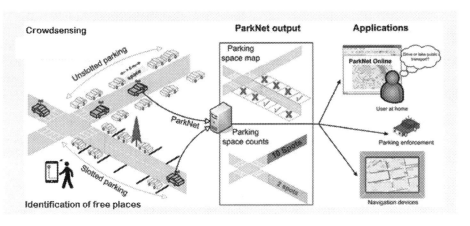

Fig. 4. Users notification about free parking places, based on a crowdsourcing mechanism approach

To avoid spam we need more notifications to extract the average, deviations are treated as spam, and those users can be removed from the system. To avoid the creation of different logins, users are validated based on the fiscal number.

5 Eco-Parking Development

We incorporate the most advanced techniques of data visualization, especially for what concerns the ease of discrimination of the target of interest vs. the rest of the picture.

The application is developed in the Java language and available for installation on devices with the Android operating system. The application can be obtained through the following link [20].

The Google Firebase platform was used to create a NoSQL Cloud Firestore data base with great flexibility, with the possibility of performing very complex database queries with minimal server performance. An authentication system has been created in the application that is interconnected with the Firestore database that establishes the connection between the user and the entries in the database that the user performs. The Maps API, was used to implement the map in the application, and with extensive API exploration, it was possible to modify and add features. The search was used as a reference to the Autocomplete Places of Google that presents suggestions related to search criteria entered by the user. An internal link has been implemented between the search module, map module, and database module so that they can communicate seamlessly with each other.

The application requires that location permissions be given, as it collects information from the user's current geo-location. When you start the application for the first time, you will be prompted to give these permissions. The application requires registration since it is necessary to identify the users who contribute the information. In addition, to better organize and structure the database, it was also decided to record the database data. If you already have an account, you can log in by clicking the "Log In" button at the bottom of the screen, see Fig. 5. All fields are required. If during the registration process the user does not fill in one of the fields, it will be duly identified with a red color. If you already have an account, this login screen will have to identify you with the email and password that you used during the registration process. During confirmation of the personal data between the server and the application, a progress bar will be displayed. If there is a failure in authentication, a notification balloon will be presented to the user. Otherwise, the application will proceed to the main screen of the application. The main application screen consists of the map and the menu bar that contains a search bar. Since it is an application that presents the user with the location of the searched place and presents information on the number of available parking places, it has been chosen to simplify as much as possible so that the user can get the desired result without having to click and navigate a lot in the application until you get the result. In the lower left corner is the button that centralizes the map at the user's current position. In the bottom right corner the zoom feature. The search bar is centered on the menu bar containing the button that expands the menu (left button) and the voice search button. Clicking the menu button displays the screens available in the application. To simplify the use of the App, the whole focus was given to the main screen ("Search for Parking"), (see Fig. 6(a)). If one wants to enter information about the number of vacant spots in a particular location, he can do so by selecting the "Insert Parking" menu option. The Developer Board is only used by the application developer to facilitate the tests he needs to perform. For identification purposes, the user data is displayed at the top of the menu (name and email that was used during the registration process). During the search process, entering characters into the search bar will give the user suggestions about what the user has entered. A limitation was applied in the survey in relation to Country (Portugal) and city (Lisbon), since the focus of the test was only the city of Lisbon. When choosing one of the search suggestions/results, the screen centers the selected location by placing a pin in that location. During the search process, entering characters into the search bar will give the user suggestions about what the user has entered.

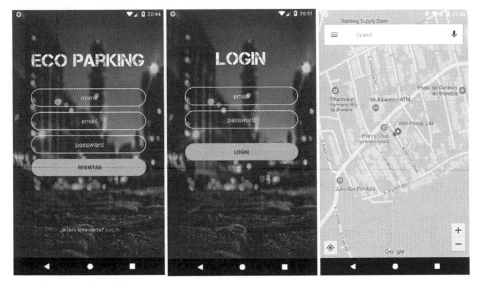

Fig. 5. Application main screen with login and the search screen (Color figure online)

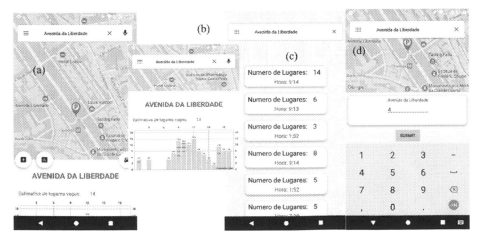

Fig. 6. App info: (a) statistics about a street, (b) detailed statistics through the time, (c) free parking space with a time window and (d) screen of a user input about free places in a street

If the user selects the "Statistics" button (see Fig. 6(b) and (c)), the list of existing information will be displayed with the number of vacancies identified with the time it was entered. If the option to register the number of vacant posts from the "+" button is chosen from the side menu, the following screen will be displayed identifying the location in question and the field of insertion of the vacancy number. By submitting information (see Fig. 6(d)), it will be sent to the server and can be instantly queried by performing a search.

6 Conclusion

We show a collaborative network of beacon data collection to implement a parking control approach without the existing of a dedicated solution and also a collaborative approach to marking empty park space. Users win free minutes parking places, authorities saves on control process and also users receive information about free parking places., save time and money on looking for then.. also CO_2 is decrease because less Km were performed by drivers in the parking process. We implemented one of the first approach using blockchain platforms to handle this collaborative transaction. Users can participate in this process and collect free parking minutes for their own usage. This proposal needs a complete electronic solution for parking payment and needs beacons that are not implemented in every vehicle, but the economic benefits are considerable because there is not the need of a dedicated infrastructure. The current payment solution can be adapted for the connection between vehicle plate number to a beacon reference. Identification of free parking places is essential information to handle the problem of guidance of drivers to free parking places. Again, a significant advantage of this system is that it can work without large investments on sensors or other related equipment.

Future Work - A large scale testing will be explored to explore the potential of gamification with a large number of involved users.

References

1. Dowling, C.F., Tanner, R., Lillian, Z.B.: How much urban traffic is searching for parking? (2017)
2. Estatísticas dos Transportes 2011, edição de 2012 do INE
3. Mimbela, L.Y., Klein, L.A.: A summary of vehicle detection and surveillance technologies used in intelligent transportation systems. Tech. report, New Mexico State University (2007). http://www.fhwa.dot.gov/ohim/tvtw/vdstits.pdf
4. Mouskos, K.C., Boile, M., Parker, N.: Technical solutions to overcrowded park and ride facilities. Final Report, FHWANJ-2007-01, University Transportation Research Center-Region 2. City College of New York (2007). http://www.nj.gov/transportation/refdata/research/reports/FHWA-NJ-2007-011.pdf
5. Cheung, S.Y., Coleri Ergen, S., Varaiya, P.: Traffic surveillance with wireless magnetic sensors. In: Proceedings of the 12th ITS World Congress, San Francisco, 6–10 November 2005, pp. 1–13 (2005)

6. Lenz, J.E., Edelstein, A.S.: A review of magnetic sensors. IEEE Sensors J. **6**, 631–649 (2006)
7. Wolff, J., Heuer, J., Haibin, T., Weinmann, G., Voit, M., Hartmann, S.: Parking monitor system based on magnetic field senso. In: Proceedings of the Intelligent Transportation System Conference, Toronto, Ontology, 17–20 September 2006, pp. 1275–1279 (2006)
8. San Francisco Park. http://sfpark.org/
9. Mathur, S., et al.: ParkNet: drive-by sensing of road-side parking statistics. In: ACM MobiSys (2010)
10. Noor, H.H.M.H., Badiozaman, M.H., Daud, H.: Smart parking reservation system using short message services (SMS). IEEE (2009)
11. Geng, Y., Cassandras, C.G.: New smart parking system based on resource allocation and reservations. IEEE Trans. Intell. Transp. Syst. **14**(3), 1129–1139 (2013)
12. Reddy, P.D., Rao, A.R., Ahmed, S.M.: An intelligent parking guidance and information system by using image processing technique. IJARCCE **2**(10), 4044–4048 (2013)
13. Rashid, M.M., Musa, A., Rahman, M.A., Farahana, N., Farhana, A.: Automatic parking management system and parking fee collection based on number plate recognition. Int. J. Mach. Learn. Comput. **2**(2), 94 (2012). Published 2014
14. Al-Kharusi, H., Al-Bahadly, I.: Intelligent parking management system based on image processing. World J. Eng. Technol. **2**, 55–67 (2014). 4799-8802-0/15 ©2015 IEEE
15. Khan, W.Z., Xiang, Y., Aalsalem, M.Y., Arshad, Q.: Mobile phone sensing systems: a survey. Commun. Surv. Tutor. **15**, 402–427 (2013)
16. Zhang, Y., van der Schaar, M.: Reputation-based incentive protocols in crowdsourcing applications. In: Proceedings of IEEE INFOCOM, pp. 2140–2148, March 2012
17. Delot, T., Cenerario, N., Ilarri, S., Lecomte, S.: A cooperative reservation protocol for parking spaces in vehicular ad hoc networks. In: Mobility Conference (2009)
18. Myers, K.A., Tapley, B.D.: Adaptive sequential estimation with unknown noise statistics. IEEE Trans. Autom. Control **21**(4), 520–523 (1976)
19. http://www.dgterritorio.pt/ficheiros/cadastro/caop/caop_download/caop_2014_0/areasfregmundistcaop2014_2. Accessed Sept. 2018
20. App Download link. https://iscteiul365-my.sharepoint.com/:u:/g/personal/ngvii_iscte-iul_pt/EQjjAxRiulROrXseEQMFoMBWx1puOqzHehGMzH8fX5zA?e=qGpkUL

A Low-Cost Smart Parking Solution for Smart Cities Based on Open Software and Hardware

Carlos Serrão[1]([✉]) and Nuno Garrido[2]

[1] Information Sciences, Technologies and Architecture Research Center
(ISTAR-IUL), ISCTE – Instituto Universitário de Lisboa,
Ed. ISCTE, Av. das Forças Armadas, 1649-026 Lisbon, Portugal
carlos.serrao@iscte-iul.pt
[2] Instituto de Telecomunicações (IT-IUL), ISCTE – Instituto Universitário
de Lisboa, Ed. ISCTE, Av. das Forças Armadas, 1649-026 Lisbon, Portugal
nuno.garrido@iscte-iul.pt

Abstract. Traffic management and car parking on modern cities continues to be a problem both for citizens and for city officials. The increasing number of vehicles flowing into the city drain the existing scarce parking resources, and the increase in time spent looking for a parking spot leads to more congestions, parasitic traffic, whilst augmenting fuel consumption and air pollution. In this paper we present an integrated flexible solution developed to help address this issue, using open hardware and software components to develop a low-cost smart parking system suitable for contemporary metropolitan cities. The smart parking solution is based on Arduino boards for the sensors network and on Raspberry Pi single-board computers for the gateway devices, integrated through specific developed software components and a mobile application for the end-users.

Keywords: Smart parking · Smart cities · Prototype · Parking · Arduino · Raspberry Pi · Android · iOS

1 Introduction

Modern cities must deal with different problems and challenges. One of the most important challenges of modern cities is the number of vehicles that cross the city borders every day creating major problems that citizens and city authorities have to face on a daily basis. It is important to find appropriate solutions capable of improving the quality of the city's life and therefore IT has helped the creation of a new type of smart cities. This has been regarded as the answer to some of the major city problems and is slowly changing the citizens way of interacting with their cities. "A city that monitors and integrates conditions of all of its critical infrastructures, including roads, bridges, tunnels, railways, subways, airports, seaports, communications, water, power, even major buildings, and that can better optimize its resources, plan its preventive maintenance activities, and monitor security aspects while maximizing services to its citizens" can be described as a smart city (Chourabi et al. 2012).

© ICST Institute for Computer Sciences, Social Informatics and Telecommunications Engineering 2019
Published by Springer Nature Switzerland AG 2019. All Rights Reserved
J. C. Ferreira et al. (Eds.): INTSYS 2018, LNICST 267, pp. 15–25, 2019.
https://doi.org/10.1007/978-3-030-14757-0_2

Parking and parking management systems have always been amongst some of the major cities concerns. City officials have conducted long term studies on the smart parking concept and of which might be the social, economic, political and environmental impact such systems may cause. Nevertheless, the large investment that is required on this type of systems has created political problems in the cities for their widespread adoption.

The purpose of this paper is to present a prototype of an integrated low-cost system based on open hardware and software components and designed to address the needs of the cities that require monitoring and measurement, not only of the parking areas, but also of other environment data such as mobility, pollution, temperature and humidity.

As part of the research conducted to address the problem of creating a hardware and software solution for this problem a prototype was developed and will be succinctly described on this paper. This prototype integrates hardware components to operate as parking sensors, and gateways that integrate the different parking sensors in a parking area, it also includes all the necessary software for the components to operate and communicate with the backend, and finally a mobile application that is used by end-users to find and give driving directions to existing free parking spots.

The first part of this paper introduces the smart parking topics and determines its importance in the context of smart cities and how they can contribute to solve some of the parking problems cities and city officials have to face. The second part makes a small overview over some already existing intelligent parking solutions that were developed and are being used on the context of smart cities. In the third section of the paper the proposed system is presented as well as the different components and how they are integrated. The tests and results from the developed solution are discussed on the following section, and in the final section of the paper we present some conclusions and point out some future work that needs to be accomplished.

2 Smart Cities Intelligent Parking Solutions

As previously referred, many cities around the world are already implementing or considering the future implementation of smart parking solutions to solve some of the existing problems with parking pressure over their existing parking equipment.

Many different studies have been conducted around the world about this theme that refer the importance of improving the existing parking systems and the way they are used and managed in order to provide benefits to smart cities (Pham et al. 2015; Giuffrè et al. 2012; Mohd et al. 2009). The pressure of the number of vehicles either existing on the cities or crossing its borders everyday needs to be tackled. This has contributed to the development of innovative parking technologies (Fraifer and Fernström 2016).

There are already some examples of smart cities using intelligent parking solutions that try to address the parking problems cities have to deal with. In (Pham et al. 2015) the authors make a proposal to create a system based on an IoT network that can help drivers to find free parking spaces at the lowest possible cost based on different metrics, considering the geolocation of the vehicle, the distance between the parking areas and the total number of free slots in the parking area. If the car park is full, the driver is redirected to another location until he can park the vehicle. Each car park uses WSN (Wireless Sensor Network) (Hancke and Hancke Jr 2012) technology which monitors the parking lots through RFID (Akyildiz and Kasimoglu 2004). The system works in real-time and gives the user the choice of the most suitable parking place, sending directions to the destination. Whenever a vehicle enters or exits the park, the data is updated by communicating with the parking lot WSN.

SmartParking Systems has presented another solution that consists of an advanced navigation system that signals the availability of a parking spot and directs the user towards it (Smart Parking Systems 2017). This system is based on the LoRaWAN technology (Adelantado et al. 2017) making it capable of connecting sensors over long distances, requiring minimal structure while delivering optimal battery life. This offers advantages such as mobility, security and optimized location/positioning, as well as cost savings. This system provides also a smartphone and a tablet application that permits the user to see real-time parking spaces and helps drivers to choose the best location without having to move around to check available parking spots. Time wasted in finding available spots is eliminated; the user saves time and the traffic in residential areas is relieved. The user can pay for parking easily using the application that is associated with a credit card.

There are other systems that can be used to implement intelligent parking solutions and help the management of the existing parking areas in the city, however the referred ones are amongst some of the most relevant ones. In the following section, the developed low-cost intelligent parking solution based on open hardware and software is presented.

3 Low-Cost Intelligent Parking System

The objective of this paper is to describe the implementation of a low-cost intelligent parking solution based on open hardware and software. The developed prototype also regarded scalability and upgradability issues that can allow some of the components currently on the system to be replaced by others in the future, to better adequate to the specific city parking solution requirements.

The architecture of the system depicted on Fig. 1 is composed of a set of components that work in an integrated manner to provide the necessary functionalities required by the intelligent smart parking solution.

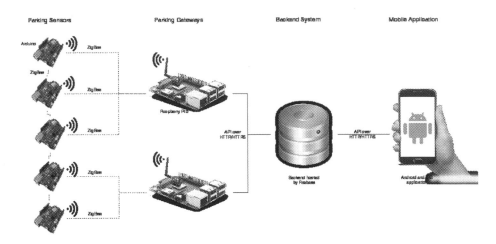

Fig. 1. Integrated smart parking solution architecture

The major components of the system are:

- Parking sensors: the hardware and software cells required to implement the detection of vehicles on the different parking spots;
- Parking gateways: the hardware and software hubs that manage and integrate a set of parking sensors on a parking area and connect the collected data with the system backend, through an Internet connection;
- Backend system: web-based system that is responsible for collecting information from the different gateways, process that information and provide the required information to the mobile application;
- Mobile application: the end-user mobile application that supplies information to the end-user about the availability and location of parking spaces.

In the following sections the different components of the system will be presented and described in detail, specifying their major functionalities.

3.1 Parking Sensors

One of the major components on any smart parking solution is the component capable of detecting the presence of a vehicle on the parking spot, thus allowing the signaling of the availability of the parking place to the system. For this specific prototype, the implementation of the parking sensor is based on an Arduino board integrated with an infrared proximity sensor used to detect the presence of a car over the parking spot. This sensor can detect the presence of obstacles based on the reflection of infrared radiation emitted by a transparent LED and collected by a photoelectric device. This is a basic and low-cost solution used only for prototyping purposes and may not be adequate for use in a final smart parking system, since different things may incorrectly trigger the device and emulate a parked car. The basic different hardware components that integrate the parking sensor are the Arduino Uno R3 board, a Xbee 2mW Wire Antenna, an infrared sensor, a Shield (connector between the Xbee Antenna and the

Arduino board) and a power supply. The developed sensor is only used to simulate one of the many parking sensors that can be applied for this smart parking solution, it is not a real issue for the smart parking system because one of the objectives is to provide the ability to support any kind of sensor (or groups of sensors) capable of accurately detecting a parked car. The proximity sensor is integrated within an Arduino board to implement the necessary logic switch for the parking sensor.

To implement a wireless communication meshed network between the different parking sensors, XBee was the selected data transceiver used to enable the communication between the different sensors and the gateways using the ZigBee protocol. For the prototype sake all devices were configured as Router (Silicon Laboratories 2018), due to the existence of only three sensors in the sensor network and thus increasing the radius of communication between the sensors and the gateway. Although this configuration is not the most efficient in terms of energy consumption, the sensors energy consumption is extremely low and increasing the range of the sensor relative to the gateway is an important implementation aspect of the system that justifies the followed approach.

The Arduino board integrates the different components of the sensor and enables the communication obtaining the sensor status and sending the data to the gateway. To achieve this, specific software was developed for the Arduino UART controller that allows the initialization of the variables inherent to the proximity sensor and the XBee transceiver. The sensor software starts by initializing the different elements that are part of parking sensor. Firstly, the proximity sensor is initialized by receiving as arguments the identifier of where the sensor is connected, and the type of the connected element (in this case, 'INPUT', because the intention here is to obtain the state of the sensor as data input for the Arduino board). After this process, the baud rate (bit per second) of the data transmission is also defined. After this initial process the sensor enters in a loop mode that enables its execution until some shutdown will need to be conducted. The diagram Fig. 2 displays the different states that might occur during the looping on the Arduino software.

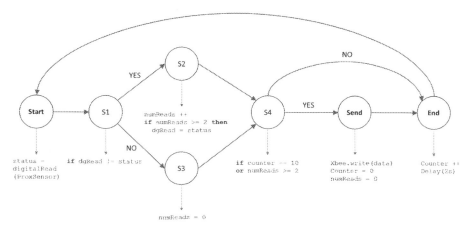

Fig. 2. State machine and pseudocode diagram of the Arduino loop function.

The looping part of the Arduino software contains the logic that handles the collection, processing and communication of data. The first state of this loop is called 'Start' and is responsible for gathering the status of the proximity sensor by calling function 'digitalRead()' and saving it to a 'status' variable. State 'Send' contains the function 'Xbee.write()' which is responsible for sending the data through the XBee to the parking gateway. The variables 'counter' and 'numReads' respectively specify a counter for each iteration of the cycle, and the number of readings in which the previous state of the sensor represented by 'dgRead' is different from the current state indicated by the variable 'status'. The goal is to ensure that there are no false detections. The variable 'numReads' must be greater than or equal to 2 (corresponding to the 'S4' state), assuring the first change of status was confirmed by a second iteration of the cycle, thus guaranteeing a true detection. This allows the sensor to respond immediately when sensing a consistent status change while avoiding constantly sending redundant information and thus save important energy. The counter can be set to send data every 10 iterations even if there are no state changes, informing the gateway that the sensor is active on the network thus providing fast battery failure detection. The last function of the software implements a delay of two seconds before returning to the first instruction of the cycle, therefore setting the sampling rate of the sensor cell cycle. After connecting all elements, the result of the parking sensor is displayed in Fig. 3.

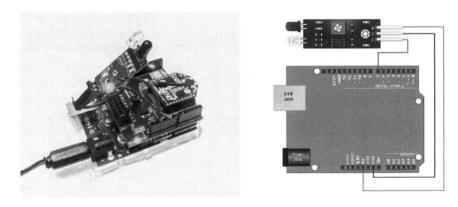

Fig. 3. Prototype proximity sensor and IR sensor connection to the Arduino (Vxlabs 2018).

3.2   Parking Gateway

The parking gateway is one of the most important components on the system and it will be responsible for allowing the communication of the parking sensors network with the management backend system, through the Internet (using a REST API, through HTTP/HTTPS). The gateway component is also composed by hardware and specifically designed software to implement its functionality. The hardware component that was selected to implement this gateway prototype was the Raspberry Pi 3, running on the Raspbian Linux operating system. The basic hardware components of the parking gateway are a Raspberry Pi 3, a USB Wi-Fi or 4G adapter, a Xbee 2mW Wire Antenna, a Socket (connector between the Xbee Antenna and the Raspberry Pi) and a power supply. The following image (Fig. 4) represents the gateway prototype and depicts the connection of the XBee transceiver to the GPIO ports of the Raspberry Pi (Electronics For You 2016). This will enable the gateway to communication with the neighboring sensor network.

The GPIO ports of the Raspberry Pi are set to use a baud rate of 115200 to connected to the XBee, coherently with the settings of the sensors XBee devices. Since for the backend part of the system, Firebase will be used, on the gateway software the Firebase API needs to be initialized and will be used to send the collected data. The software developed for this gateway also implements a loop that enables the gateway to run forever until it is shutdown. Within this loop the information from the sensors will be collected from the XBee device. This data will then be transferred to a vector which separates a string from a defined character. After this, the correct reception of the data is verified and then the information regarding each specific sensor is sent to the backend database.

Fig. 4. Gateway prototype and connecting of the XBee transceiver to the Raspberry Pi (Electronics For You 2016).

3.3 Backend System

For the system to work, the backend of the prototype is based on the online Firebase platform. This platform was selected because it provides the essential services needed for a faster prototype development, however it may be replaced by any other backend platform if the basic necessary backend services are guaranteed.

In the gateway component, authentication is initially performed on Firebase followed by the API initialization, which later allows the use of functions for collecting and sending data to the database.

In the configuration of a Firebase project, chunks of code are provided for introduction into the Android, iOS, and Web application projects that allow Firebase API initialization.

Access to the Firebase backend database is performed through a REST API served through the HTTP/HTTPS protocols.

3.4 Mobile Application

The final objective of a smart parking solution integrated on a smart city is to provide the necessary intelligent and intuitive tools for citizens to easily and quickly find ways to improve their lives through the usage of affordable technologies.

In this specific case, the objective is to provide the end users with a simple tool to access the most convenient parking slot available at a given time and give the means to find their way to the available parking spot. Due to the growing usage of mobile technologies, the best solution was the development of a mobile smart parking application. To produce a multiplatform mobile application (available on Android and iOS), an hybrid mobile development framework - Ionic Framework (Ionic Framework 2018) was selected. After finalizing the design and export of the created project through the Ionic Creator website (Ionic Creator 2018), the Google Maps library was added to the project scope so that the user could navigate the map in search of parking zones represented by custom markers.

Using the mobile application, it is possible to check the number of available spots in a given period represented by a number inserted in the markers of each zone, as shown in Fig. 5. This number will be updated depending on the state changing of the sensors for a given zone. Whenever the user presses a marker, he will be taken to another screen that displays in more detail the information about the selected zone, i.e. the list of parking spots and their current state, and information about the parking zone. If the user selects a spot, the screen with the previous map will appear again, but, in this case, the map shows the route from the driver's location to the destination, and this operation can be confirmed or cancelled. There is another way to search for parking zones and it is in the second tab located at the bottom of the screen. The side menu offers completeness to the application, showing the most relevant sections of the application and each one was implemented separately.

Fig. 5. Application prototype layout.

All data generated and modified by the user is subsequently updated in the database, where each registered user has a reserved section. This is possible by calling methods implemented in the Firebase API library. During the application execution, information about the parking status in each zone can be updated in real-time, because of the listener implemented that can detect if the database has changed.

4 Functional Prototype

As proof of concept for this work, a fully functional prototype was implemented and tested. The proposed prototype consists of two gateways as depicted in Fig. 6, one on the right side and another on the left side, simulating two separate hubs managing two different parking zones, with a total of three parking sensors (two on the right and one the left), and a mobile application for the end-user running on an Android phone (on the bottom).

For testing purpose, one of the gateways is powered by a photovoltaic cell driving a lithium polymer rechargeable power bank, the other gateway runs on a common 5 V USB charger and the parking sensor cells are supplied by 9 V batteries.

For the parking sensor cells, we used infrared sensors as a simple solution for the prototype, that can be easily replaced by a magnetic sensor, specific for the detection of vehicles.

The system was first tested on the software console of the Arduino, and also checked in real-time through the Firebase console. The system is coherent and robust, and the components interconnect correctly as expected demonstrating full functionality and showing status changes on the end-user application in real-time with the sensor stimulation.

Fig. 6. Complete smart parking prototype test setup.

5   Conclusions

This paper presents a fully scalable low-cost open hardware and software smart parking system for parking management in smart cities alternative to existing studies with less flexible and more costly solutions.

The system consists of sensor cells, parking gateways, a web-based backend database, and an end-user mobile application. This is a complete and integrated system designed for flexibility and allowing diverse component implementation alternative to those selected for the functional prototype, such as other types of sensors, data communication methods, front-end software or backend solutions.

We propose the use of low-cost general-purpose Arduino and Raspberry Pi boards for the implementation of parking sensors and gateways, respectively. The prototype demonstrates the use of ZigBee technology for the communication between the physical elements of the system as a suitable scalable solution and efficient in terms of energy savings and cost. The cost of the implemented prototype is relatively low, when compared with other solutions existing on the market. The total cost of each parking sensors is estimated in around 40 euros, while the cost of the parking gateway is around 75 euros. These represent the costs of the individual components used to assemble both the parking sensors and parking gateway and does not consider any economy of scale effect (as the number of hardware components increases, the price of each individual components lowers). Moreover, it is also important to notice that since all the hardware and software used on the solution are open it does not require a specific company for its implementation allowing anyone to be able to build the parking sensors integrating different types of hardware components. The cost calculation for the solution do not include data communication costs nor the maintenance and operation costs, because they highly depend on the different solutions adopted.

The parking sensor network responds to changes in real-time using the communication between the physical components and allowing the mobile application to show the availability of parking spaces available for the user, even in areas with the highest occupancy and daily demand.

This smart parking system can improve the existing approaches or unveil new solutions that can satisfy the citizens and change the paradigm of traffic and parking as one of the biggest problems in the context of smart cities.

Acknowledgements. This project was partially funded by FCT | UID/MULTI/4466/2016.

References

Adelantado, F., Vilajosana, X., Tuset, P., Martínez, B., Melià, J.: Understanding the limits of LoRaWAN. IEEE Commun. Mag. **55**, 34–40 (2017)

Chourabi, H., et al.: Understanding smart cities: an integrative framework. In: 2012 45th Hawaii International Conference on System Science (HICSS), pp. 2289–2297. IEEE, January 2012

Electronics For You: XBee interfacing Raspberry Pi Model 2 (2016). https://electronicsforu.com/electronics-projects/XBee-interfacing-raspberry-pi-model-2/2. Accessed 15 Nov 2017

Fraifer, M., Fernström, M.: Investigation of smart parking systems and their technologies (2016)

Giuffrè, T., Siniscalchi, S.M., Tesoriere, G.: A novel architecture of parking management for smart cities. Procedia-Soc. Behav. Sci. **53**, 16–28 (2012)

Hancke, G.P., Hancke Jr., G.P.: The role of advanced sensing in smart cities. Sensors **13**(1), 393–425 (2012)

Akyildiz, F., Kasimoglu, I.H.: Wireless sensor and actor networks: research challenges. Ad Hoc Netw. **2**(4), 351–367 (2004)

Mohd, I., Leng, Y.Y., Tamil, E.M., Noor, N.M., Zaidi, R.: Car park system: a review of smart parking system and its technology. Inf. Technol. J. **8**, 101–113 (2009). https://doi.org/10.3923/itj.2009.101.113

Ionic Creator (2018).https://creator.ionic.io/

Ionic Framework: Build amazing apps in one codebase, for any platform, with the web (2018). https://ionicframework.com/

Silicon Laboratories: What is the difference between an end device, a router, and a coordinator? (2018). https://www.silabs.com/community/wireless/zigbee-and-thread/knowledge-base.entry.html/2012/07/02/what_is_the_differen-1Yze. Accessed 4 Nov 2017

Smart Parking Systems: Shape the future of tomorrow's cities (2017). http://www.smartparkingsystems.com/. Accessed 19 Dec 2016

Pham, T.N., Tsai, M.F., Nguyen, D.B., Dow, C.R., Deng, D.J.: A cloud-based smart-parking system based on internet-of-things technologies. Digital Object Identifier, pp. 1581–1591 (2015). https://doi.org/10.1109/access.2015.2477299

Vxlabs: Which jumper to set on the ITEAD XBee shield v1.1 for use with a 3.3 V Arduino (2018). https://vxlabs.com/2018/03/23/which-jumper-to-set-on-the-itead-XBee-shield-v1-1-for-use-with-a-3-3v-arduino/. Accessed 25 Oct 2017

Collaborative Gamified Approach
for Transportation

Ana Lúcia Martins[1,2(✉)], João Carlos Ferreira[1,3,4], and Rui Maia[4,5]

[1] Instituto Universitário de Lisboa (ISCTE-IUL), Lisbon, Portugal
almartins@iscte-iul.pt
[2] Business Research Unit (BRU-IUL), Lisbon, Portugal
[3] Information Sciences, Technologies and Architecture Research Center
(ISTAR-IUL), Lisbon, Portugal
[4] Inov Inesc Inovação – Instituto de Novas Tecnologias, Lisbon, Portugal
[5] Instituto Superior Tecnico, Lisbon, Portugal

Abstract. Transportation-related costs are responsible for a large portion of the logistics cost. This is particularly important in city logistics process where it is not easy to aggregate deliveries. Fleet management if often based on efficiency criteria which does not always is compatible with customers' service requests. Models supported by ICT, blockchain and gamification tools are developed to raise collaboration and share of resources in urban logistics process, in a kind of "Logistics-as-uber" concept, where operators share resource and ICT system support than giving advice, handle transactions. The discussion is provided on how such a framework can contribute to simultaneously reduce logistics costs, improve service delivery, reduce traffic in cities and reduce pollution.

Keywords: Fleet management · Logistics · Transportation · Collaboration · Gamification

1 Introduction

In recent years, there has been a great concern of local authorities and the community in general, regarding issues related to the high flow of polluting vehicles circulating in large cities, causing several adverse effects on the quality of life of those who share the urban space. A good percentage of these vehicles are intended for passenger transport (private and collective), although many of the vehicles that circulate every day in cities aim to ensure the distribution of different types of goods in the cities. The growing awareness and concern of local authorities and the general public about the high levels of pollution and noise present in large cities and the resulting health problems, as well as the problems of congestion in urban centers, provides great motivation to question and rethink the way merchandise is transported in the first and last mile of the collection and delivery steps. The activity of urban logistics, which aims to ensure the distribution of goods in cities, has a significant contribution to the quality of life in these places and is also fundamental for the urban economy. In addition, merchandise flows in cities are increasing, with high growth prospects, either because of the growth of the e-commerce business or because of an increase in the population in urban areas.

© ICST Institute for Computer Sciences, Social Informatics and Telecommunications Engineering 2019
Published by Springer Nature Switzerland AG 2019. All Rights Reserved
J. C. Ferreira et al. (Eds.): INTSYS 2018, LNICST 267, pp. 26–38, 2019.
https://doi.org/10.1007/978-3-030-14757-0_3

In parallel, there are increasing restrictions on accessibility (restrictions on access for certain types of vehicles, establishment of own areas for loading/unloading/transfers, restrictions on access to pedestrian zones, creation of urban tolls, establishment of temporary access windows, among others), often in areas of high concentration of services and commerce, causing many difficulties to urban logistics service providers, among which the uncertainty regarding the service time due to the congestion of the road infrastructure and the difficulties of parking. In practice, the problem of urban logistics is characterized by a rather high degree of complexity. One of the primary sources of complexity is the fact that there are several Stakeholders with different and sometimes contradictory objectives. On the one hand, there are local and central authorities, urban planners and residents whose main concern is centered on sustainability issues in cities. On the other hand, there are customers, suppliers and distribution companies whose focus is on reducing costs and increasing efficiency.

In the current scenario, most of urban logistics cargo are carried by private companies, using dedicated fleets (typically vans and trucks) using with fuels derived from Petroleum, leading to the associated CO_2 emissions. In this context, the problem is exacerbated by a large number of parcels (both in volume and weight) to be collected and/or delivered to a large number of customers (private as well as public/private and/or retail) atomised in the cities, implying a significant challenge to simultaneously optimize daily loads to provide a service adjusted to the needs of the clients and optimize the available resources. In parallel, the transport of passengers in the city is mostly assured by a dedicated public or private network of buses, taxis, electric cars and/or metro. Throughout the daily operation, there are significant variations in the number of passengers using a transport service, although the transport network continues to operate uninterruptedly throughout the day, albeit with less frequency during some periods. This leads to poor performance of the transportation system regarding capacity utilization, creating challenges for fleet and driver management. The need to minimize the negative impacts [1] associated with the traditional distribution of goods within cities motivated the definition of this research work.

Recent data indicate that most of the world's population lives in areas that are considered urban [2]. This situation leads to higher traffic intensity and congestion, which are exponentiated if there are parking difficulties. CO_2 emissions are a direct consequence, and the European Commission [3] estimates that on average 8%–15% of traffic in urban areas is the result of transportation of parcels. One management approach is to postpone or anticipate the movement of at part of this load to periods with lower traffic intensity, usually evening or night periods.

Increasing the size and density of urban areas raises issues of mobility of people and goods. The concept associated with it, smart mobility, is one of the current topics in international forums and recent studies [1, 4]. Mobility management systems have not kept pace with emerging growth and challenges, leading to longer path times and more congested communication routes. The entry and exit of goods in urban space are usually carried out independently by each issuer or receiver involved. This situation prevents cargo aggregation and rationalization of the number of vehicles in urban space, as well as the use of roads without concern to avoid periods of greater congestion. Within the concept of mobility in zones of high urban density, logistic activity places continuously higher restrictions on other users of the city. Of these, the most important are pollution (sound and atmospheric) associated with transport, the use of infrastructures initially intended for other purposes (roads, car parks), and the resulting congestion caused by loading and unloading activities. Smart goods mobility aims to make more efficient use of means of transport and communication routes, as well as to reduce CO_2 emissions. In order to mitigate these problems, the present project intends to contribute with technological solutions that allow increasing the sustainability of the distribution of goods within the cities, maintaining, however, the service quality of this distribution according to the needs of supply; that is, to rationalize the distribution process - economically, spatially and temporally - by reducing the flow of goods but maintaining the service level of deliveries. The general objective of current work is to create a system of merchandise management, as well as its efficient collection and reception, contributing to increasing the smart mobility of cities. In this context, the aim is to develop a platform to add goods that require to be moved, improve the occupation of the vehicles used and manage the cash flows, in parallel with more efficient and effective management of the loading and unloading places with prior reservation of spaces using a platform created for this purpose.

We developed a collaborative gamified an online platform oriented to logistics in urban areas, as kind of "Logistics-as-uber" concept, which allows:

(1) To operate as a collaborative broker where there are companies with goods transport needs (buyers) and freight companies with space still available in their vehicles (sellers). The buyer defines the nature of the merchandise, the volume and the weight of the goods, the delivery time-window, the point of origin of the goods and the point of delivery of the goods. Then the buyer receives service proposals from sellers (delivery window, price, and type of transport). The platform, taking into account the available transport offers, will determine the best proposal is taking into account the characteristics of the requested service, providing a solution for the transport of goods similar to Uber's passenger transport solution. Associated gamification process has the mission of increasing users' participation.
(2) Companies that offer transportation services to optimize their routes and spaces in vehicles, contributing to the minimization of empty returns and non-complete loads.
(3) Dynamic price setting depending on the supply available and the degree of aggregation of goods achieved.
(4) Developing a solution that allows the management of parking spaces by creating a pre-reservation policy for a particular parking slot by the logistics operator.

2   Literature Review

Since the work is developed under four topics we analyze the state of the art as follows: (1) Collaborative platforms for sharing transport resources; (2) Reservation place loading and unloading; (3) Optimizing Routes; (4) Dynamic prices supply function and demand; (5) blockchain; and (6) gamification platforms.

2.1   Collaborative Platforms for Sharing Transport Resources

Chow et al. [5] provide an informational base model grounded on the collaboration between the different players in the supply chain. This model allows the consolidation of several cargoes and, consequently, rationalization of physical flows of goods. Such an Internet-based logistics information system, called E-logistics [6], allows for greater integration of information and is especially useful in situations involving reduced time windows and small size cargoes [7], i.e. less than full truckload, which is consistent with the moved of cargo in urban areas and for which there is currently no efficient and effective solution. The aggregation of these loads, through an information platform, allows the reduction of transportation costs and the number of vehicles required to handle this load. These aggregation principles are used by large carriers, but not by individual approaches that often do not contemplate urban logistics.

There are already conceptual models for the development of collaborative platforms that allow the integration of loads in urban spaces [4]. However, there are no systems implemented due to the tendency of the market to function individually. Cargo consolidation works well outside the cities where there is a high volume of goods and with individual loads of high dimension for which large carriers have their own systems. However, within the urban environment, this type of approach has not been successful because of the volume of the business is smaller and more atomized and, therefore, not attractive from a commercial point of view. In urban logistics, it is common to have small carriers that often lack information systems because of low levels of activity. It has been proved that collaboration between partners [1] in a supply chain context, aiming at improving collective performance, requires visibility of the system [8]. Therefore, a solution based on collaboration and resource sharing between different carriers could be beneficial for both the carriers and the environment.

Information systems and communication networks are essential factors for the development of collaborative relationships [9]. The degree of collaboration between partners can be diverse, ranging from a simple exchange of information to the development of strategic alliances [9, 10]. The exchange of information online allows for faster coordination between partners or between autonomous players, enabling collaboration and mutual gains even in situations of previous commercial ignorance among these partners. An informational meeting point does not currently exist for goods. However, its absence in the market causes that today loads within the cities end up being moved using inefficient solutions.

Information-based systems used by the large carriers allow better utilization of available vehicle capacity, thereby reducing the unit cost of transport [11]. However, this type of optimization requires high volumes of customer orders to be effective regarding delivery windows, a situation that presents itself as a challenge for small, individual companies. One way to overcome this challenge is by being able to aggregate parcels. Reservation os space for loading and unloading cargo

Applied cases in urban logistics are scarce in part because of the difficulty of real tests is performing. Also, there are specific laws that do not allow easy replication. In literature, the Green Paper on Urban Mobility [10] is one of the research work to raise attention to this problem and was the basis for three major initiative: CIVITAS I (2002), CIVITAS II (2005) and CIVITAS PLUS (2008) (www.civitas-initiative.net).

Another example is STRAIGHTSOL project (http://www.straightsol.eu) with seven cases. One of this initiatives took place in Lisbon in the area of parking for load/unload of goods, but unfortunately, this process stopped due to missing laws and high investments.

In terms of academic work, most of the research is oriented to urban freight distribution at European level, most of then oriented to the load/unload process, the need for reservation space to avoid road occupancy and consequently congestion:

– One work of Ambrosi [11] shows a comparative study of nine countries, where is highlighted applied methodologies and results obtained.
– At Reims, France, a project shows the time restriction scheme that foresees time delivery windows for each delivery vehicle entering the inner-city area [12].
– In 20005, rules for delivery times for urban logistics process were attempted in Maribor, Slovenia [13]. Around 1000 violations with the lower value (85€) would be identified, and the total benefits would be 85K€.
– At Aalborg, Denmark, a case-study to improves delivery efficiency and working conditions for freight distributors, and reduced numbers of freight vehicles in the city centre (aggregation process) [14].
– In Spain, Barcelona another study on cargo transport management measures that can bring useful results and improvement to the process. The associated process was SMILE (Street Management Improvements for Loading/unloading Enforcement). About 100,000 urban logistics deliveries are made using the urban road as a place for loading and unloading the goods, requiring four thousand additional loading and unloading places to accommodate all this operation.
– Winchester study was concerning the benefits of offering reservation of loading and unloading places in urban areas [15].
– Also, [16] shows that parking areas are essential in urban centres, but the reality shows that this does not exist in many municipalities.
– In work [17] again the creation of urban logistics spaces for the distribution of goods can reduce the number of cargo vehicles using the roads in search of a parking space.

Some other research works on urban logistics centres were oriented to the identification of urban consolidation centres (UCCs) [18]. These more specific studies have been of great help when planning to implement initiatives has the example in Bilbao [19]. Although still in its infancy, there is already evidence that organizing parking areas in municipalities can lead to the reduction of environmental hazards and the volume of traffic. Nonetheless, the lack of coordinated efforts from the stakeholders involved is limiting the success of these initiatives.

2.2 Optimization of Routes

It is intended to take advantage of the opportunity to apply and adapt academic models of route optimization to the transport situations explored in the project, namely the so-called vehicle routing problem (VRP), usually referred to model and optimize vehicle routes in a logistic context [3]. With adequate optimization, in addition to other benefits, savings of more than 10% in transport costs can be achieved [20].

Among the routing problem approaches, one is focused on defining the route each vehicle has to follow without exceeding its capacity (both regarding cargo and availability of time). The rout is only completed when the vehicle returns to its origin. This routing problem is known as the Vehicle Routing Problem (VRP) and was initially introduced by Dantzig and Ramser [20]. Among these, the improvement heuristic from [21, 22], VRPH, applications using the program made available by [23], is a very recent one regarding the heuristic techniques it uses. This metaheuristic can perform several types of local research in the vicinity of initial solutions generated by the heuristic of Clark and Wright [22] and also to the diversification of solutions, returning, in the end, the best solution found. Because it is a heuristic improvement process, the routes obtained by VRPH are at least as good as Clarke and Wright's. VRPH hs been used to identify the best route for a specific case, minimizing its distance (see, for instance, [24, 25]).

2.3 Dynamic Prices Supply Function and Demand

There is a decision support system for the dynamic calculation of prices and promotions for stocks [1]. These authors created mathematical models that satisfactorily covered the interdependencies between products and the modeling and optimization of the demand in support systems decision to calculate prices. Setting prices dynamically, due to its non-deterministic nature, is complex. Several models can be found in the literature to address these issues [26–31].

Transportation is the logistic activity that directly impacts on-time delivery and customer service quality, but at the same time, it can strongly influence logistical costs. Setting prices in freight transportation involve trade-offs between these issues and models are required to address them simultaneously.

2.4 Blockchain

Blockchain can play an important role in this collaborative process taking into account that is able to handle distributed transactions without a central supervision entity. This approach has been applied with success in several areas, as for example microgrid, addressing incentive issues while respecting operational constraints [32] and on the management of complex system without centralized supervision [33]. Also blockchains supports monetary transactions based on the concept of cryptocurrencies, such as Bitcoin [33], giving in this case the possibility of performing transportation payments based on agreed conditions without the intervention of a central entity, based on a shared list of blocks of transactions [32], with resilience because there is not a central structure and low cost there is no third parties with commissions involved. Blockchain also can handle cyber-attacks, communication dropouts, and participants joining/departing the network.

In our case the collaborative negotiation can be programmed and handle in the associated smart contract supports monetary transactions in a transparent based on pre-defined rules. This smart contract tries to reflect prices based on aggregation level and changes on distribution timeline and distance based on pre-defined heuristics. The first step is the transportation operator defines the transportation price based on time and distance covered. Based on the aggregation to define a price point agreement, and then the defined amount of money (digital money) is sent to a predefined address that works as an escrow account.

Blockchain creates a security measurement environment using the Trusted Platform Module (TPM), Trusted Execution Environment (TEE), Secure Element (SE), or any similar component could be introduced in smart meters supported by a remote verification service [32].

2.5 Gamification Platforms

Gamification is the strategy of interaction between people towards a pre-defined goal based on the offer of incentives that stimulate the engagement of the public. In this collaborative is important to motive the user under the pre-defined goal and gamification approaches with monetary rewards play an important role. It rewards collaborative behavior with recognition and visibility within the community [34, 35]. The community is maintained under pre-defined goals through users' high engagement and flexibility behavior. We use our experience in several fields applied, energy to motivate user behavior change towards sharing available resources.

3 Platform

The proposed platform in this project is intended to fill the gap in the solutions available in the market, either in the lack of simultaneous integration of several actors, (TMS) used for transport management and planning [36], planning loads and looking for possibilities of consolidation of these for later coordination of loads and discharges [37].

This limitation is exceeded by the present project because, although it is intended for the aggregation of parcels, these are originated in a multiplicity of simultaneous actors generating an aggregate volume with sufficient scale to generate efficient movements of goods. The collaborative solution represented by the platform will allow small players to be integrated that would otherwise be separated from the possibility of goods integration.

The relationship between the logistical integration systems referred to above is centered on the sharing of information and resources between operators. Consequently, the position of this proposal is as follows:

1. A modeling solution that follows the above principles can be found in Leung et al. [38], who proposed a virtual market for operators in the air transport sector where there is logistical integration. This model has no direct application to the problem that is addressed in the present work since it is limited to the aggregation of the load in a controlled environment but can be a partial reference for the solution to be developed. This project will overcome this gap in the market, allowing consolidation with other modules and the possibility of a larger scale use than the current models.

2. Reinheimer and Bodendorf [39] addressed the integration of information between elements of the supply chain and advocate that access to the system should be decentralized, i.e. it should allow access by all players (load transmitters and carriers) individually and easy way. This access is not easy and is limited in the current solutions, intending the present project to fill this absence of solutions in the market.

3. Logistics Brokerage Systems (LBS) is another variety of logistics integration system, in which there is the open integration of information for the transport of goods, and that offers its users financial links, prices, an indication of available space, reservation of transport capacity of door-to-door goods and a single payment point [1]. This model, however, in essence, does not involve the possibility of coordination with entities in the destination of the flow for scheduling of temporal slots of space for loads and discharges. The platform to be developed with this project will overcome this limitation by providing a transportation solution that also integrates coordination with spaces for loading and unloading.

4. While TMS is a more closed system for individual firms, Chen et al. [36] introduced a road freight transport platform (HFTP), which is operated by a fourth party logistics player and is open to industry. Applied in the technical scope, HFTP intends to serve as a network between the owners of the cargoes to be handled and the transport companies (not necessarily logistics operators). This is a feature that will be included in the platform resulting from this project, making it possible to fill a gap in the market.

Given the specificities of the collaborative platform for sharing transport resources, we aim to create open services that optimize transport routes and the packaging of the goods to be transported, depending on the volume and weight, taking into account the diversity of transport vehicles). To this problem, to treat as a whole using multiobjective optimization functions, we want to combine the temporal constraints of the deliveries (defined by the clients) and the traffic restrictions in the cities (a type of vehicles and eventual temporal windows). The heuristic algorithms to be developed and incorporated in the platform, capable of providing efficient routes in real time, will also have to consider the fact that the same route has associated several loading and unloading operations (collection and delivery). This particularity constitutes additional difficulties in the planning of the different loading and unloading periods and in the occupation of packing space. We will apply a decision system to the calculation of the price. Although the authors do not know of the existence of a decision support system for the calculation of dynamic prices applied to the freight transport theme, there are, however, in the literature examples of similarly complex challenges.

It is in this perspective that we intend to develop a model-oriented decision support system, emphasized in statistical access and manipulation and optimized for the dynamic calculation of prices. The goal is for the system to define a strategy (dynamic price determination) that assists decision making that maximizes utility over time. In order to do this, it will be necessary to describe the complexity of the reality of price formulation through specially designed mathematical models. Dynamic pricing, given its complex and non-deterministic nature, will be addressed through the most appropriate techniques and modeling and analysis tools available [30, 31]. This approach will aim to build a model that satisfies the requirements and can be integrated into the platform. This dynamism of prices will tend to lower the values and the consequent demand for the customer of this type of services. This process will work in a similar way to Uber's prices, where price is a function of demand. In this process, the price will be a function of the integration achieved.

Figure 1 illustrates our approach. It is grounded on an installation of steemit (https://steemit.com), where an aggregated system based on an intelligent decision support system (SIAD) collect users' goods transportation needs and operators' offers. A BID system calculates pricing and a gamified approach tries to incentive users' flexibility with lower prices.

In order for the proposed distribution channel to ensure the distribution of the goods, after the request of the service by a customer that intends to send merchandise to one or more locations within the city, the provider platform (the service provider that is the owner of the system that will be developed in the project) should allocate the goods to a passenger transport operator and define, among other issues, where it should be delivered (from a set of strategically pre-defined locations in the outskirts of the city or a reduced set of locations in the city, such as terminals of passenger transport operators), assuring this way the first transfer of the goods from a delivery perspective. In the next step, the goods are transported by the passenger transport operator to a location inside the city and as close as possible to its final destination (at a stopping point for the transportation operator) to be collected by micro-logistics operators, that (e.g. standard bicycles and/or electric bicycles, electric trailers, electric logistic trains and minivans) will move the goods from that location to their final destination using a fleet of electric vehicles), thus verifying the second transfer of the goods. To physically collect the goods, the same system can be used, in reverse order, or the customer can make arrangements to have them available at the location of the logistics operator. It is emphasized that in this last stage of the journey, the merchandise to be delivered to the various endpoints will be integrated into the daily operations of the micro-logistics company, and it can be delivered shortly after its collection or not, depending on the operational arrangements that are made by the micro-logistics company. However, the micro-logistics company is responsible for assuring the service level agreed upon with the end customer. It is also important to mention that, in addition to the fleet to be used by the micro-logistics operator, this more ecologically friendly solution is much more beneficial in terms of environmental impact and noise levels than the traditional fleets, has fewer access restrictions and usually is better accepted by the population that interacts with it.

The intelligent decision support system (SIAD) that it is proposed in this project will allow the management of real-time transport operations in a coordinated and synchronized way, in time and space, of the whole network of vehicles in operation. This synchronization assumes a preponderant role in cargo loading/unloading/transfer points. In addition, this system also ensures real-time re-planning of transport operations in order to respond to extraordinary events or incidents (such as the micro-logistics operator is not at the place of unloading of the goods when of the arrival of the

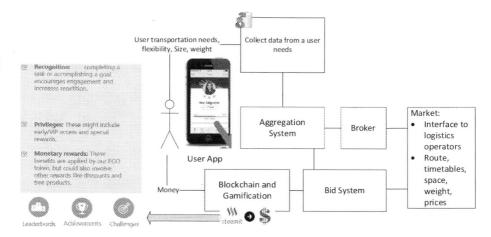

Fig. 1. Overview of main platform modules

transport operator's vehicle in the event of a breakdown or accident, or if the customer for whom the goods are intended to is not at the place of delivery at the time of delivery). To this end, it will be necessary to ensure the continuous monitoring of the whole network of vehicles [1] involved in the process (both the vehicles of the transport operators and those of the micro-logistics operators).

4 BID System and Smart Contract

Transportation publicity their offer based on available space and weight associated time window and route. This could be pre-defined transportation that does not go fully or new ones. The BID price is also defined and the availability to perform a change on original route and times. This is a basis to load gamified platform, where end-users express their transportation needs (space, weight, time and destination). The system tries to fit and suggests possible operators routes with availability and cost. End-user needs to check the availability the best to fit their needs, usually with a need of change time. This part is accounted on this platform where behavior change is quantified in a gamified approach of points. Operators receive request about the possibility of route changes. This is done in a pre-defined time windows. After an agreement, the system quantifies behavior change from operators and end-user towards the common goal of sharing transportation resources. This approach is implemented in the Steemit platform module. To ensure users' data privacy, data is stored without being directly related to the user. Those users who change behavior towards the aggregation win points that can be used on this dynamic pricing creation and this gives a price reduction [1]. After this process, the blockchain accounts the transactions between several possible end-users towards some transportation.

5   Use Case

Since this initial set up, a city distribution process was not possible to come live yet, we apply the current approach to a sharing approach in the automotive industry in Portugal. As most of the logistics flows are inbound, and outbound trucks go less full. Consequently, the goal was to invite other companies to share transportation synergies mainly those that use outbound flows (export companies). A set of potential companies was invited to use the platform in a shared transportation approach. In a first phase, potential partners were contacted directly and invited to upload their transportation needs to the system. Example of these suppliers are: (1) Colepccl; (2) Corticeira Amorim; (3) Grohe; (4) Karmann Ghia; (5) Simoldes; (6) Labsfal, among others. A detailed information about this process can be found at [40]. Transactions were performed on Steemit, and prices were calculated based on the aggregation and initial transportation pricing.

This collaborative approach allowed a reduction in transportation cost of by one quarter in 2014. Some of the procedures used can be applied to city logistics. A pilot in Lisbon is intended to go live next year.

6   Conclusion

In this research work a new paradigm for the transportation of goods taking into account the power of ICT platforms mainly blockchain and gamification platforms to raise collaboration towards the sharing of transportation resources. Sharing approach is fundamental to savings, sustainable approaches. In spite of this ICT approach, this type of collaboration system works well with a considerable number of users to increase matching possibilities. It is our intention to add an interface to include commercial delivery companies, to be used in the case of having a limited number of users present and no matching is possible. In addition, this approach can be used to fulfill this dedicated transportation.

It is our intention to add an interface to include commercial delivery companies, to be used in the case of having a limited number of users present and no matching is possible. Additionally, this approach can be used to fulfill dedicated transportation.

References

1. Ferreira, J.C., Martins, A.L., Pereira, R.: GoodsPooling: an intelligent approach for urban logistics. In: De Paz, J.F., Julián, V., Villarrubia, G., Marreiros, G., Novais, P. (eds.) ISAmI 2017. AISC, vol. 615, pp. 55–62. Springer, Cham (2017). https://doi.org/10.1007/978-3-319-61118-1_8
2. Demographia: Demographia World Urban Areas, 11th Annual edn (2015)
3. MDS Transmodal Limited: DG MOVE, European Commission: Study on Urban Freight Transport, Final Report (2012)

4. Souza, R., Goh, M., Lau, H.-C., Ng, W.-S., Tan, P.-S.: Collaborative urban logistics – synchronizing the last mile: a Singapore research perspective. In: Procedia – Social and Behavioural Sciences, vol. 125, pp. 422–431 (2014)
5. Chow, H.K.H., Choy, K.L., Lee, W.B.: A strategic knowledge based planning system for freight forwarding industry. Expert Syst. Appl. 33, 936–954 (2007)
6. Graham, D., Manikas, I., Folinas, D.K.: e-Logistics and e-Supply Chain Management: Applications for Evolving Business. ISI Global, Hershey (2013)
7. Christopher, M.: Logistics and Supply Chain Management, 5th edn. Pearson, London (2016)
8. Lynch, K.: Collaborative logistics networks – breaking traditional performance barriers for shippers and carriers. White paper, Nistevo, Minnesota, USA (2001). (http://www.idii.com/wp/col_logistics.pdf)
9. Audy, J., D'amours, S., Lehoux, N., Rönnqvist, M.: Coordination in collaborative logistics. In: International Workshop on Supply Chain Models for Shared Resource Management, Brussels (2010)
10. Kadlubek, M.: The selected areas of e-logistics I Polish e-commerce. Procedia – Comput. Sci. 65, 1059–1065 (2015)
11. Ambrosini, C., Patier, D., Routhier, J.-L.: Urban freight establishment and tour based surveys for policy oriented modelling. Proceedia – Soc. Behav. Sci. 2(3), 6013–6026 (2010)
12. Littiere, H.: Example 3.3.3: control of delivery areas in Reims (France). In: BESTUFS – D 2.2 Best Practice Handbook (2006): Control and Enforcement in Urban Freight Transport, pp. 45–46 (2006)
13. Politic, D.: Example 3.3.6: management of pedestrian zones (Slovenia). In: BESTUFS – D 2.2 Best Practice Handbook (2006): Control and Enforcement in Urban Freight Transport, pp. 54–56 (2006)
14. Mikkelsen, B.: City-Goods Delivery Co-operation (2012). http://www.eltis.org/discover/case-studies/city-goods-delivery-co-operation. Checked 08 May 2017
15. McLeod, F., Cherrett, T.: Loading bay booking and control for urban freight. J. Int. Logistics Res. Appl. 14(6), 385–397 (2011). https://doi.org/10.1080/13675567.2011.641525
16. Dablanc L.: Freight transport for development toolkit: urban freight. The International Bank for Reconstruction and Development/The World Bank (2009)
17. Awasthi, A., Proth, J.M.: A systems-based approach for city logistics decision making. J. Adv. Manag. Res. 3(2), 7–17 (2006)
18. Browne, M., Piotrowska, M., Woodburn, A., Allen, J.: Literature Review WM9: Part I - Urban Freight Transport, Green Logistics Project. Transport Studies Group, University of Westminster (2007)
19. Oliveira, B.R.P.: Simulação de um espaço logístico urbano para a distribuição de mercadorias em Belo Horizonte. Monografia (Graduação em Engenharia de Produção). UFMG (2012). (in Portuguese)
20. Dantzig, G.B., Ramser, J.H.: The truck dispatching problem. Manag. Sci. 6, 80–91 (1959)
21. Groer, C., Golden, B., Wasil, E.: A library for local search heuristics for vehicle routing problem. Mathelatical Programmim Computation 2, 79–101 (2010)
22. Clarke, G., Wright, J.R.: Scheduling of vehicle routing problem from a central depot to a number of delivery points. Oper. Res. 12, 568–581 (1964). https://doi.org/10.1287/opre.12.4.568
23. Huang, S.-H., Yang, T.-H., Tang, C.-H.: Fleet size determination for a truckload distribution center, 48, 377–389 (2014)
24. Hassold, S., Ceder, A.: Public transport vehicle scheduling featuring multiple vehicle types. Transp. Res. Part B 67, 129–143 (2014)
25. Laporte, G.: The vehicle-routing problem – an overview of exact and approximate algorithms, 59(3), 345–358 (1992)

26. Coase, R.: The nature of the firm. Economica **4**(16), 386–405 (1937)
27. Hall, R.W., Racer, M.: Transportation with common carrier and private fleets – system assignment and shipment frequency optimization. IIE Trans. **27**(2), 217–225 (1995)
28. Gudmundsson, S.V., Walczuck, R.: The development of electronic markets in logistics. Int. J. Logistics Manag. **10**, 99–113 (1999)
29. Novais, P., Carneiro, D.: Interdisciplinary Perspectives on Contemporary Conflict Resolution, pp. 1–363. IGI Global, Hershey (2016). https://doi.org/10.4018/978-1-5225-0245-6
30. Carneiro, D., Novais, P., Neves, J.: Conflict Resolution and its Context. From the Analysis of Behavioural Patterns to Efficient Decision-Making, pp. 1–279. Springer, Cham (2014). https://doi.org/10.1007/978-3-319-06239-6. ISBN 978-3-319-06238-9
31. Gomes, M., Oliveira, T., Carneiro, D., Novais, P., Neves, J.: Studying the Effects of Stress on Negotiation Behaviour, Cybernetics and Systems, vol. 45, no. 3, pp. 279–291. Taylor & Francis Ltd., Abingdon (2014). http://dx.doi.org/10.1080/01969722.2014.894858. ISSN 0196-9722
32. Fernández-Caramés, T.M., Fraga-Lamas, P.: A review on the use of blockchain for the internet of things. IEEE Access (2018). https://doi.org/10.1109/access.2018.2842685
33. Crosby, M., Pattanayak, P., Verma, S., Kalyanaraman, V.: Blockchain technology: beyond bitcoin. Appl. Innov. **2**, 6–10 (2016)
34. Morschheuser, B., Hamari, J., Koivisto, J.: Gamification in crowdsourcing: a review. In: Proceedings of the 2016 49th Hawaii International Conference on System Sciences (HICSS), Koloa, HI, USA, 5–8 January 2016, pp. 4375–4384 (2016)
35. Hansch, A., Newman, C., Schildhauer, T.: Fostering Engagement with Gamification: Review of Current Practices on Online Learning Platforms. Elsevier, New York (2015)
36. Chen L., Taudes, A., Chao, W., Hou, H.: A highway freight transport platform for the chinese freight market—requirements analysis and case study. In: 2011 IEEE Forum on Integrated and Sustainable Transportation Systems Vienna, Austria, pp. 344–350 (2011)
37. European Commission (2007). https://ec.europa.eu/transport/themes/urban/urban_mobility/green_paper_en. Checked 08 May 2017
38. Leung, L.C., Cheung, W., Hui, Y.C.: A framework for a logistics e-commerce community network: the Hong Kong air cargo industry. IEEE Trans. Syst. Man Cybern. Part A: Syst. Hum. **30**, 446–455 (2000)
39. Reinheimer, S., Bodendorf, F.: A framework for electronic coordination in the air cargo market. Inf. Soc. **15**, 51–55 (1999)
40. Ferreira, J.C., Martins, A.L.: Transportation synergies in inbound logistics flow at automotive assembler plant. In: Pawar, K.S., Potter, A., Lisec, A. (ed.) 22nd International Symposium on Logistics (ISL 2017), pp. 561–568. Centre for Concurrent Enterprise, Nottingham University Business School, Ljubljana

Case Studies and Simulation

Improving Fleet Solution – A Case Study

Ana Lúcia Martins[1,2(✉)], Ana Catarina Nunes[1,3], Rita Pereira[1],
and João Carlos Ferreira[1,4]

[1] Instituto Universitário de Lisboa (ISCTE-IUL), Lisbon, Portugal
almartins@iscte-iul.pt
[2] Business Research Unit (BRU-IUL), Lisbon, Portugal
[3] Centro de Matemática, Aplicações Fundamentais e Investigação Operacional
(CMAFcIO-Universidade de Lisboa), Lisbon, Portugal
[4] Information Sciences, Technologies and Architecture Research Center
(ISTAR-IUL), Lisbon, Portugal

Abstract. Transportation management is a logistical activity with a high impact on a company's ability to compete in the market. Although the focus on cost reduction is the most usual concern with this activity, lead times and the quality of the service provided should also be considered depending on the market to be served. The goal of this research was to compare different fleet alternatives for a specific construction materials company and discuss which scenario is the most suited to fulfil the company's customer service policy. A case study approach was developed, and four alternative scenarios were considered. These were compared both regarding the costs they involve, which was analysed using a vehicle routing problem heuristic, and the quality of the customer service they allow, which was assessed based on their ability to provide flexibility in the fleet occupancy rate to respond to unexpected orders. Evidence showed that the current fleet solution is not adequate and investment should be made only if the demand level increases, otherwise outsourcing should be considered along with a minimum level of the self-owned fleet.

Keywords: A case study · Fleet management · Logistics · Transportation · VRPH

1 Introduction

Transportation is considered a typical logistics activity [1] and is probably the most visible logistics activity. Decisions at this level influence the company's ability to compete in the market. Its value to the customer is widely recognised [2–5]. Finding the best fleet solution to each company at any given moment is a challenge that is never completely fulfilled.

The current economic world scenario presents itself as an additional challenge to companies. Although keeping their customer service level is critical in commercial terms and owning a private fleet is considered as a "strategic asset" [6], cost reduction is currently a survival issue.

Literature is rich in terms of research focused on route optimization, either for private fleet see, for instance, [7, 8], or for a dual option of private fleet and outsourced

J. C. Ferreira et al. (Eds.): INTSYS 2018, LNICST 267, pp. 41–52, 2019.
https://doi.org/10.1007/978-3-030-14757-0_4

transportation services see, for instance, [9, 10] or even just focused on fleet size see, for instance, [11]. This perspective, although also aiming for lead time fulfilment, has its optimization routines based on cost (which can be transportation and/or inventory costs) and/or distance/time reduction. It is possible to research focused on the fleet replacement issue [12], but the focus is still on cost reduction. Not much can be found on the trade-off between the quality of the logistics service provided and the cost the system has to support to deliver it. This is the gap in the literature that the present research aims to reduce.

This research emerged from the request of a Portuguese construction materials company to have its fleet solution analyzed. This company is considered a medium size one. Its main activity is the production and distribution of plaster for construction and porcelain industry. It holds a factory warehouse, and three large warehouses spotted in populous regions from where it supplies its customers. Transportation in bulk is outsourced as loads are random and always in full. Packed products, which represent 82% of products sold, are moved using both the company's fleet and outsourcing. The company's customer service policy aims for due dates fulfilment and a lead time of up to one week. Due to the economic crisis in Europe, the company was not able to renew its fleet but is currently challenged by the fact that it is old and has high maintenance costs.

This research aims to compare and discuss different fleet alternative scenarios for packed product's transportation taking into consideration the company's customer service policy.

In order to fulfil the goal, a literature review focus on the relevance of logistical value and fleet solution. A case study approach is considered taking into consideration [13] recommendations. Firstly, the company is briefly characterized as to identify customer service challenges and scenarios are developed taking into consideration both the company's desire and best practices from literature. Then data from one year of deliveries is analyzed using a vehicle routing problem heuristic (VRPH). Lastly, both quantitative and qualitative analysis is conducted to better fulfil the goal of this research.

2   Literature Review

There are several ways in which a company can generate value to its customers with its offer. One of them is using its logistical system [14]. In fact, it is argued that as long as logistics is "managed as an integrated effort to achieve customer satisfaction at the lowest cost possible", it will create value [15]. This value creation, or the logistics value proposition of a company, should be defined according to an individual or selected customer group [15] and as a result of the trade-off between the time the logistics system requires to respond to the desired value proposition, the cost of the logistic system has to support to perform it, and the quality of the logistic service provided that should be considered in terms of the availability, support and commitment provided to the customer [4, 14].

Customer service, as the set of activities that provide product availability in a way that customers recognize as valuable, requires availability, operational performance and service reliability [5]. On-time delivery, in-full delivery and error-free deliveries are common measures of customer service. These are part of the product surrounding services that customers require when they purchase a product, and although they only represent a small part of the cost of product ownership for the customer [5], they represent a very high impact in terms of purchasing decision (20–80 rule).

Transportation is the logistic activity that directly impacts on-time delivery and customer service quality, but at the same time, it can heavily influence costs. It is known that costs increase with distance travelled but decrease with increased cargo load [5]. This means that companies in search for cost reduction tend to focus on fleet and routing solutions that allow them higher occupancy rates. As a consequence, they might be sacrificing customer service levels, which is of high impact when commodities are involved [15].

There are several routing problem solutions each aimed at situations with specific characteristics. These are highlighted by several authors see, for instance, [16–18] and [17] provide a literature review on the referred variances as well as on exact resolution methods and heuristics. Although whole linear programming is popular, it is sometimes unpractical due to computer capacity constraints to deal with the dimension and complexity of real situations [5]. As so, heuristics have become more popular.

Among the routing problem approaches, one is focused on defining the rout each vehicle has to follow without exceeding its capacity (both in terms of cargo and availability of time). The rout is only completed when the vehicle returns to its origin. This routing problem is known as the Vehicle Routing Problem (VRP) and was initially introduced by Dantzig and Ramser [19]. Among these, the improvement heuristic from [20, 21], VRPH, applicable using the program made available by [28], is a very recent one in terms of the heuristic techniques it uses. This metaheuristic can perform several types of local research in the vicinity of initial solutions generated by the heuristic of Clark and Wright [22] and also to the diversification of solutions, returning, in the end, the best solution found. Because it is a heuristic improvement process, the routes obtained by VRPH are at least as good as Clarke and Wright's. VRPH also provides routes for VRP in which not only vehicle capacity constraints are considered but also maximum distance ones for each vehicle.

Research has mostly been focused on cost reduction, basically on finding the best fleet size see, for instance, [11, 23], or identifying the best route for a specific case see, for instance, [24, 25].

The required trade-off within the logistics attributes [5] and the influence the transportation option has on the company's competitive position in the market have not been the focus of much research. In fact, not much has been published in this area, and even the "make-or-buy" decision is mostly based on cost, as argued by Coase [26], even if service quality is also mentioned see, for instance, [27].

Although the use of private fleets was mentioned in the past as the option to obtain lower costs or higher service levels than the ones available from for-hire carriers, the development of logistics service providers reduced, and most times even eliminated, the relevance of the argument. Nonetheless, arguments in favour of keeping private fleets remain, as long as they are properly supervised in terms of the costs they implicate, as the value it can bring in terms of customer satisfaction and visibility is of a strategic nature [6], but not much research is focused on customer service using cost as a relevant but secondary concern.

3 Methodology

3.1 Scenarios

In order to access the most adjusted solution for the company's fleet, several scenarios were developed and compared. These were developed based not only on the scenario the Company is considering (Scenario 2) but also on taking into account other possible solutions (Scenarios 3 and 4). They are as follows:

- Scenario 1 – Company's current situation: self-owned fleet composed of one 24.5 tons vehicle and two 16.5 tons vehicles, and outsourcing deliveries are performed whenever this fleet is insufficient. With this scenario, the current company costs are evaluated (it is the reference scenario).
- Scenario 2 – Solution proposed by the Company: a new 24.5 tons vehicle substitutes the two 16.5 tons vehicles, and outsourcing whenever needed. The company will consequently have two 24.5 tons vehicles. The age of the two 16.5 tons vehicles, which will reach their lifespan in the medium term, motivates this scenario.
- Scenario 3 – Reduce the self-owned fleet: discard the two 16.5 tons vehicles, keeping the 24.5 tons vehicle, and outsourcing when needed. The present Portuguese economic situation and forecasts about the end life of the two 16.5 tons vehicles substantiate this scenario.
- Scenario 4 – Full outsourcing of deliveries: discard all the self-owned fleet. Many companies have been increasingly outsourcing their transportation needs, which explains this scenario.

The age of the current vehicles of the company is shown in Table 1.

Table 1. Characterization of the fleet

Vehicle	Age (years)
16.5 tons (1)	24
16.5 tons (2)	22
24.5 tons	8

3.2 Steps in the Analysis

This study was developed considering the company's consignment notes for a full year associated with products delivered from its factory warehouse. Additionally, and in order to access qualitative information, informal interviews with the manufacturing director and the transportation operations coordinator were conducted. This initial phase allowed evaluating the company's customer service policy and competitive positioning.

In the second phase, and according to the objectives of the research, the aim was to determine individual customer demand for each day of the year and their delivery location based on the collected data. All the outsourced deliveries of bulk products or products transported by the customer were excluded from the analysis as they do not occupy the fleet under analysis.

Daily routes were determined for each scenario, minimizing transportation costs. The heuristic method VRPH [20, 21, 28] was used to deal with the limited capacity of the vehicles and the legal driving times allowed. The vehicle routes planning started running the interface GenRoutes for 24.5 tons vehicles since the VRPH heuristic determines trips for the VRP, which assumes homogeneous capacity vehicles. Thus, for each day, initial vehicle trips not exceeding 24.5 tons nor 1080 km were obtained (this last limit is detailed in the next sub-chapter).

As a result of this planning, for each scenario, day and vehicle, the number of trips performed, the delivered quantity and the travelled distance (in kilometres) were obtained. Then, based on this information, the total cost related to each scenario was computed, taking into account the associated fixed and variables costs, the purchase vehicle costs (when applied), and the outsourcing costs. All data needed to compute the referred costs was made available by the company.

Finally, in order to accomplish the objective of this research, the advantages and disadvantages of each scenario are outlined according to the established criteria, namely the cost and customer service policy.

3.3   Data Collection and Treatment

This study was conducted considering the Company's deliveries for one full year. Completion of deliveries was assumed for the day they were actually delivered, i.e., the possibility to fulfil the delivery after that day was not considered. According to the company, this year is a good representation of its current delivery level. All the data needed to be was registered in Microsoft Excel worksheets. This included, for each delivery: document number; order date; deliver date and time; vehicle registry; customer name and address; delivery place; products details: reference, description, and quantities.

Data was then summarized regarding its usage by the VRPH software to determine the daily vehicle routes. For each day, this included the identification of the customers to serve (identification of customer and delivery location) and the demand level in kilograms. It was also considered:

- a matrix with the distances between all pairs of delivery locations, including the production center (based on a distance matrix between all pairs of councils);
- legal driving times per day;
- data for each vehicle (average velocity and maximum cargo weight per trip).

The 9 h driving time per day and per driver agreement between the Company and its drivers were converted into kilometres assuming a 60 km/h average driving time, resulting in a maximum of 540 km per driver per day. However, since two drivers are available for each type of vehicle and adding the fact that they may perform trips together, twice of 540 km were considered, as it is used by the company, resulting in 1080 km per day per type of vehicle.

Products can be divided into two categories regarding shape, volume and weight, with consequences in its packaging solutions for distribution purposes. One product category considers homogeneous products, which are high-density products disposed of in standard pallets; the other category considers heterogeneous products, which are low weight and small size ones, and these have a residual volume per delivery.

Almost all products distributed are from the homogeneous category. Their high density suggests that vehicles' weight capacity is reached before the cargo volume limit. Furthermore, these are good stability and easy handling products.

On the contrary, heterogeneous products are residual in terms of volume per order. Adding to this, the fact that they are low weighted and small-sized leads them to have no significant impact on cargo weight and volume. In practice, the Company places these small bags manually on the top of the pallets of homogeneous products. This motivated the exclusion of the heterogeneous products from the analysis.

3.4 Costs

In order to evaluate the total cost associated with each scenario, the following information was obtained from the Company:

- fixed costs of each vehicle: driver, insurance;
- variable costs of each vehicle: fuel, tolls, and maintenance and repair;
- outsourcing prices;
- acquisition cost of a 24.5 tons vehicle, in the conditions the Company would be willing to acquire it – second-hand vehicle but in good conditions.

The costs for 2017 were assumed. For the variables costs, the 2017 costs were actualized from the real costs in 2015. Increases of 41% in cost for fuel, 3% for tolls, and 5.15% for maintenance and repair were considered, based on the information obtained, respectively, from the Portuguese National Council for Energy and Geology, from the company running the highways in Portugal, and the National Institute of Statistics.

3.5 MatLab Interface to Generate Daily Routs

An interface software GenRoutes was developed using the MatLab programming language to generate daily trips. First, GenRoutes reads all the data collected in the excel files. Afterwards, for each day, GenRoutes calls the VRPH software. VRPH produces the trips for that day, and GenRoutes writes that solution to an excel file.

3.6 Vehicle Route Planning for Each Scenario

On a daily basis, each vehicle may perform a route not exceeding the legal driving time. This route is composed of one or several trips, each of them not exceeding the vehicle's weight capacity. Each trip must start and end at the production centre and may visit one or more customers.

Each of the 16.5 tons vehicles may perform one shift a day, since one driver is allocated to each, whereas the 24.5 tons vehicle may execute two shifts a day, due to the two drivers allocated to it. It is worth to point out that the allocation of drivers to vehicles is flexible.

The cost evaluation for each scenario is based on its routes planning. For each scenario, the fleet characteristics are considered, namely the number of vehicles and their weight capacities.

The vehicle routes planning started running the GenRoutes interface, considering a weight capacity limit of 24.5 tons and a maximum of 1080 km per trip. Thus, for each day, initial vehicle trips not exceeding 24.5 tons nor 1080 km were obtained. Afterwards, these trips were used to define, for each day, the routes planning for the Company's own fleet in each scenario, as described hereafter.

For each scenario and day, and taking the number of vehicles and their capacities into account, the steps carried out were:

1. allocate the initial trips to the vehicles, as far as 1080 km length is not exceeded for each vehicle. The deliveries not allocated to any vehicle are outsourced;
2. identify the trips, the weight quantity delivered and the kilometres associated with each vehicle, as well as the weight quantity delivered by outsourcing;
3. determine the cost per trip and the outsourcing cost.

- Scenario 1 – Company's current situation (one 24.5 tons vehicle, and two 16.5 tons vehicles): the initial trips are allocated to the 24.5 tons vehicle, as far as the 1080 km length is not exceeded. The deliveries not allocated to this vehicle have then to be allocated to 16.5 tons vehicles. Thus, GenRoutes is run again, now for the remaining deliveries and assuming 16.5 tons of weight capacity and 1080 km of length. This followed literature recommendation [16], for cases with heterogeneous vehicles;
- Scenario 2 – Situation proposed by the Company: a new 24.5 tons vehicle substitutes the two 16.5 tons vehicles, and outsourcing whenever needed. The age of the two 16.5 tons vehicles, expecting its end life in medium future, motivated this scenario. Procedures were performed as for Scenario 1, but only for the two 24.5 tons vehicles. Cargo exceeding the weight capacity of these vehicles or the 1080 km limit in the distance was considered for outsourcing.
- Scenario 3 – Reduce the self-owned fleet: discard the two 16.5 tons vehicles, keeping the 24.5 tons vehicle, and outsourcing when needed. The present economic world situation and forecasts about the end life of the two 16.5 tons vehicles substantiate this scenario. Procedures were conducted as for scenario 1 except for its second part (the allocation to the 16.5 tons vehicles, as they do not exist in this scenario).
- Scenario 4 – Totally outsource deliveries: discard all the self-owned fleet. Many companies have been increasing outsourcing their transportation needs, which explains this scenario. Costs considered based on the prices the outsourcing companies offered.

4   Case Study Analysis

4.1   Customer Service Criteria

Despite being the only plaster manufacturing company in the country, other payers share this market and the Company directly competes with other companies. The Company thus reinforces customer service and product quality as a means to obtain the customer's preference.

The Company uses the following criteria in its internal policy:

- price per deliver: varies depending on the delivery zone;
- minimum dispatched quantities: one pallet;
- maximum response times: two working days for complete cargos, and 5–7 working days otherwise;
- cargo occupancy rate: minimum of 70%, with exceptions for small distances or special customers, but with no less than 50% occupancy rate;
- incoterms: the Company assumes the responsibility for the products until they arrive at the customer, supporting loss and damage costs, except for outsourcing.

As competition is fierce in this type of business and unplanned deliveries due to last minute request are usual, the Company also wants to have the ability to fulfil these orders. Consequently, the 70% vehicle occupancy rate is relevant for the Company.

4.2   Product Delivery

Due to the irregularity of the ordered quantities and customers locations, vehicle routs have to be planed daily. Presently, routes are derived based on the professional experience of the transports operations manager. Figure 1 presents examples of daily routes.

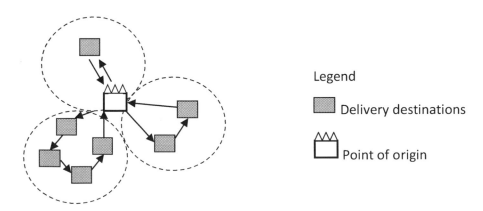

Fig. 1. Current rout types performed by the company

4.3   Findings

Taking into consideration the criteria previously defined, the results for each scenario under analyses, specified per vehicle (or outsourcing), number of kilometres per year, tons carried per year, variable fixed and total cost are shown in Table 2.

Each scenario was also analyzed in terms of the average occupancy rates of the vehicles so that the flexibility of the solution and its consequent impact on customer service quality might be assessed. The average occupancy rates per vehicle in each scenario are shown in Fig. 2.

Table 2. Total annual cost per scenario

Vehicles	Kms travelled	Quantity transported (tons)	Variable cost (€)	Fixed cost (€)	Total cost (€)
Scenario 1 - Company's current situation					
24.5 tons	112,823	6,526	85,420	41,744	127,164
16.5 tons	110,168	5,163	43,532	40,006	83,538
Outsourcing	13,680	1,220	36,681	–	36,681
Total annual cost (€)			165,634	81,750	247,384
Scenario 2 - Solution proposed by the company					
24.5 tons	238,421	12,586	149,354	91,202	240,556
16.5 tons	n.a.	n.a.	n.a.	n.a.	n.a.
Outsourcing	4,446	323,000	7,564	–	7,564
Total annual cost (€)			156,918	91,202	248,120
Scenario 3 - Reduce self-owned fleet					
24.5 tons	177,822	10,356	113,298	41,744	155,042
16.5 tons	n.a.	n.a.	n.a.	n.a.	n.a.
Outsourcing	34,656	2,553	97,687	–	97,687
Total annual cost (€)			210.985	41.744	252.730
Scenario 4 - Totally outsourced deliveries					
24.5 tons	n.a.	n.a.	n.a.	n.a.	n.a.
16.5 tons	n.a.	n.a.	n.a.	n.a.	n.a.
Outsourcing	141,219	12,909	369,659	–	369,659
Total annual cost (€)			369,659	–	369,659

(Legend: n.a. - not applicable)

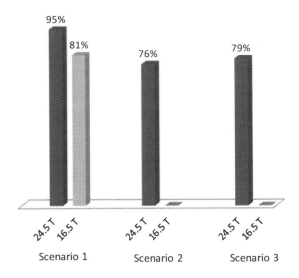

Fig. 2. Average vehicle occupancy rate in each scenario

5   Discussion

The analysis in Table 2 is solely based on cost. Nonetheless, the Company has a dual goal: reduce costs and provide good quality customer service, for which flexibility of the solution has to be taken into consideration when deciding which one is the most adjusted for the Company's present and future.

Although the tendency to outsource [5], Scenario 4 – totally outsourced deliveries, is the most expensive one with a cost 46.3% higher than the second most expensive scenario. Adding to the cost situation, this Scenario of total outsourcing, although allowing the Company to use a specialized company to perform delivery, prevents the company to contact the customer during product delivery directly and makes it lose control over the pipeline during transportation, therefore limiting customer service quality [5, 14]. Both arguments support that Scenario 4 should not be adopted by the Company.

If the decision was to be based solely on costs, Scenario 1 – maintaining the current fleet solution, presents itself as the most economic, although Scenario 2 – selling the two small vehicles and purchasing a new 24 tons vehicle, shows almost the same level of cost. In fact, Scenario 2 is only about 0.3% more expensive than the first one, but it involves the purchase of a new vehicle that requires less maintenance and downtime. At the same time, according to (Legend: n.a. - not applicable), Scenario 2 provides the company with lower vehicle occupancy rates, with is to say that it has more flexibility to receive urgent orders and fulfil them immediately. Scenario 1 is based on three vehicles, two of which are old and more probable to breakdown. As so, Scenario 2 is preferable to Scenario 1, allowing more consistent on-time deliveries and a larger capacity buffer for urgent deliveries.

Taking into consideration the decrease in construction activity in Europe due not only to the economic crisis but also the fact that it is said that in Portugal a new crisis may emerge shortly, investing in new vehicles might seem like a risk. As so, Scenario 3, of keeping only the 24 tons vehicle, might present itself as an intermediate solution while the crisis lasts. In fact, this Scenario is less than 2% more expensive than Scenario 2, but has the advantages of not requiring immediate investment in a new vehicle and keeping similar buffer capacity (see Fig. 2) as Scenario 2, allowing flexibility for urgent orders. At the same time, it shows more dependency of outsourced companies, but it can be considered as a lesser evil during this uncertain economic period when compared to the need to invest in new equipment.

6   Conclusion

This case study is based on the request from a specific company from the construction industry that has undertaken the challenges of the economic crisis and wanted to find a better fleet solution that would not only allow it to keep distribution cost low but also to fulfil demanding customer service criteria in terms of flexibility and on-time deliveries.

Taking into consideration the previous discussion, Scenario 3 – keeping a single 24 tons vehicle, is recommended for the Company as the Scenario to be implemented immediately, but Scenario 2 – purchasing an additional 24 tons vehicle, should be considered in the future when the construction industry starts to show recovery from the Economic crisis. Consequently, this article provides contribute to practice.

Although much research has been conducted on the fleet cost minimization (see for instance, [11, 23]) or route optimization (see, for instance, [24, 25]), this research aimed for a gap in literature in which not only the cost perspective is considered but also the quality of the service provided is taken into consideration. As so, this articles also contribute to literature.

As a single company was analyzed, findings cannot be generalized to other companies [13]. Nonetheless, it would be interesting that similar research is conducted in other companies that run their own transportation fleet to access if the findings from the present research are only applicable to the analyzed Company or in fact, they show a tendency that when contact with the final customer is relevant costs might be overruled.

Acknowledgments. This work is supported by National Funding from FCT - Fundação para a Ciência e a Tecnologia, under the project: UID/MAT/04561/2019.

References

1. CSCMP (2014). http://cscmp.org/. Accessed 23 Jan 2014
2. Porter, M.: Competitive Advantage. The Free Press, New York (1985)
3. Poist, R.F.: Evolution of conceptual approaches to designing business logistics systems. Transp. J. **26**(1), 55–64 (1986)
4. Christopher, M.: Logistics and Supply Chain Management – Creating Value Adding Networks, 4th edn. Financial Times – Prentice Hall, Upper Saddle River (2011)

5. Rushton, A., Croucher, P., Baker, P.: The Handbook of Logistics and Distribution Management, 4th edn. Kogan Page Limited, London (2010)
6. Pitt, B., Reiss, M., Hirsch, S.: Private fleet management: from necessary evil to strategic asset. Logistics Management, November 2011
7. List, G.F., et al.: Robust optimization for fleet planning under uncertainty. Transp. Res. Part E **39**, 209–227 (2003)
8. Lee, Y.H., Kim, J.I., Kang, K.H., Kim, K.H.: A heuristic for vehicle fleet mix problem using tabu search and set partitioning. J. Oper. Res. Soc. **59**, 833–841 (2008)
9. Potvin, J.Y., Naud, M.A.: Tabu search with ejection chains for the vehicle routing problem with private fleet and common carrier. J. Oper. Res. Soc. **62**, 326–336 (2011)
10. Dondo, R., Cerdá, J.: A cluster-based optimization approach for the multi-depot heterogeneous fleet vehicle routing problem with time windows. Eur. J. Oper. Res. **176**, 1478–1507 (2007)
11. Braysy, O., Dullaert, W., Hasle, G., Mester, D.: An effective multirestart deterministic annealing metaheuristic for the fleet size and mix vehicle-routing problem with time windows. Transp. Sci. **42**(3), 371–386 (2008)
12. Hritonenko, N., Yatsenko, Y.: Fleet replacement under technological shocks. Ann. Oper. Res. **196**, 311–331 (2012)
13. Yin, R.: Case Study Research. Sage, Thousand Oaks (2009)
14. Christopher, M., Peck, H.: Marketing Logistics. Butterworth-Heinemann, Oxford (2003)
15. Bowersox, D.J., Closs, D.J., Cooper, M.B.: Supply Chain Logistics Management, 3rd edn. McGraw-Hill, New York (2010)
16. Ballou, R.: Business Logistics/Supply Chain Management. Pearson Prentice Hall, New Jersey (2004)
17. Toth, P., Vigo, D.: The Vehicle Routing Problem. SIAM Monographs on Discrete Mathematics and Applications. Society for Industrial and Applied Mathematics, Philadelphia (2002)
18. Golden, B., Raghavan, S., Wasil, E.: The Vehicle Routing Problem. Springer, Heidelberg (2008). https://doi.org/10.1007/978-0-387-77778-8
19. Dantzig, G.B., Ramser, J.H.: The truck dispatching problem. Manag. Sci. **6**, 80–91 (1959)
20. Groer, C.: Parallel and serial algorithms for vehicle routing problems. Ph.D. thesis, University of Maryland, USA (2008)
21. Groer, C., Golden, B., Wasil, E.: A library for local search heuristics for vehicle routing problem. Math. Program. Comput. **2**, 79–101 (2010)
22. Clarke, G., Wright, J.R.: Scheduling of vehicle routing problem from a central depot to a number of delivery points. Oper. Res. **12**, 568–581 (1964). https://doi.org/10.1287/opre.12.4.568
23. Huang, S.-H., Yang, T.-H., Tang, C.-H.: Fleet size determination for a truckload distribution center. J. Adv. Transp. **48**, 377–389 (2014)
24. Hassold, S., Ceder, A.: Public transport vehicle scheduling featuring multiple vehicle types. Transp. Res. Part B **67**, 129–143 (2014)
25. Laporte, G.: The vehicle-routing problem – an overview of exact and approximate algorithms. Eur. J. Oper. Res. **59**(3), 345–358 (1992)
26. Coase, R.: The nature of the firm. Economica **4**(16), 386–405 (1937)
27. Hall, R.W., Racer, M.: Transportation with common carrier and private fleets – system assignment and shipment frequency optimization. IIE Trans. **27**(2), 217–225 (1995)
28. Groer, C.: VRPH software (2010). http://sitesGoogle.com/sites/vrphlibrary

Challenges in Object Detection Under Rainy Weather Conditions

Sinan Hasirlioglu[1,2(✉)] and Andreas Riener[1,2]

[1] Technische Hochschule Ingolstadt, CARISSMA, 85049 Ingolstadt, Germany
Sinan.Hasirlioglu@carissma.eu
[2] Johannes Kepler University Linz, 4040 Linz, Austria
http://www.carissma.eu

Abstract. Intelligent vehicles use surround sensors which perceive their environment and therefore enable automatic vehicle control. As already small errors in sensor data measurement and interpretation could lead to severe accidents, future object detection algorithms must function safely and reliably. However, adverse weather conditions, illustrated here using the example of rain, attenuate the sensor signals and thus limit sensor performance. The indoor rain simulation facility at CARISSMA enables reproducible measurements of predefined scenarios under varying conditions of rain. This simulator is used to systematically investigate the effects of rain on camera, lidar, and radar sensor data. This paper aims at (1) comparing the performance of simple object detection algorithms under clear weather conditions, (2) visualizing/discussing the direct negative effects of the same algorithms under adverse weather conditions, and (3) summarizing the identified challenges and pointing out future work.

Keywords: Object detection · Camera · Lidar · Radar · Perception · Rain · Adverse weather condition · Vehicle safety · Autonomous driving

1 Introduction

Active and integral safety systems rely on data given by surround sensors such as camera, lidar, and radar. Using the obtained information, control systems can take over forward and sideways guidance of vehicles in order to assist the driving task or to prevent imminent accidents. These systems could thus be regarded as precursors on the way to autonomous driving. However, each surround sensor has limited capabilities under certain circumstances, especially under adverse weather conditions [11,12]. Water droplets in the air cause scattering and absorption effects and limit sensor performance. Note that incorrect detections and classifications increase the risk of an accident.

Each sensor type outputs raw data with different physical unit and quantity. In this work, we focus on images of camera sensors, point clouds of lidar sensors,

© ICST Institute for Computer Sciences, Social Informatics and Telecommunications Engineering 2019
Published by Springer Nature Switzerland AG 2019. All Rights Reserved
J. C. Ferreira et al. (Eds.): INTSYS 2018, LNICST 267, pp. 53–65, 2019.
https://doi.org/10.1007/978-3-030-14757-0_5

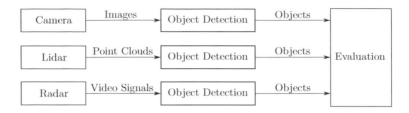

Fig. 1. Procedure for investigating the weather effects on object detection algorithms. Each surround sensor type is analyzed individually.

and video signals of radar sensors. Figure 1 shows the general procedure for investigating weather effects on object level. The effects are sensor specific and must be investigated individually.

Object detection algorithms process raw sensor data to detect objects in the surrounding. The camera algorithms used in this work output bounding boxes with corresponding classification scores. In case of lidar, the algorithms group points into ground plane and obstacles. Lastly, the radar algorithms detect objects when the received intensity exceeds an adaptive threshold value.

Outline

This paper aims to present challenges under rainy conditions. Object detection algorithms that process data from two identical scenarios with various weather conditions are investigated. Even minor changes in sensor data can lead to major challenges in the detection task. Therefore, testing algorithms under adverse weather conditions is mandatory to ensure safe autonomous driving.

This paper is organized as follows. Section 2 gives an overview on related work done in the field of object detection under adverse weather conditions. Further, Sect. 3 describes the experimental setup and used object detection algorithms for each sensor type. Section 4 discusses the results and challenges under rainy conditions where Sect. 5 presents the scientific contribution of this paper.

2   Related Work

In this section, we will present the related work with focus on object detection under adverse weather conditions. Today, the robustness is mainly tested in clear weather conditions, while only little research is focusing on adverse conditions.

2.1   Camera

Garg and Nayar published several works about the effects of rain on camera. In [5], a geometric and photometric model for refraction and reflection from a single raindrop was presented. It was shown that raindrops redirect light from a large field of view (approx. 165°). Therefore, the brightness of raindrops does not depend absolutely on their background. However, falling drops result in rain streaks which depend on their background and the exposure time of the camera

[6]. A method in order to reduce the effects of rain by setting the camera parameters (exposure time, F-number, distance of the focal plane) was presented in [7]. More practical work was presented by Duthon et al. [2] in which they generated artificial rain in the laboratory and investigated the impact of rain by using the Harris Corner Detector. The authors showed that lower rain intensities (approx. 40 mm/h) has nearly no influence on the Harris feature, whereas higher intensities (approx. 130 mm/h) strongly impact the feature. The authors in [12] showed that raindrops lead to increasing mean intensity of the image and decreasing contrast, where the rain conditions are also generated by a rain simulator.

This work focuses on the influence of rain on object detection, in which we investigate the detection (based on histogram of oriented gradients (HOG) features) and classification (based on AlexNet) separately.

2.2   Lidar

Wojtanowski et al. [19] showed that the impact of atmospheric extinction on lidar is much more crucial than the impact of surface wetness. The light propagating through the medium of rain gets strongly attenuated which drastically decreases the sensor performance. Rasshofer et al. [15] showed that water drop reflections could result in false positive scan points, especially in the near field (<10 m). By using an indoor rain simulator, they investigated the maximum detection range with different target reflectivities, sensors, and rain intensities. The higher the rain intensity and the lower the target reflectivity, the shorter the detection range. The authors in [12] showed that in case of high rain intensity the false positives dominate which may hide the object completely. Using the multi echo technology, object points can still be detected but with drastically decreased intensity. Note that the sensor behavior is strongly hardware-dependent, due to the fact that internal signal processing is unknown.

This paper focuses on the influence of rain on the clustering process of standard algorithms and presents additional challenging secondary effects.

2.3   Radar

The influence of rain on automotive radar sensors have been studied in [13], where a reduction of the millimeter-wave signal can be observed. An electromagnetic wave traveling through rain will be absorbed, depolarized, scattered, and delayed in time. Unlike lidar sensor, strong performance degradation can be detected when a water film covers the radome. Gourova et al. [8] presented experimental data of a standard automotive radar sensor and demonstrated the detectability of strong rain, generated with a rain simulator. They conclude that raindrops are especially visible in the near field (2–3 m). The authors in [12] showed that the radar cross section values of surrounding objects decrease in rainy scenarios and can lead to incorrect classification.

In this work, we focus on the influence of rain on adaptive threshold algorithms, that are used for detecting objects based on the received intensity.

3   Materials and Methods

In this section, we present the experimental setup used for gathering data from surround sensors and the object detection algorithms.

3.1   Experimental Setup

Measurements are performed in the CARISSMA test facility which is equipped with an indoor rain simulator capable of simulating various intensities and drop size distributions over a length of 50 m. Rain is generated by different full cone nozzle combinations. For this work, a rain intensity of 100 mm/h is selected to make the effects clearly visible.

The sensor setup is placed in front of the rain simulator due to the fact that not all sensors are waterproof. The images are recorded by an uEye camera (U3-3250LE-C-HQ) with a resolution of 1.92 MP and a 6 mm focal length lens. Lidar measurements are performed using a Velodyne VLP-16 sensor, which outputs a point cloud with 16 layers. The video signals are output of the Inras RDL-77G-TX2RX16 radar. We set the sweep bandwidth to 300 MHz and the ramp slope to 10 MHz/μs, which results in a range resolution of 0.5 m. The measurements are performed with and without rain. For reproducible results, we use a standardized Euro NCAP Vehicle Target (EVT) [16] which is placed at a distance of 10 m from the sensors without a lateral offset. This setup is imitating an urban car-following scenario. Figure 2 shows the test area in both conditions without a target. Further, it is assumed that the rain is distributed uniformly in the sensor's field of view.

Fig. 2. CARISSMA test facility with an indoor rain simulator that enables measurements from identical scenarios with various weather conditions. The full cone nozzles produce many small water drops which lead to decreased visibility. It is assumed that the rain is distributed uniformly in the sensor's field of view.

3.2   Object Detection Based on Camera

In this work, objects are detected in images by combining a cascade object detector [18] based on HOG features [1] with a pre-trained AlexNet model [14]. The cascade object detector provides the bounding box which defines the region of interest (ROI) for the classification based on AlexNet. Figure 3 shows the result of object detection and classification under clear conditions. The camera output is cropped to the size of 640×480 pixels.

Fig. 3. Detection using a cascade object detector based on HOG (left) and classification based on AlexNet model (right), which results in a score of 0.89.

Cascade object detection is a machine learning approach, in which a HOG-based object detector is trained by a set of positive and negative images. In this work, we provided 233 positive images of rear views of different vehicles and 380 negative images without vehicles. Training the cascade detector is applied in form of simple stages where each stage is considered to be a weak learner. Each stage is trained by using all provided positive samples and a part of the negative image set. More negative samples are automatically generated from detections in the provided negative images. In this way, each new stage will be trained to correct mistakes done by previous stages, which results in a robust detector at the end. We defined 50 stages and 50% false positive rate to achieve our results.

For classification, a transfer learning on AlexNet neural network is implemented, which is an approach to reuse a pre-trained model or network and customize it for another task. The pre-trained AlexNet model has been trained on more than a million images and can classify 1000 object categories [14]. Relevant objects in traffic scenarios are obstacles such as vehicles, pedestrians, or traffic signs. Via transfer learning, the newly created model will classify only these relevant objects. The final three layers of the model use features extracted from the initial layers for classification. Therefore, only weight values of the final layers are tuned, whereas those of the initial layers are constant.

3.3   Object Detection Based on Lidar

Lidar sensors provide position and signal strength (intensity) information of each single scan point of the point cloud. In this paper, we focus on two basic algorithms that process position information. The ground plane segmentation is based on a variant of the random sample consensus (RANSAC) [4,17], whereas the clustering is based on a density-based algorithm.

The ground plane detection algorithm groups data into inliers and outliers where the former one is determined by a chosen model. Here, we used the z-plane as model input to determine the ground plane and subtract it from the original point cloud. Therefore, a new point cloud is generated containing only obstacle scan points. Note that the segmentation process in complex real world scenarios is more challenging due to up and down gradients of the roads.

Clustering of lidar scan points into objects or obstacles is performed using the density-based spatial clustering of applications with noise (DBSCAN) algorithm [3], which groups points that are close to each other based on a distance measure (e.g., Euclidean distance) and minimum number of points. The algorithm marks points, which are not in dense regions as outliers. Figure 4 shows the results under clear weather conditions.

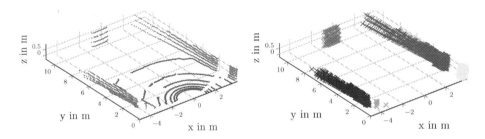

Fig. 4. Point cloud after ground plane segmentation (left) and clustering (right). The multi-layer lidar sensor detects the target vehicle with four layers, which are clustered correctly and highlighted in pink. (Color figure online)

The left image shows the segmented point cloud, where the magenta points belong to the ground plane and the green points to objects and obstacles in the surrounding. The image on the right side shows the results of the clustering process, where all green points from the left image are divided into groups and marked with different colors. It can be seen that the algorithms perform well under clear weather conditions. All ground reflections are detected and separated from the initial point cloud. The target object is clustered clearly and highlighted in pink. The remaining clusters originate from the barriers (see Fig. 2).

3.4   Object Detection Based on Radar

This work focuses on object detection based on reflected intensity from surrounding objects. In addition to direct target reflections, the sensor receives reflections from unwanted objects (also called clutter). Adaptive threshold algorithms based on different constant false alarm rate (CFAR) techniques are implemented for filtering unwanted signals and detecting objects of interest. We focus on cell averaging (CA-CFAR), cell averaging smallest of (CASO-CFAR), cell averaging greatest of (CAGO-CFAR), and order statistic (OS-CFAR) methods.

In CFAR systems, target decisions are performed using the sliding window technique, where the data of a reference window enter an algorithm for calculating the decision threshold T based on clutter power Z and scaling factor S. For estimating Z, the sliding window is split into leading and lagging part. CA-CFAR uses the average of the averaged two parts as the clutter power Z. CASO-CFAR and CAGO-CFAR combine the neighboring parts by selecting the minimum (CASO) or the maximum (CAGO). The OS-CFAR method sorts all cells inside the sliding window in ascending order and selects one certain value as Z. A more detailed overview is given in [9] and [10]. The results based on the radar output can be seen in Fig. 5.

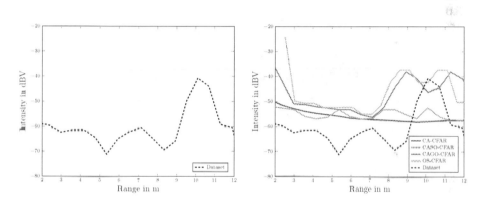

Fig. 5. Video signal under clear conditions, in which the target is positioned at a distance of 10 m (left) and the corresponding CFAR thresholds (right).

The left image shows the video signal in clear weather conditions. It can be seen that the target object at a distance of 10 m causes the highest reflections. The remaining reflections are considered as clutter. The image on the right side shows the result of the object detection based on CFAR algorithms. The sliding window size is chosen as N = 6 and the scaling factor as 0.85. For OS-CFAR, the reference cell value is chosen as 5th maximum. All CFAR techniques can detect the target vehicle. Note that a lower threshold can lead to closer object position.

4 Experimental Results and Discussion

In this section, we present the influences of rain on object detection algorithms, introduced in the previous section, and discuss potential challenges.

4.1   Camera

The results of the object detection can be seen in Fig. 6. The left image shows the detection without rain with a classification score of 0.89. The image on the right shows the detection with rain, where the score is decreased by 21%. Further, it can be seen that the bounding box is shifted to the left by 13 pixels and increased in size by 6%. Note that incorrect position or size estimations can lead to incorrect crash severity predictions. If the target is placed at a distance of 30 m, the algorithms detect exclusively false positives for both conditions, as they are classified by the AlexNet model as background. Hence, raindrops have a direct negative influence on image features and therefore on the object detection task.

Fig. 6. Object detection without rain (left) and with rain (right). The score decreases from 0.89 to 0.70. The bounding box is shifted to the left by 13 pixels and covers a 6% larger region.

For a more in-depth analysis, we visualize the distribution of oriented gradients under both weather conditions. It is known, that rain decreases the image contrast and creates blurry effects. Figure 7 shows the histograms of the gray scaled images of the target vehicle without (left) and with (right) rain. The ROI is limited to the vehicle region. The channels spread over 0 to 180° using nine bins. It can be seen that the gradient magnitudes decrease drastically and result in a new histogram shape. The total magnitude (sum of all bins) decreases under rainy conditions by 49%, which originates from smaller intensity changes around edges and corners. It can therefore be concluded that rainy conditions affect raw sensor data and limit the general sensor performance.

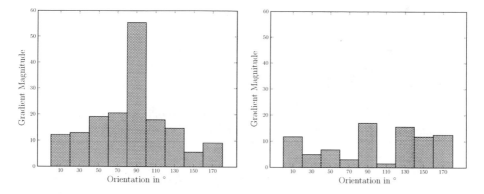

Fig. 7. Comparison of HOG histograms in clear (left) and rainy (right) conditions. The bins represent nine orientation angles. The total magnitude decreases in rainy conditions by 49%.

4.2 Lidar

Rainy conditions are directly related to falling water drops and wet ground. The left image in Fig. 8 shows the direct influence of rain on the lidar measurement. The number of target vehicle scan points decreases by only 4%. However, some transmitted light beams are deflected by the wet ground plane and form a mirror image of the target vehicle below the ground. Therefore, an object at a distance of 10 m is detected with 8 layers. This effect also occurs in images of camera sensors in a weakened form (see image on the right of Fig. 6). Note that false positive scan points, due to ground reflections, lead to missing ground plane points. False positive scan points can also originate from falling drop reflections, which are mainly visible in the near field.

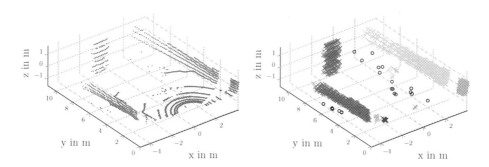

Fig. 8. Point cloud under rainy conditions including ground plane segmentation (left) and clustering (right). Raindrop reflections can lead to false positive clusters, whereby ground reflections can form a mirror image of the target vehicle. (Color figure online)

The image on the right side of Fig. 8 shows the result of clustering in rainy conditions. The ground reflections cause a mirror image whose scan points are close to the real target reflections. Therefore, the algorithm clusters these points to one object which is highlighted in red. The size is increased to about twice. Moreover, falling drop reflections can also be close to each other and result in clusters. Two false positive objects can be detected between sensor and target vehicle. The majority of the raindrops reflections are detected as noise.

Further, rainy conditions affect the intensity of scan points. Absorption and scattering processes reduce the amount of power, which is backscattered to the receiver. Figure 9 illustrates different histograms under clear and adverse weather conditions to show the influence in detail. Note that the intensity value depends on the incident angle. A small angle to the vertical means that the intensity value is likely to be higher in comparison to a large angle.

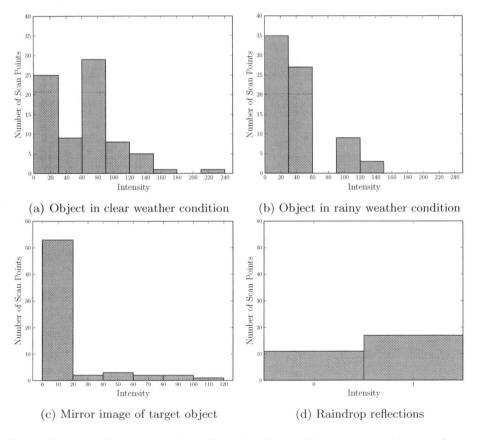

(a) Object in clear weather condition

(b) Object in rainy weather condition

(c) Mirror image of target object

(d) Raindrop reflections

Fig. 9. Intensity histograms of specific point clouds. The intensity of target object reflections in clear weather condition is represented in (a). Rain leads to decreasing object intensity (b), low intensity mirror image below the ground (c), and low intensity raindrop reflections (d).

The intensity histogram of the target vehicle under clear conditions shows a wide range due to varying incident angles (see Fig. 9(a)). In case of rain, the intensities decrease and the bars are shifted to the left (Fig. 9(b)). The resulting mirror image contains mainly scan points with low intensities, but also some points with higher intensities (see Fig. 9(c)). The falling water drop reflections are limited to values between 0 and 1 (Fig. 9(d)). Therefore, a simple intensity-based filtering is associated with loosing true positive scan points. It can be concluded that rain leads to challenging segmentation and clustering tasks.

4.3 Radar

Raindrops scatter the transmitted wave back to the sensor which is visible in the measured video signal. Figure 10 shows the received signal and adaptive thresholds under clear and adverse weather conditions.

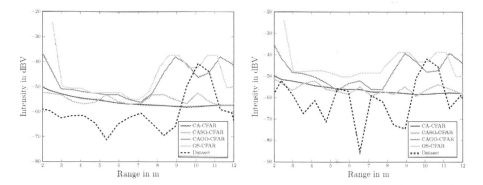

Fig. 10. Video signal (black dotted line) and different CFAR threshold values under clear (left) and rainy (right) conditions.

The left image shows the measured video signal (black dotted line) and the performance of different CFAR algorithms in clear conditions, where the image on the right shows the performance in rainy conditions. It can be seen that the video signal in rainy conditions has higher intensity in the near field which decreases with distance. The object reflection decreases by 1.23 dB due to extinction caused by water particles, but can be neglected in this work.

In clear conditions, all algorithms can detect the target object at 10 m precisely. The increased near field reflections under rain lead to changes in threshold values. CASO-CFAR detects a false positive object at a distance of approx. 2.5 m. At a distance of approx. 5 m CASO-CFAR, CAGO-CFAR, and CA-CFAR output incorrect detections. Further, CASO-CFAR detects two more false positive objects at distances of approx. 6 and 7 m. The target object is visible for each algorithm. The OS-CFAR performs best without any false detections. Hence, it can be concluded that adaptive threshold algorithms have possibilities of false detections in non-homogeneous environment (with more clutter peaks).

5   Conclusion

Intelligent safety systems are reliant on data from surround sensors such as camera, lidar, and radar. Using this information, control systems can take over the forward and sideways guidance of vehicles in order to assist the driver or to prevent imminent accidents. It is known that sensor signals suffer much attenuation while propagating through the atmosphere, especially under adverse weather conditions. This paper presents the influence of rain on basic object detection algorithms for camera, lidar, and radar sensors. Initial static tests show that each sensor can generate false positive objects due to changed weather condition. The problem is that incorrect environmental perception, especially in the area of integral safety, can result in incorrect actions and hence severe accidents.

Camera sensors suffer mainly from decreased gradient magnitudes, which result in changed position and size of the bounding boxes during the detection task. Further, the classification scores can decrease which represent the increasing uncertainty. Lidar sensors can generate false positive scan points or even false positive objects from raindrop reflections. Moreover, the wet ground can lead to deflections of the laser light which can result in mirror images below the ground. These effects increase the complexity of ground plane detection and scan point clustering. Radar sensors receive the backscattered waves from raindrops which lead to increased reflection intensities in the near field. Scattering and absorption processes result in decreased object intensity, which can be neglected within close distances. Changes in received intensity are associated with changes in threshold values, so that three of four algorithms under test generate false positive objects.

Future work includes the use of additional detection algorithms for all types of surround sensors. Furthermore, different objects enable the investigation of false classifications in detail. More in-depth analysis is intended by varying the rain intensity from low to extremely high. Finally, dynamic tests can increase the level of realism and include the benchmark of tracking algorithms.

Acknowledgment. We applied the SDC approach for the sequence of authors. The authors would like to thank the master students Al-Bahr Ayad Ameen Sadeq, Altinbas Selim, Intriz Ercan, Ladva Ronak Madhavji, Malaviya Ujval Jaysukhbhai, and Nguyen Huu Anh Huy for implementing the detection algorithms and analyzing the influences on object-level. This work is supported under the FH-Impuls program of the German Federal Ministry of Education and Research (BMBF) under Grant No. 13FH7I01IA.

References

1. Dalal, N., Triggs, B.: Histograms of oriented gradients for human detection. In: 2005 IEEE Computer Society Conference on Computer Vision and Pattern Recognition (CVPR 2005), pp. 886–893. IEEE (2005)
2. Duthon, P., Bernardin, F., Chausse, F., Colomb, M.: Methodology used to evaluate computer vision algorithms in adverse weather conditions. Transp. Res. Procedia **14**, 2178–2187 (2016)

3. Ester, M., Kriegel, H.P., Sander, J., Xu, X.: A density-based algorithm for discovering clusters a density-based algorithm for discovering clusters in large spatial databases with noise. In: Proceedings of the Second International Conference on Knowledge Discovery and Data Mining, KDD 1996, pp. 226–231. AAAI Press (1996)
4. Fischler, M.A., Bolles, R.C.: Random sample consensus: a paradigm for model fitting with applications to image analysis and automated cartography, vol. 24, pp. 381–395. ACM, New York (1981)
5. Garg, K., Nayar, S.K.: Photometric model of a rain drop. CMU Technical report (2003)
6. Garg, K., Nayar, S.K.: Detection and removal of rain from videos. In: Computer Vision and Pattern Recognition (2004)
7. Garg, K., Nayar, S.K.: Vision and rain. Int. J. Comput. Vis. **75**(1), 3–27 (2007)
8. Gourova, R., Krasnov, O., Yarovoy, A.: Analysis of rain clutter detections in commercial 77 GHz automotive radar. In: 2017 European Radar Conference EURAD, pp. 25–28 (2017)
9. Rohling, H.: Radar CFAR thresholding in clutter and multiple target situations. IEEE Trans. Aerosp. Electron. Syst. **AES–19**(4), 608–621 (1983)
10. Rohling, H.: Ordered statistic CFAR technique - an overview. In: 2011 12th International Radar Symposium (IRS), pp. 631–638 (2011)
11. Hasirlioglu, S., Doric, I., Kamann, A., Riener, A.: Reproducible fog simulation for testing automotive surround sensors. In: 2017 IEEE 85th Vehicular Technology Conference (VTC Spring), pp. 1–7. IEEE (2017)
12. Hasirlioglu, S., Kamann, A., Doric, I., Brandmeier, T.: Test methodology for rain influence on automotive surround sensors. In: 2016 IEEE 19th International Conference on Intelligent Transportation Systems (ITSC), pp. 2242–2247. IEEE (2016)
13. Hassen, A.A.: Indicators for the signal degradation and optimization of automotive radar sensors under adverse weather conditions: Zugl.: Darmstadt, Techn. Univ., Diss., 2006. Berichte aus der Hochfrequenztechnik, Shaker, Aachen (2007)
14. Krizhevsky, A., Sutskever, I., Hinton, G.E.: ImageNet classification with deep convolutional neural networks. In: Proceedings of the 25th International Conference on Neural Information Processing Systems - Volume 1, NIPS 2012. pp. 1097–1105. Curran Associates Inc., USA (2012)
15. Rasshofer, R.H., Spies, M., Spies, H.: Influences of weather phenomena on automotive laser radar systems. Adv. Radio Sci. **9**, 49–60 (2011)
16. Sandner, V.: Development of a test target for AEB systems. In: 23rd International Technical Conference on the Enhanced Safety of Vehicles (ESV): Research Collaboration to Benefit Safety of All Road Users (2013)
17. Torr, P., Zisserman, A.: MLESAC: a new robust estimator with application to estimating image geometry. Comput. Vis. Image Underst. **78**(1), 138–156 (2000)
18. Viola, P., Jones, M.: Rapid object detection using a boosted cascade of simple features. In: Proceedings of the 2001 IEEE Computer Society Conference on Computer Vision and Pattern Recognition, CVPR 2001. pp. I-511–I-518. IEEE (2001)
19. Wojtanowski, J., Zygmunt, M., Kaszczuk, M., Mierczyk, Z., Muzal, M.: Comparison of 905 nm and 1550 nm semiconductor laser rangefinders' performance deterioration due to adverse environmental conditions. Opto-Electron. Rev. **22**(3), 183–190 (2014)

Simulation and Testing of a Platooning Cooperative Longitudinal Controller

Vadym Hapanchak[(✉)], António Costa, Joaquim Macedo, Alexandre Santos,
Bruno Dias, M. João Nicolau, Bruno Ribeiro, Fábio Gonçalves,
Oscar Gama, and Paulo Araújo

Algoritmi Center, Department of Informatics, University of Minho,
Campus de Gualtar, 4710-057 Braga, Portugal
b7768@algoritmi.uminho.pt, {costa,macedo,alex,bruno.dias}@di.uminho.pt,
joao@dsi.uminho.pt, {b7214,b7207,b2583}@algoritmi.uminho.pt,
pjnaraujo@gmail.com
http://algoritmi.uminho.pt

Abstract. Previous studies have shown that the ITS solution called *platooning* allows the autonomous collaborative driving and can improve traffic safety and throughput. Traffic flow is optimized by Cooperative Adaptive Cruise Control (CACC), which allows for the automatic short-distance vehicle following, using inter-vehicle wireless communication in addition to onboard sensors. This paper presents the platooning vehicle longitudinal controller evaluation using simulation environment. The employed controller uses IEEE 802.11p technology for vehicle-to-vehicle (V2V) communications on Vehicular Ad hoc Network (VANET). To evaluate the CACC the Veins simulation framework was used and the complete simulation setup is described in this paper. The presented analysis expound the methodology to verify controller safety and stability characteristics within the different traffic scenarios and platooning maneuvers using the simulation.

Keywords: VANET Simulation · ITS · IVC · CACC · Platooning ·
Cooperative driving · IEEE 802.11p

1 Introduction

As the statistics show, the majority of the road fatal accidents occurs on high speed roads [Eurostat], and that makes focusing on improving vehicles and infrastructure safety for the high-speed traffic an important issue. In addition, the traffic congestion problem, caused by the increased number of vehicles, affects the efficiency of the road transportation system. To help solve these problems, a more efficient use of currently available means of transportation is needed. Therefore, the set of Intelligent Transportation Systems (ITS) solutions is proposed, that contributes to improving traffic flow stability and safety. One promising ITS

© ICST Institute for Computer Sciences, Social Informatics and Telecommunications Engineering 2019
Published by Springer Nature Switzerland AG 2019. All Rights Reserved
J. C. Ferreira et al. (Eds.): INTSYS 2018, LNICST 267, pp. 66–80, 2019.
https://doi.org/10.1007/978-3-030-14757-0_6

application that deals with traffic congestion, safety and fuel saving, is called *platooning*. The highway traffic is organized into groups of close-following vehicles: platoons. Platooning enables the vehicles to drive in groups at a small distance, autonomously and safely, following the leader vehicle, driven by a professional driver, that is able to lead the platoon [1,3,7]. This is a complex ITS application that is composed of two different parts, i.e. the vehicle control system and Inter-Vehicular Communication (IVC) system. The vehicle control, which allows for the automatic short-distance vehicle follow, is carried out by the Cooperative Adaptive Cruise Control (CACC) system. The CACC technology uses wireless communication in addition to onboard sensors to improve system reactivity. The focus in this paper is the CACC longitudinal control system that automatically regulates the vehicle acceleration to guarantee the desired distance to the preceding vehicle. Regarding communication technologies, short range DSRC and vehicular LTE are currently both presented as a possible common solution for ITS applications. Eventually combined into hybrid communication system. Nevertheless, the current paper focus on IEEE 802.11p Vehicle-to-Vehicle (V2V) communications technology for Vehicular Ad hoc Network (VANET).

2   Related Work

The research community presents several versions of a vehicle longitudinal controller, which exploits wireless communication. This section provides a brief overview of available publications that cover the subjects related to V2X applications, with special attention to advanced applications (e.g. Platooning and CACC).

The use of feedback control systems on vehicles is covered on R. Rajamani *Vehicle Dynamics and Control* [2] book. It is intended to serve as a useful resource to researchers who work on the development of such control systems. Also, this book provides a comprehensive coverage of vehicle control systems and the dynamic models used in the development of these control systems.

Ploeg et al. [4,5] describe the design and practical validation of a CACC system. Focusing on the feasibility of implementation, a decentralized controller design with a limited communication structure is proposed (a wireless communication link with the preceding vehicle only). A necessary and sufficient condition for string stability is derived. For a velocity-dependent inter-vehicle spacing policy, it is shown that the wireless communication link enables driving at small inter-vehicle distances, whereas string stability is guaranteed.

This paper widely uses the work presented in Segata Ph.D. thesis [1,6]. Its first contribution is the design of PLEXE, an extension for the vehicular simulation framework Veins that enables research studies on various platooning aspects, including design and evaluation of control algorithms, communication protocols, and applications. The same work presents a platooning control algorithm that can be adapted to network conditions. Also, this work proposes a set of undirected information broadcasting (beaconing) protocols that specifically take into account the application requirements.

Amoozadeh et al. [3] present a developed platoon management protocol for CACC vehicles based on wireless communication through VANET. The validity

and effectiveness approach is shown by means of simulations, using different platooning setting. The idea of organizing traffic in platoons is originally proposed in
[9] by PATH for Intelligent Vehicle Highway System (IVHS) and was successfully
demonstrated by National Automated Highway Systems Consortium (NAHSC)
using real cars in 1997. They propose a system architecture where control tasks
are arranged in a five-layer hierarchy. Physical, regulation and coordination layers are distributed among controllers on each vehicle, whereas link and network
layer control groups of vehicles.

The CACC approach presented by Gehring et al. [10] is based on distance
measurement between the vehicles and on a vehicle to vehicle communication but
does not need road infrastructure. A two layered control structure is proposed.
Therefore, a robust platoon controller is introduced for the outer control loop
by use of sliding mode control design. Practical results of a platoon consisting
of 7 trucks show that by use of the proposed control concept string stability can
be achieved.

Milanês et al. [11] describe the design, development, implementation and
testing of a CACC system. The design of the system is based on controllers that
determinate the maneuvers in the platoon [18]: the leader vehicle approaching maneuver and the car-following regulation maneuver. The solution aims to
reduce significantly the gaps between the vehicles, taking advantage of information exchanged using DSRC wireless communication. Additionally, the CACC
improved the response time and platoon stability, when in comparison to the
ACC system, proving that the system may be able to improve traffic flow and
capacity.

3   Control Theory

The automated vehicle control system can be divided into lateral (steering) and
longitudinal (speed) controllers. In this paper we will discuss only the vehicle longitudinal controller. This system is able to maintain automatically the
intended speed by sending a signal to the vehicle control unit that tells the
engine to speed up or to slow down. In a platoon, the controller objective is to
realize a desired distance to the preceding vehicle. This desired distance may
be an increasing function of vehicle velocity in order to take safety aspects into
account. The control system actuation is normally delayed due to the internal
mechanical dynamic. When the controller advise the car to accelerate, it needs
to send the signal to the engine control unit, that, in the end, accelerates the
car. This process is clearly not immediate and is referred to as actuation lag.
The typical actuation time is around 0.5 s [1] and it includes the engine response
delay, sensors/sampling delay, etc.

3.1   String Stability

String stability is a property of a cascaded system, characterizing the evolution of the effects of disturbances over the interconnected systems. Thereby,

string stability is a fundamental platoon propriety used to analyze the car following control logic. The attenuation of disturbances across the vehicle string is an essential requirement for vehicle platooning control algorithm [2,3,5]. For a graphical demonstration of string stability consider Fig. 1, which shows the vehicles speed as a function of time, representing stable and unstable behaviour. Figure 1(b) demonstrate that the rear vehicle can not attenuate disturbance induced by the vehicle in front, that leads to the unstable behaviour of the 2nd car. This instability (strong speed oscillation) may lead to vehicles collision. The controller string stability can be proved if any disturbance induced by the preceding vehicle is not amplified towards the end of the platoon.

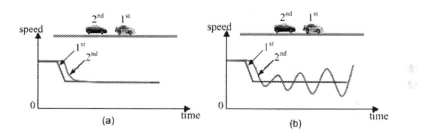

Fig. 1. String stability propriety: (a) stable (b) unstable [15]

3.2 Cooperative Adaptive Cruise Control

Automatic vehicle following based on data exchange by means of wireless communication, in addition to the data obtained by radar, is commonly referred to as *Cooperative Adaptive Cruise Control (CACC)*, illustrated in Fig. 2. The main idea is to share information such as acceleration, speed, position, etc., through wireless communication, to improve the reactivity of the longitudinal controller, by reducing the delay of the response to the preceding vehicle behaviour. The messages are transmitted several times per second using IEEE 802.11p technology. Due to this additional V2V communication CACC is able to achieve string stability at time gaps significantly smaller than 1 s. Furthermore, each vehicle can obtain information from the vehicles around using the wireless communication.

3.3 CACC Logic

The used controller is a predictive controller employing a one-vehicle look-ahead communication topology. The longitudinal control algorithm is based on the work described in [5]. In brief: CACC employs wireless V2V communication, in addition to onboard sensors, to share real-time vehicle data that may improve controller reactivity and enable car-following at closer distances. The advantage here is gained by communicating the *desired* acceleration of the preceding vehicle

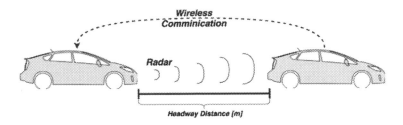

Fig. 2. Schematically depicted CACC system concept

instead of the actual one. The desired longitudinal acceleration represents the intention of the vehicle in front and can be determined based on driver's pedal signals or controller command. The reason for choosing this controller is the fact that the one-vehicle look-ahead topology is the easiest to understand and has the simplest possible communication structure. Thereby it has the highest probability of being implemented for the real world. According to [5], the control formula is defined as:

$$\Delta a = T_g^{-1}(-a_c + K_p(d - L - T_g V) + K_d(V_p - V - T_g a_r) + a_p)T_s \qquad (1)$$

where K_p, K_d is the controller design parameters, d actual distance to preceding vehicle, L standstill distance, V_p velocity of the preceding car, a_r and V is the own vehicle acceleration and speed, a_p is the preceding vehicle acceleration, a_c is the own vehicle controller acceleration calculated on previous step, Δa delta acceleration, T_g pretended time headway and T_s is the controller execution period. Then, the indented vehicle acceleration is given by:

$$a = a_c + \Delta a \qquad (2)$$

This model does not hold for limit situations, such as emergency braking, which are characterized by nonlinear behavior due to complex braking system dynamics. However, such situations can be handled with sending a specific message using other ITS solution like *collision avoidance system*.

4   Simulation Setup

Simulation is a better solution to evaluate the performance of the designed vehicle control system before starting implementing the real prototype. Every test on simulation can be easily accomplished and repeated for posterior analysis. PLEXE [6,8] allows the simulation of automated car-following systems (i.e. platooning). It provides realistic vehicle dynamics and several cruise control models. This framework enables a detailed simulation of wireless communication among the vehicles, together with realistic mobility. PLEXE is Veins-based [12], also coupling the OMNeT++ network simulator with the SUMO road traffic simulator, meaning that users can benefit from a fully detailed IEEE 802.11p and

IEEE 1609.4 DSCR/WAVE network stack for realistic simulation of vehicular networks. Moreover, it extends SUMO by implementing several cruise control models and realistic engine dynamics. Due to these benefits, PLEXE framework was chosen to perform all the following simulation tests. We adopt the common beacon format and the standard message dissemination procedure used on PLEXE. *Beacons* in ITS application are single-hop periodic broadcast messages, transmitted by every vehicle. The information received by means of this beacons (i.e. acceleration, position, speed, etc.) is then used to feed automated controller.

To perform the evaluation of the vehicle cooperative longitudinal controller, an highway simulation scenario was chosen. CACC is supposed to be used mostly outside the city roads, thus the urban scenarios are not covered in this paper. This simple use case represents four lines straight highway road with unidirectional traffic flow. Figure 3 shows a part of the highway with a platoon of six vehicles. Each vehicle has an assigned ID, where platoon leader ID is equal to 0, first follower vehicle has ID equal to 1, and so on. A homogeneous platoon was assumed for this study, assuming that all vehicles in the string show identical dynamic behaviour and implements the same engine model.

The OMNeT++ network simulator represents vehicles in the form of communication nodes, as shown in Fig. 3(a). All nodes send periodic beacons to perform information exchange. Each node has the same position as the vehicle in the traffic simulation. This is achieved by means of TraCI server provided by SUMO. On every simulation step OMNeT++ node pass received beacon data to the SUMO. Then, SUMO uses this information as input for the CACC controller to calculate velocity and acceleration. The resulting values are used to estimate the position of the vehicle. SUMO returns this position to OMNeT, which moves its nodes accordingly.

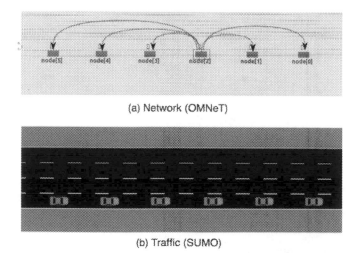

(a) Network (OMNeT)

(b) Traffic (SUMO)

Fig. 3. Screenshot of network (a) and traffic (b) simulation environment

In this simulation setup, the free-space path loss model and Nakagami-m distributed fading model is considered. The beacon message work on top of the IEEE 802.11p (PHY)/IEEE 1609.4 (MAC) models provided by Veins and send beacons on Control Channel (CH) only. The channel central frequency is 5.89 GHz with data rate of 6 Mbit/s and transmission power of 100 mW. Other configuration parameters are listed in Table 1. The vehicles inside the platoon should follow the preceding vehicle at predefined time-gap spacing. Larger platoon sizes can increase maximum road utilization, but also affect platoon flexibility and traffic flow stability. There is no exact size limit defined, although some researches [7,11] recommends a maximum platoon size up to 10 to 20 vehicles.

Table 1. Default simulation settings

	Parameter	Value
Communication	Free space path loss model (α)	2.0
	PHY/MAC model	IEEE 802.11p/1609.4
	Frequency	5.89 GHz(CCH)
	Bitrate	6 Mbits/s
	Access category	AC_VI
	Beacon size	150 B
	Beacon frequency	10 Hz
	Transmit power	20 dBm
	Sensitivity	−94 dBm
	Thermal noise	−95 dBm
	CCA-threshold	−65 dBm
Mobility	Platoon size	6
	Car length	4 m
	Intra-platoon time-gap	0.5 s
	Max Speed	150 km/h
	Max acceleration	2.5 m/s^2
	Max deceleration	6 m/s^2
CACC	Kp	0.2
	Kd	0.7
	Ks	0.4
	Reaction time (τ)	0.5 s
	Standstill distance	2 m
	Operating frequency	100 Hz

5   Controller Evaluation

This section presents controller tests in a simulation environment. Analyzing controller behavior in different scenarios allows verifying its stability, safety and performance characteristics. Simulation permits fast controller analysis using different configuration parameters during the tests. However, the simulation may reduce the system realism due to the use of simplified models. For this basic tests an ideal wireless communication is considered (i.e. no packet losses). The leader introduces all movement disturbance and the followers should correctly react to these changes.

5.1   Comparison with ACC

The longitudinal controller is tested against Adaptive Cruise Control (ACC) system provided by PLEXE framework. ACC is an optional cruise control system, that uses the additional devices (radar or LIDAR) and automatically adjusts the vehicle speed to maintain a safe distance from vehicles ahead. The controllers are compared by looking at the velocity profiles as a function of time using the same time-gap spacing for both. Figure 4 shows the vehicles speed over the time, illustrating the benefits of IVC-based controller against a purely sensor-based system. ACC controlled vehicles have increased disturbance introduced by the leader. This means that under these conditions ACC control system is not string-stable and make cause vehicle collision. The additional information received via wireless communication ensures CACC controller string stability on small spacing.

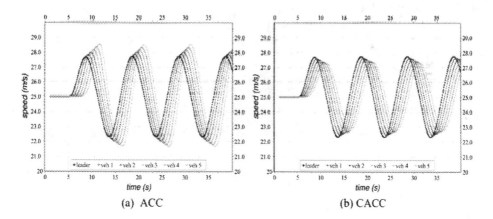

(a) ACC   (b) CACC

Fig. 4. Comparison between ACC and CACC showing string stable (b) and string unstable (a) behavior

5.2   String Stability Properties

String stability is an essential requirement of the vehicle-following control systems. Using the standard approach to analyze string stability, the implemented simulation scenario continuously changes the leader speed in sinusoidal mode. A constant headway time policy is used to calculate the desired inter-vehicle

distance, which is related to the vehicle speed. Sinusoidal disturbance frequency
is set to 0.1 Hz with 10 km/h of oscillation amplitude. The controller string-
stability evaluation was provided using different headway times, see Fig. 5. It
clearly shows a tradeoff between selected headway time and attenuation capabilities of the controller. A tracking lag can be observed by looking at how the
velocity of one vehicle is out of phase with its predecessor.

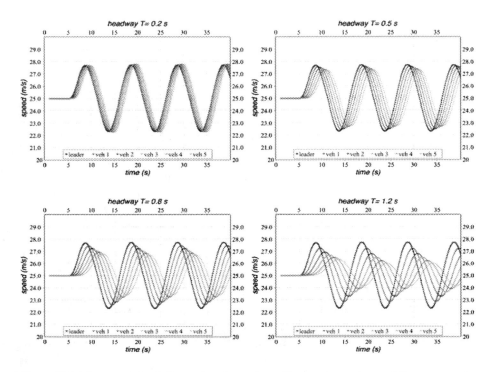

Fig. 5. Vehicles speed for different headway time, illustrating string-stability properties

5.3   Desired vs Real Acceleration

Using wireless communication, the CACC can also obtain the *desired* acceleration of the front vehicle to control the external input. Unlike *real* acceleration,
the desired acceleration represent future information about the intended vehicle behavior. Using the desired acceleration instead of the actual one gives an
advantage in term of system reactivity. Clearly, this information cannot be measured by any sensor. Figure 6 compares behavior of the resulting platoon when
preceding vehicle sends the actual and desired acceleration using the same headway time. Then it was analyzed with respect to string stability, from which it
appears that sharing the desired acceleration increases the performance in terms
of minimizing the inter-vehicle distance while guaranteeing string stability.

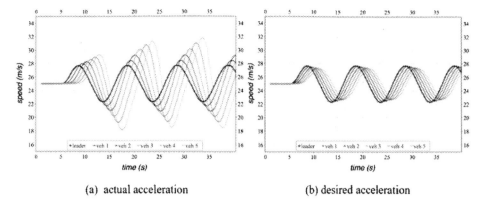

(a) actual acceleration   (b) desired acceleration

Fig. 6. Speed profile when sending actual (a) and desired (b) acceleration

5.4   Basic Analysis

It has been shown that CACC is string stable for time-gaps smaller than $T = 1\,$s, besides the other simulation experiments must be performed to validate the longitudinal controller. There are numerous possible traffic scenarios that can be implemented, so this work is focused on extreme situations, like sudden braking or fast acceleration. By analyzing the behaviour of the controller in extreme maneuvers the performance can be tested in terms of stability and robustness. Figure 7 shows the result obtained for these scenarios that represent acceleration, speed and distance profiles of a platoon with five vehicles and a leader.

Figure 7(a) shows the *Accelerate and Brake* scenario, where all platoon vehicles depart from the rest position. The leader vehicle continuously accelerates for 5 s and then brakes until complete stop, using the maximum possible deceleration. The initial inter-vehicle distance is 2 m. The leader accelerates from the standstill with the constant acceleration of $2.5\,\text{m/s}^2$ and all the followers attempt to reach the desired distance and speed. After 5 s the leader achieves the velocity of about 45 km/h and applies maximum deceleration ($-8\,\text{m/s}^2$) until full stop is reached. This particular scenario is pretty demonstrative, since after maximum acceleration it comes to the maximum deceleration and all vehicles come to a stop safely.

Figure 7(b) shows the second example, the platoon travels on the freeway with the constant speed of 90 km/h. The leader performs a sudden break, constantly decelerating ($-8\,\text{m/s}^2$) until full stop. The followers correctly track its behavior without causing any collision. All the vehicles were able to come to a full stop and converge at the predefined standstill distance of 2 m. In both scenarios a tracking lag can be observed, in spite of it, every platoon vehicle can safely track leader motion in short distance following.

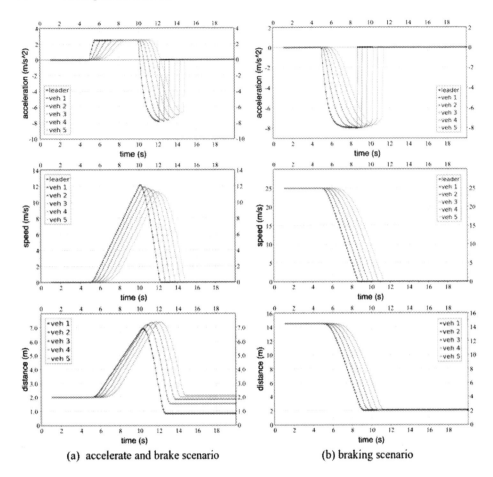

(a) accelerate and brake scenario   (b) braking scenario

Fig. 7. Simulation experiments to validate the longitudinal controller

5.5   CACC Maneuvering

So far, it has been demonstrated that the CACC is able to maintain platoon
string stable behaviour if choosing an appropriate headway time. Intra-platton
distance depends on platoon cruise speed: the higher the speed the larger the
distance. However, a platoon needs to be modified during its course, therefore,
it should support basic platoon maneuvers (e.g. vehicle join, vehicle leave, lane
change, etc.). Moreover, a platoon needs interact with other vehicles on the
road. For these reasons, CACC equipped vehicle must be able to maintain the
desired fixed distance to the preceding vehicle and the longitudinal controller
must provide those capabilities.

To support these features the original controller was extended introducing a new input variable and a new configuration parameter to the controller logic. This new input variable on the control loop represents the desired distance to the front vehicle. The new configuration parameter was called $Gain(G)$ characterizes the internal controller dynamics, i.e. define how fast the vehicle reaches the desired distance. Basically the controller need to transform the desired distance into the time-gap indicated in seconds on every execution step. The simple transformation algorithm is represented in the following:

if $d_i > 0$ **and** $V_p > 0$ **then**
  if $d_i > d$ **then**
    $H \leftarrow (d + G)/V_p$
  else
    $H \leftarrow d_i/V_p$
  end if
end if

where d_i is the pretended distance in meters, d is the actual distance to the preceding vehicle, V_p is the preceding vehicle speed, G is the defined gain parameter and H is the required headway time. Figure 8 provides a simple example of platooning join by side maneuver and the Fig. 9 shows the acceleration, distance and speed profiles of the platoon vehicles. The vehicle on the side wants to join the platoon, so in order to make the lane change possible, the vehicle in the middle of platoon must create enough space at the front of the preceding vehicle. Here, the main task of the longitudinal controller is to guarantee the desired fixed distance to the front vehicle, independently of the leader behaviour. The CACC of the other followers, which are already platoon members, does not change the operation state and just maintain headway distance. When $G = 10$, see Fig. 9(a) the controller responds faster and conclude the maneuver at around 20 s. The fast maneuver CACC-settings leads to undesirable oscillations and might result in an uncomfortable driving for the passengers. Figure 9(b) shows a successful longitudinal maneuver when $G = 1$. After 35 s vehicle 2 creates the required gap to let the joiner enter the platoon. The gain parameter (G) manage the controller reactivity. It is clear that G must be tuned to meet a good trade-off between convergence time and driving comfort.

Fig. 8. Graphical representation of platooning join by side maneuver

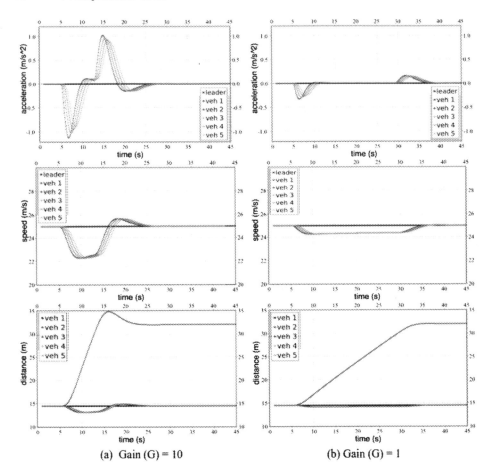

Fig. 9. Platoon vehicles behaviour for different CACC parametrization. Controller reaching the desired distance faster (a) and slowly (b).

6   Conclusion and Future Work

The CACC system may improve car-following performance using the additional data (e.g. acceleration) exchanged between the vehicles through a wireless communication link. Consequently, the controller can react faster to the behaviour of the vehicle in front. This paper describes the process of CACC testing using the simulation environment. It was possible to conclude that the used longitudinal controller is able to work safely and efficiently, ensures a vehicle following at a close distance, together with traffic flow stability. Finally, the performance of the longitudinal controller employed for basic platoon operations was demonstrated. The presented results allow determining the parameters under witch CACC confirms its string stability and robustness.

The future work could be extended by improving the CACC in order to take into account the existence of road gradient and bend, since all the simulation testes was realized on the straight road. The implemented controller uses the information received from the directly preceding vehicle only. However, recently proposed CACC solutions have introduced multi-vehicle communication topology to improve the controller performance. This additional information from the other platoon vehicles may improve controller robustness against communication impairments. The controller evolution section provides the basic controller tests in simulation environment. Nevertheless, the other traffic scenarios should be also analyzed. The simulation scenario could be improved using the real road topologies, rather than straight road. Furthermore, stimulation may take into account heterogeneous traffic (i.e., vehicles with possibly different dynamic characteristics).

The CACC performance strongly depends on the availability of communicated information of the preceding vehicle. However, IEEE 802.11p wireless communication is not flawless i.e. collisions on the shared wireless medium may cause packet loss. Therefore the impact of communication impairments, such as transmission delays and packet losses, should be investigated. The presented simulation setup uses only the strictly periodic beaconing approach, however the dynamic beaconing strategy can be tested for the future work. For example, the beaconing frequency may vary according to the vehicle speed variation. Further research on the impact of communication losses on CACC performance is needed. Moreover, the increased network traffic also requires a careful analysis.

Acknowledgements. This work was sponsored by the Portugal Incentive System for Research and Technological Development. Project in copromotion no. 002797/2015 (INNOVCAR 2015-2018), and also by COMPETE: POCI-01-0145-FEDER-007043 and FCT - Fundação para a Ciência e Tecnologia within the Project Scope: UID/ CEC/ 00319/2013.

References

1. Segata, M.: Safe and efficient communication protocols for platooning control. Ph.D. thesis, University of Trento, University of Innsbruck (2016)
2. Rajamani, R.: Vehicle Dynamics and Control, 2nd edn. Springer, Heidelberg (2012). https://doi.org/10.1007/978-1-4614-1433-9. Varaiya, P.: Smart cars on smart roads: problems of control. IEEE Trans. Autom. Control **38**(2), 195–207 (1993)
3. Amoozadeh, M., Deng, H., Chuah, C.N., Zhang, H.M., Ghosal, D.: Platoon management with cooperative adaptive cruise control enabled by VANET, 04 January 2015
4. Ploeg, J.: Analysis and design of controllers for cooperative and automated driving. Ph.D. thesis. Technische Universiteit Eindhoven, Eindhoven (2014)
5. Ploeg, J., Scheepers, B., van Nunen, E., van de Wouw, N., Nijmeijer, H.: Design and experimental evaluation of cooperative adaptive cruise control. In: IEEE International Conference on Intelligent Transportation Systems (ITSC 2011), pp. 260–265. IEEE, Washington, DC, October 2011

6. Segata, M., Joerer, S., Bloessl, B., Sommer, C., Dressler, F., Lo Cigno, R.: PLEXE: a platooning extension for Veins. In: IEEE Vehicular Networking Conference, VNC 2015 (2014). https://doi.org/10.1109/VNC.2014.7013309
7. Robinson, T., Chan, E., Coelingh, E.: Operating platoons on public motorways: an introduction to the sartre platooning programme. In: 17th World Congress on Intelligent Transport Systems, pp. 1–11 (2010)
8. PLEXE Homepage. http://plexe.car2x.org/. Accessed 15 May 2018
9. Varaiya, P.: Smart cars on smart roads: problems of control. IEEE Trans. Autom. Control. **38**(2), 195–207 (1993)
10. Gehring, O., Fritz, H.: Practical results of a longitudinal control concept for truck platooning with vehicle to vehicle communication. In: Proceedings of the IEEE Conference on Intelligent Transportation Systems, 9–12 November 1997, pp. 117–122 (1997)
11. Milanês, V., Shladover, S.E., Spring, J., Nowakowski, C., Kawazoe, H., Nakamura, M.: Cooperative adaptive cruise control in real traffic situations. IEEE Trans. Intell. Transp. Syst. **15**(1), 296–305 (2014)
12. Veins Homepage. http://veins.car2x.org. Accessed 15 May 2018
13. Ploeg, J., Shukla, D.P., van de Wouw, N.: Controller synthesis for string stability of vehicle platoons. IEEE Trans. Intell. Transp. Syst. **15**(2), 854–865 (2014). https://doi.org/10.1109/TITS.2013.2291493
14. Guvenc, L., et al.: Cooperative adaptive cruise control implementation of team mekar at the grand cooperative driving challenge. IEEE Trans. Intell. Transp. Syst. **13**(3), 1062–1074 (2012)
15. Lei, C., van Eenennaam, E.M., Wolterink, W.K., Karagiannis, G., Heijenk, G., Ploeg, J.: Impact of packet loss on CACC string stability performance. In: 2011 11th International Conference on ITS Telecommunications, St. Petersburg, pp. 381–386 (2011)
16. Öncü, S.: String stability of interconnected vehicles: network-aware modelling, analysis and experiments. Ph.D. thesis. Technische Universiteit Eindhoven, Eindhoven (2014)
17. Michele Segata et al.: Supporting platooning maneuvers through IVC: an initial protocol analysis for the JOIN Maneuver. In: 2014 11th Annual Conference on Wireless On-demand Network Systems and Services (WONS), pp. 130–137. IEEE (2014)
18. Ribeiro, B., et al.: Simulation and testing of a platooning management protocol implementation. In: Koucheryavy, Y., Mamatas, L., Matta, I., Ometov, A., Papadimitriou, P. (eds.) WWIC 2017. LNCS, vol. 10372, pp. 174–185. Springer, Cham (2017). https://doi.org/10.1007/978-3-319-61382-6_14

ROM-P: Route Optimization Management of Producer Mobility in Information-Centric Networking

Low Xian Wee[1], Zhiwei Yan[2], Yong Jin Park[1(✉)], Yu-Beng Leau[1],
Kashif Nisar[1], and Ag Asri Ag Ibrahim[1]

[1] University Malaysia Sabah, Kota Kinabalu, Malaysia
yjp@ieee.org
[2] China Internet Network Information Center, Beijing, China

Abstract. In recent times, ICN (Information-Centric Networking) attracts interest as an auspicious future Internet architecture, which resolves problems of the current TCP/IP architecture. However, one of challenging problems is how to support producer mobility for explosively increasing mobile devices as well as vehicular communications. This paper proposes efficient producer mobility scheme with devices dynamically moving, considering route optimization. Our scheme, called ROM-P, uses auxiliary FIB (Forward Information Base), referred to BIT (Binding Information Table), which is located on top of FIB and contains producer mobility information. The features of the proposed scheme are: (i) distribute anchor points, which reduces system failure caused by anchor damage and (ii) enable caching using the same data name in comparison with our previous work [3].

Keywords: Information-Centric Networking (ICN) · Producer mobility · Route optimization

1 Introduction

The current TCP/IP Internet has severe challenges in aspects of security, scalability, and mobility. ICN (Information Centric Networking) attracts great interest as a promising future Internet architecture. The TCP/IP uses host-centric paradigm where IP protocol plays a central role and uses location-dependent address to establish communications. On the other hand, ICN takes data-centric paradigm and uses data names to access data instead of IP address as in TCP/IP [1], whereas NDN (Named Data Networking) [2] is the most typical implementation. This paradigm shift produces potentials to cope with the above- mentioned challenges in TCP/IP. However, ICN also has challenging problems to be solved. One of them is producer mobility [5] which is crucial particularly in explosively increasing mobile devices as well as coming connected cars, although consumer mobility is naturally supported in ICN based on its per-packet stateful data plane and caching mechanism. If a producer node moves, the corresponding node cannot continue to communicate with it. Some of routers should be informed about new network attachment information in some way.

J. C. Ferreira et al. (Eds.): INTSYS 2018, LNICST 267, pp. 81–91, 2019.
https://doi.org/10.1007/978-3-030-14757-0_7

We published a paper [3], referred to as EPMS, which is the first paper realizing route optimization in NDN. It makes use of prepended data name method and supports producer mobility as well as the route optimization by creating and maintaining BIT (Binding Information Table) at Home Access Router (AR-H), Foreign Access Router (AR-F), and Consumer Access Router (AR-C), respectively. As these access routers play a role of anchors, EPMS belongs to anchor-based approach. However, it has downside because the failure of the anchor means dysfunction of BIT table and makes EPMS fatal. Furthermore, a different name is used for caching before and after prepending data name. This paper proposes ROM-P which improves these drawbacks by (i) distributing anchors and (ii) using the same data name in caching, which is anchor-less approach. Performance evaluation shows advantage of ROM-P.

2   Design Principle

2.1   Producer Mobility Management

The mobility operations begin after the Mobile Producer (MP) moves from the AR-H to the AR-F (Fig. 1). When the MP moves and attaches to AR-F, it transfers its previous prefix to the AR-F. When receiving the MP prefix, an entry is made in the AR-F's BIT, which shows the binding information of the AR-F prefix and MP prefix. Accordingly, the AR-F transfers to AR-H a Point-of-attachment Update (PU) message, where the PU message, using an Interest packet, is a control message which has the AR-H prefix of MP (/h.com) as the data name, and also includes the MP prefix (/h.com/alice) and AR-F's prefix (/f.com) in additional fields (which will be mentioned later in 2.4).

When the AR-H gets the PU message, it sends back a Point-of-attachment Update Acknowledgement (PUACK), using a Data packet with AR-F's prefix as its data name, to the AR-F in order to show that the redirecting path between the AR-H and AR-F was established. Then the AR-H gets the binding information of the AR-F prefix of the MP, MP's prefix, and incoming PU face number (f0) for its BIT.

When a consumer asks for the content of the MP, an Interest packet is transferred to the AR-H (Fig. 2). In this operation, FIB is referred at each router for forwarding. Then, the AR-H looks for its BIT entry first and gets the forwarding face (f0) if there is a positive match. The AR-H sends the Interest packet to the AR-F. When the Interest packet arrives at the AR-F, it is transferred to the MP. When the corresponding Data packet is transferred back from the MP, the AR-F forwards it to the AR-H by checking its PIT (Pending Interest Table). The AR-H forwards the Data packet to the consumer in the same way.

If there are several routers between AR-F and AR-H, the PU message updates the entry of each BIT on the intermediate routers in the same way like updating the BIT entry of AR-H (Fig. 3). As shown in Fig. 3, when an intermediate router i (IR-i) receives PU, a new entry is created and the incoming face number (fi) is also recorded. Upon PU's arrival at AR-H correctly, PUACK is sent back to AR-F along the reversed path. In this scheme, an Interest packet which is a data request from a consumer looks

up BIT and can be forwarded between AR-F and AR-H. As the BIT entry gives
forwarding information, looking up FIBs are omitted.

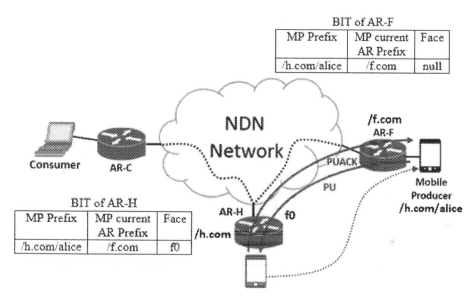

Fig. 1. Creation of BIT at the AR-H and the AR-F

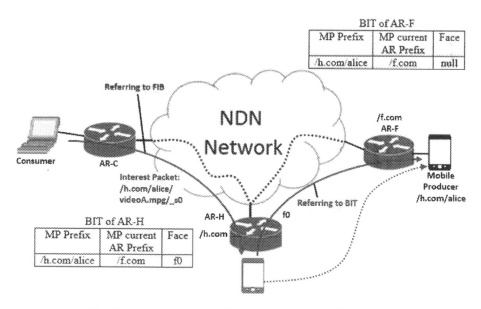

Fig. 2. Interest forwarding from consumer to AR-F via AR-H

2.2   Successive Handover Management

The MP is likely to move successively. Figure 4 shows that it moves into AR-F and then AR-G. PU message is transferred to the AR-F from AR-G and the AR-F's BIT entry is revised like Fig. 4 and PUACK is sent back. In ROM-P, the PU is not further sent to the AR-H. It is assumed that entries of BITs are soft-state. They will disappear after a certain period, if they are not refreshed. When the MP stays in AR-G over a pre-defined time threshold, PU is generated through AR-G toward AR-H to refresh the BIT entries on their path. PUACK is returned when the PU successfully arrives at AR-H.

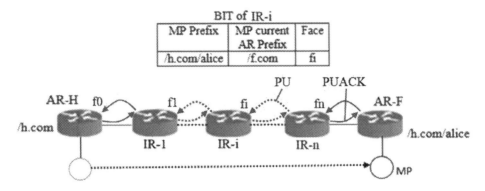

Fig. 3. BIT in intermediate routers between AR-F and AR-H

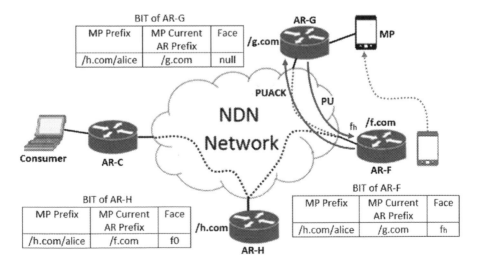

Fig. 4. Successive handover of MP

2.3   Route Optimization

The route optimization uses a piggybacked Data packet like EPMS. In the case of Fig. 2, when MP sends out the Data packet after movement, the binding information (/h.com/alice; /f.com) is placed in the additional header field of the Data packet. This Data packet is sent to the consumer through AR-H. When it reaches the AR-C, the AR-C's BIT makes a new entry for the biding information (Fig. 5).

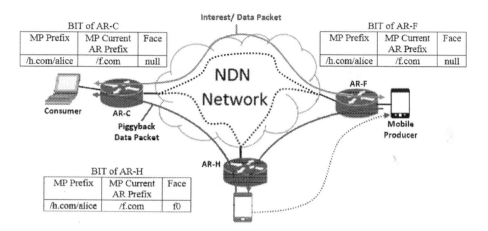

Fig. 5. Route optimization

Afterward when the consumer transfers the following Interest packets to the MP, the AR-C prepends the data name with the AR-F prefix, and the data name-prepended Interest packet (/f.com/h.com/alice) is directly sent to the MP. Then the Data packet is sent back to the AR-C and the consumer.

2.4   Control Message Format

When we refer to the NDN packet formats [2], the control messages in ROM-P are shown in Fig. 6. The "Guiders" field of the Interest packet and "MetaInfo" field of the Data packet have some additive information such as "message type", "AR-F prefix", and "MP prefix". The message type specifies normal Interest/Data packet or PU/PUACK packet. The PU packet contains "signature" for security. In this manner the control messages can make use of the original NDN packet formats.

3   Evaluation

Once PU and PUACK messages are exchanged, a new entry of BIT is created in AR-H, AR-F, and their intermediate routers. As the entry has the field of a forwarding face number, Interest packets which are data requests by a consumer don't need to look up FIB for forwarding in the intermediate routers between AR-H and AR-F. As the size of

FIB is usually much larger than that of BIT, the table look-up time is a lot reduced by ROM-P. Meanwhile, BIT is first checked in routers before looking up FIB. When a route optimization path is via AR-H or one of the by-pathed routers, the above-mentioned advantage is obtained. This is likely to happen, if MP moves in a limited area.

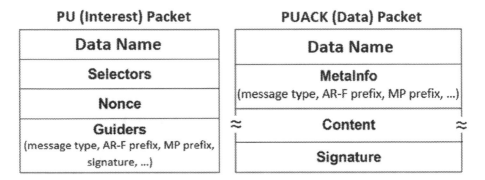

Fig. 6. Packet format

If new consumers connected to AR-H, AR-F and their intermediate routers want to the MP's data, they just need to generate Interest packets, where there are no need for PU and PUACK messages. Because there already exists the corresponding entry of BIT in their routers. When the original consumer moves to one of those routers like Fig. 7, the same is true. However, in EMPS these are not possible, since it has no face field in BIT entries. Therefore, PU/PUACK messages have to be used and the process about data name prepending is done in ARs.

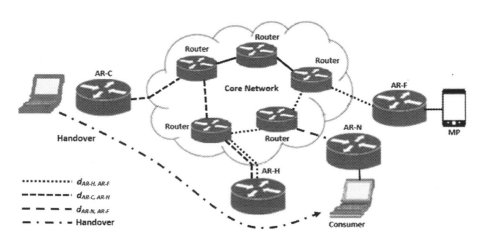

Fig. 7. Relocation of consumer between AR-H and AR-F

Performance evaluation is made about successive handovers in ROM-P in comparison with EPMS.

3.1   Network Mobility Model

As a network mobility model, the fluid-flow mobility [7] model is chosen, due to its suitability for a mobile terminal with a static speed and moving direction. MP moves in any direction within the range of (0, 2) with a uniform distribution probability. Table 1 contains the parameters and notation used, which is referred from [3] with slight modification. r_c (mobiles/s) is the cell crossing rate as shows below [8]:

$$r_c = (\rho * v * l)/\pi \tag{1}$$

in which l denotes the perimeter of a cell (m), and v (m/s) and ρ (mobiles/m^2) show the average velocity and density of the MP, respectively. The network model used here is shown in Fig. 8, where the wireless link is assumed to be one hop.

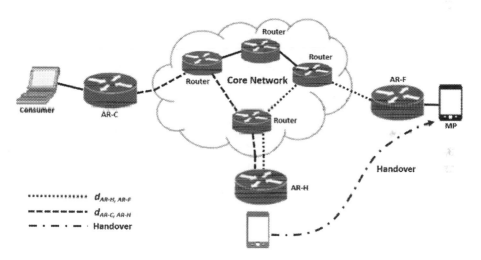

Fig. 8. Network model

Table 1. Parameters and notation

Parameter	Value	Unit	Description
l	120	M	Cell's perimeter
n	5–100		Number of cells
ω	2		Unit transmitting cost of a wireless link
μ	1		Unit transmitting cost of a wired link
P_{bu}	2		Process cost for binding update
$d_{AR-C,\ AR-H}$	$\sqrt{n}$	Hops	Distance between AR-C and AR-H
$d_{AR-H,\ AR-F}$	5–100	Hops	Distance between AR-H and AR-F

3.2   Signalling Cost

The signalling cost, represented by S, shows the cost of exchange of signalling messages, which are used for updating BIT and route optimization. It reflects the distance between two network nodes like the AR and MP, assuming that the distance indicates the number of hops. $d_{i,j}$ is the distance between network nodes i and j. μ and ω indicate the units of the transmitting cost of wired and wireless links, respectively. n is the number of cells within a domain. P_{bu} is the processing cost of binding update, which is the cost caused by making a BIT entry [3].

The signalling cost of EPMS, represented by S_o, can be calculated as the following equation:

$$S_o = (2\omega + 2 \cdot \mu \cdot d_{AR\text{-}H, AR\text{-}F} + 3P_{bu}) \cdot r_c n \tag{2}$$

The signalling cost of ROM-P, represented by S_n, is expressed as follows:

$$S_n = [2(\omega + \mu \cdot d_{AR\text{-}H, AR\text{-}F}) + PC_{BIT} \cdot (d_{AR\text{-}H, AR\text{-}F} + 1)] \cdot r_c n \tag{3}$$

where PC_{BIT} is the update cost at each intermediate router between AR-H and AR-F to create a new entry of BIT. The first term of the square bracket in Eq. (3) represents the transmission cost from the AR-H to AR-F. The second term represents the update cost for all intermediate routers between the AR-F and AR-H.

3.3   Packet Delivering Cost

The packet delivering cost contains the transmitting cost of the Interest and Data packet after the handover process, which is transmitted between the consumer and MP. The packet delivering cost of EPMS and ROM-P, represented by Do and Dn respectively, are expressed as follows:

$$\begin{aligned} Do = {} & \lambda s \cdot \overline{S} \cdot [(PC_{BIT} + PC_{FIB}) \cdot (d_{AR\text{-}C, AR\text{-}H} + 1) + (PC_{BIT} + PC_{FIB}) \cdot (d_{AR\text{-}H, AR\text{-}F} + 1)] \\ & + \lambda s \cdot \overline{S} \cdot [PC_{PIT} \cdot (d_{AR\text{-}C, AR\text{-}F})] \\ & + 2 \cdot \lambda_s \cdot \overline{S} \cdot (2\omega + \mu \cdot d_{AR\text{-}C, AR\text{-}F}) \cdot r_c n \end{aligned} \tag{4}$$

$$\begin{aligned} Do = {} & \lambda s \cdot \overline{S} \cdot [(PC_{BIT} + PC_{FIB}) \cdot (d_{AR\text{-}C, AR\text{-}H} + 1) + PC_{BIT} \cdot (d_{AR\text{-}H, AR\text{-}F} + 1)] \\ & + \lambda s \cdot \overline{S} \cdot [PC_{PIT} \cdot (d_{AR\text{-}C, AR\text{-}F})] \\ & + 2 \cdot \lambda_s \cdot \overline{S} \cdot (2\omega + \mu \cdot d_{AR\text{-}C, AR\text{-}F}) \cdot r_c n \end{aligned} \tag{5}$$

in which λ_s is a session arrival rate, $\overline{S}$ is an average session size in the unit of packet, PC_{BIT} is the update or lookup cost at BIT, and PC_{PIT} and PC_{FIB} are the lookup cost at PIT and FIB, respectively. The first terms of Eqs. (4) and (5) represent the Interest packet processing time at all routers from AR-C to AR-F. The second term represents

Data packet processing time at all routers. The last term represents the transmission time from the consumer to the MP.

Using Eqs. (1) to (5) gives the total costs for the EPMS and ROM-P, represented by Co and Cn respectively, which are as follows:

$$C_o = S_o + D_o \cdot r_c n \tag{6}$$

$$C_n = S_n + D_n \cdot r_c n \tag{7}$$

3.4 Numerical Results

Numerical results are calculated for Eqs. (6) and (7). Our ROM-P indicates better performance than EPMS. Figure 9 shows the effect of the number of cells, where $v = 1$, $\rho = 0.005$ and $d_{AR-H, AR-F} = 10$. Figure 10 shows the effect of the velocity, where n is set to 25, $\rho = 0.005$ and $d_{AR-H, AR-F} = 10$. Figure 11 shows the effect of the distance between the AR-H and AR-F, where n is set to 25, $v = 1$ and $\rho = 0.005$.

From Fig. 9, we can see that the total costs for Co and Cn do not show significant difference at the beginning. However, as the number of cell increases, the total cost of Cn becomes much lower due to the signalling cost in each intermediate router. The same phenomena are shown in Figs. 10 and 11.

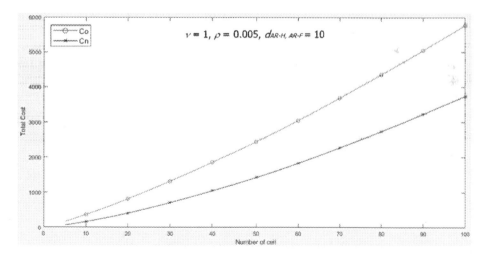

Fig. 9. Effect of the number of cells

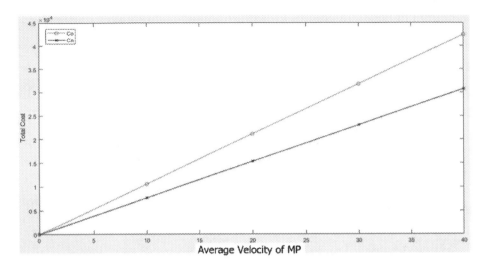

Fig. 10. Effect of MP's velocity

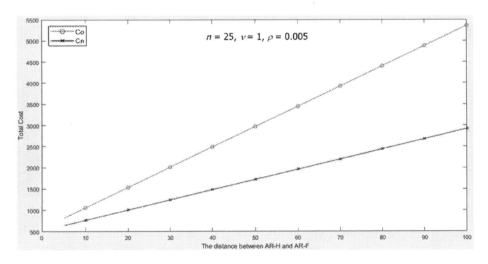

Fig. 11. Effect of the distance between AR-H and AR-F

4   Summary and Conclusion

Our scheme, ROM-P, creates a new entry on BIT in AR-H and AR-F, including their intermediate routers. In this way, BITs, namely anchors, are distributed on routers, and it reduces system failure caused by anchor damage. Caching can be made by the original data name on intermediate routers between AR-H and AR-F unlike EPMS.

An Interest packet should look up BIT first when there is no positive match in a PIT operation, and then if there is no positive match, it will look up FIB. The performance evaluation is made and shows that ROM-P is better that EPMS.

As BIT plays a role of auxiliary FIB by recording producer mobility information. In reference [4], producer movement updates FIBs of by-pathed routers but no other routers. Considering link-state routing protocols such as Named data Link State Routing protocol (NLSR) [6] like OSPF in IP protocol, all routers in the same domain have to keep the common routing database. MP movement should be immediately noticed to all the routers and the synchronization of the link-state database should be made, which means too much overhead.

Regarding the route optimization, caching is still made by prepended data name. Whether or not it should be used is dependent on sort of applications and network conditions. For example, when mobile devices are moving in high speed, the route optimization should be used. When not only is communication traffic volume or channel capacity small but redundancy of a route by route optimization is also low, the route optimization may not be used.

References

1. Xylomenos, G., et al.: A survey of information-centric networking research. Commun. Surv. Tutor. IEEE **16**(2), 1024–1049 (2014)
2. Zhang, L., et al.: Data named networking. ACM SIGCOMM Comput. Commun. Rev. (CCR) **44**, 66–73 (2014)
3. Zhang, S., et al.: Efficient producer mobility support in named data networking. IEICE Trans. Commun. **E100-B**(10), 1856–1864 (2017)
4. Augé, J., Carofiglio, G., Grassi, G., Muscariello, L., Pau, G., Zeng, X.: MAP-Me: managing anchor-less producer mobility in content-centric networks. IEEE Trans. Netw. Serv. Manag. **15**(2), 569–610 (2018)
5. Zhang, Y., Afanasyev, A., Burke, J., Zhang, L.: A survey of mobility support in named data networking. In: IEEE INFOCOM Workshop on Name-Oriented Mobility, April 2016
6. Lehman, V., et al.: A secure link state routing protocol for NDN, NDN Technical Report NDN-0037, January 2016
7. Pack, S., Choi, Y.: A study on performance of hierarchical mobile IPv6 in IP-based cellular networks. IEICE Trans. Commun. **87**(3), 462–469 (2004)
8. Zhang, X., Castellanos, J.G., Campbell, A.T.: P-MIP: paging extensions for mobile IP. Mob. Netw. Appl. **7**(2), 127–141 (2002)

Mobility and Planning

Smart Mobility: A Mobile Approach

Ricardo Faria[1,2(✉)], Lina Brito[1,2], Karolina Baras[1,2], and José Silva[1,3]

[1] Madeira Interactive Technologies Institute, Polo Científico e Tecnológico da Madeira, Caminho da Penteada, 9020-105 Funchal, Portugal
{ricardo.faria,lina.brito,
karolina.baras,jose.l.silva}@m-iti.org
[2] Universidade da Madeira, Campus Universitário da Penteada,
9020-105 Funchal, Portugal
[3] Instituto Universitário de Lisboa (ISCTE-IUL), ISTAR-IUL,
Avenida das Forças Armadas, 1649-026 Lisboa, Portugal

Abstract. The Internet of Things (IoT) is one of the key ingredients for the realization of Smart Cities. IoT devices are essential components of the Smart Cities infrastructure, as they can provide information collected from the environment through sensors or allow other systems to reach out and act on the world through actuators. IoT data collection, however, is not limited to sensors and machines, but to data from social networks, and the web. Social networks have a huge impact on the amount of data being produced daily, becoming an increasingly central and important data source. The exploitation of these data sources, combined with the growing popularity of mobile devices, can lead to the development of better solutions to improve people's quality of life. This paper discusses how to take advantage of the benefits of mobile devices and the vast range of information sources and services, such as traffic conditions, and narrow, closed or conditioned roads data. The proposed system uses a real-time collection, organization, and transmission of traffic and road conditions data to provide efficient and accurate information to drivers. With the purpose of supporting and improving traffic data collection and distribution, an Android application was developed to collect information about extraordinary events that take place in a city, providing warnings and alternative routes to drivers and helping them to improve their time management. The developed solution also exploits the existing gaps in other applications, implementing a more specific solution for the Madeira Island traffic condition problems.

Keywords: Internet of Things · Smart Cities · Smart Mobility ·
Mobile applications · Sensors · Traffic and road conditions · Route planning

1   Introduction

Over the 20th and 21st centuries, a major change has been taking place in the distribution of the world's population as a consequence of the increasing concentrations of people in highly urbanized areas known as megacities [1]. In these very large cities, the complexity of building and maintaining infrastructures, and of meeting the needs of a huge and often urban population, has reached new levels.

© ICST Institute for Computer Sciences, Social Informatics and Telecommunications Engineering 2019
Published by Springer Nature Switzerland AG 2019. All Rights Reserved
J. C. Ferreira et al. (Eds.): INTSYS 2018, LNICST 267, pp. 95–112, 2019.
https://doi.org/10.1007/978-3-030-14757-0_8

The rise of megacities has led to drastic changes in travel demand and its structure, related with a fast increase in private vehicle ownership and inadequate extensions of the public transportation system, which has also produced several problems such as traffic congestion, noise, and ambient air pollution. With this unexpected fast urban expansion, traffic has become a big challenge for most of these megacities, and as engines of the global economy, it's important that the transport network keeps those engines working efficiently. But, this continuous growth rate can be seen to have negative and positive effects, as it can create new opportunities for innovation, education, interconnectivity, and development [2, 3].

To meet the many challenges that megacities are already facing, the usual answer that keeps echoing is to create Smart Cities. So, the expectation of today's digital age is to combine cities with technological solutions, and if conceived well and designed and built well, Smart Cities could provide relief to megacities that have exceeded their optimum size [4]. This concept not only embodies its technological solutions but also its capacity to manage the information and resources to improve people's quality of life [5, 6]. Smart Cities effectively could leverage technology, infrastructure, and citizen engagement to create an urban environment that could foster economic growth and productivity, innovation, social mobility, inclusiveness, and sustainability [7].

But the Smart City vision cannot be achieved without a smart and sustainable mobility, as it is a key issue and an important motor for growth and progress, crucial for a city to function properly. As mobility problems arise, a massive research effort was gone in the direction of improving urban mobility [8]. This research effort keeps trying to improve road safety conditions and mitigate traffic congestion, especially in large, polluted, and congested cities and in harsh climates with hazardous driving scenarios.

It is difficult to understate how much private vehicles have shaped human societies since cities and infrastructures were built around this paradigm. The land transport system was mostly based on the use and ownership of private vehicles, consuming on average 85 percent of the total energy used by the transport sector [9]. But, there are too many problems related to vehicle ownership, and there is no more physical space for maintaining the 'one car, one driver' combination [10].

Smart Cities and Smart Mobility were set up to tackle the current challenges on that matter, to identify the limitations of our society, and to suggest potential solutions. The implementation of an efficient public transport system could solve part of these problems, but Smart Mobility can go one step further [11]. It could provide a comprehensive and sustainable approach by connecting the use of technology to improve the efficiency of the transport systems (e.g., reducing costs, congestion, accidents, emissions, and increasing user comfort) [12]. It also aims to address these issues by applying novel technologies such as sensing, Big Data, IoT and Ubiquitous Computing.

Smart Mobility has been advocated as one of the cornerstones of any forward-thinking city [13] and regarded as an essential component of Smart City strategies [14]. By addressing the mobility challenges facing people all over the world, Smart Mobility could potentially address the transportation needs by moving people and goods faster, seamlessly and in a convenient way, both in urban and interurban environments [15]. But Smart Mobility has many faces and focus areas depending on local contexts and different needs, which complicates the task of coordinating different, sometimes contradictory, interests in Smart City concepts. For example, residents and tourists want to reach their destinations on time, but they also want to have an exciting yet relaxed, authentic, and comfortable urban experience [16].

Smart Mobility has also gained momentum in cities around the world because of the widespread use of smartphones, and mobile devices with high computing, storage, and bandwidth capabilities, as well as sensors. In particular, the presence of onboard sensors allows the implementation of mobile applications that can provide useful information and contents to the users, according to their location and current actions [17]. Smartphones are changing the ways we travel, enabling users to consume highly personalized information at any time, in any place. The use of the above-mentioned technologies in transportation systems includes applications for various purposes, such as real-time traffic information, measurement of carbon dioxide emissions, information about roadway construction and incidents, parking availability, and navigation information for people with accessibility needs [18].

Even though smartphones and their sensors let us monitor specific physical parameters, such as the user's location or the user's activity recognition, the Internet is also another source of valuable data. If properly collected and delivered, it can contribute to solving many problems related to user's mobility in the cities. One of the most interesting research issues is to predict traffic flow by extracting traffic-related information such as congestion and incidents using textual data from the Internet. By analyzing social media, and other sources on the Internet it is possible to know beforehand, where an accident happened, or which road is closed for maintenance, helping to predict the traffic flow on those roads. It can also be made using data shared by users in many applications, such as Google Maps and Waze, or by organizations responsible for traffic management.

In their daily lives, citizens frequently experience unexpected situations while driving, like suddenly finding interrupted roads due to works or other types of extraordinary events, like sports events, happening in the city, forcing them to quickly decide which alternative road to get to the intended destination on time. Because of these situations, driving can be an emotionally stressful experience. Hernandez et al. [19] measured the stress of drivers through different types of interactions and stated that stress in large doses leads to adverse health conditions such as depression, hypertension and various forms of cardiovascular disease. So, to avoid getting stressed, a driver might prefer the least stressful route, even if it is not the fastest route.

In this sense, a platform is proposed to use technologies to support decision-making, improving user's mobility and helping citizens to optimize their time management, consequently reducing their daily stress. This platform aims to centralize all the existing information about traffic and roads condition for the Madeira Islands, a Portuguese archipelago, located in the North Atlantic Ocean, southwest of Portugal. Even though the Madeira Islands does not have a single, large megacity like London or Paris, it has its own mobility problems, which are not so different from the issues previously mentioned for other large cities. Almost half of Madeira's 270,000 population lives in Funchal, the island's capital. In this city, the narrow, cobbled streets were never meant for vehicles, usually being surprisingly congested with traffic. Road congestion is very common in many parts of the city, especially in the center at various times of the day. In the morning, for example, the main access roads are very close to their capacity, or even exceed it, leading to congestion that also affects the performance of public transport. Exploring the island to the north is also difficult because of the steep and winding terrain. Parking is also a problem felt by everyone, namely drivers and pedestrians. In almost every place in Funchal, there are more vehicles parked on the road than on legitimate parking spaces [20]. Consequently, in order to solve some of these problems, an Android application has been developed to collect traffic-related data, by using information shared by users on Facebook or in municipalities and governmental websites.

The current sources of data are obtained through Madeira Civil Protection Services [21] and from some Facebook pages [22] where users post news about accidents and other incidents on the road. Civil Protection data is more reliable than Facebook data and is used to find information about closed or conditioned roads in advance. In turn, Facebook allows us to get crowdsourced data about accidents and traffic congestion in real-time. A server collects and filters the traffic information data, obtaining the event location coordinates and distributing this data to the application. The application then notifies the users about these events and provides alternative routes if necessary. It also provides a navigational solution with additional features such as elevations, narrowness, and steepness of roads.

The remaining paper is structured in five different sections. Section 2 provides a current state of research, describing the existing systems related to this work. After the second section, there is a short description of the issues and problems that led to the development of this paper. Then the proposed system, as the design and methodologies used were described. Next, there is a discussion section to explain the obtained results, their limitations, learned lessons and directions for future improvements. Finally, a short conclusion summarizes this paper key findings.

2 Literature Survey

There is hardly a country in Europe in which urban mobility does not pose a challenge in the 21st century. Because of this problem, mobility in urban environments has become one of the most prominent research fields in the Smart City context. Therefore, different research papers and applications have been dedicated to finding solutions to those traffic-related problems.

Khatri [23] proposed a traffic monitoring system to extract traffic information data such as congestion and incidents using textual data from the Internet. To pursue this task the authors used Twitter social networking as the primary data source, in such a way that the system can detect traffic congestions and traffic incidents from the users' tweets. It extracts as much information as possible using people as sensors, instead of setting up a dedicated infrastructure for the same purpose. It follows the idea that people tend to share with others the events that occur around them, so they also share traffic-related information. By another side, Chatterjee et al. [24] created an online interface to access the dynamic real-time data from the Facebook pages about Indian cities traffic (using the Facebook API). The Facebook API helps to extract different attributes of online pages dynamically to explore the status and quality of traffic in real-time. Another example of using social media in traffic-related applications is the solution proposed by Zhang et al. [25], which consists on mining social media data to deduce useful related traffic information with a special emphasis under events, including both planned events (such as sporting games), and unplanned events (such as traffic accidents). Hence, Twitter, Facebook, Instagram, Snapchat, and other social media websites can act as new platforms for data, where people themselves act as sensors and share the information which they possess.

Similarly, the proposed platform was developed with non-traditional data sources, using Madeira Civil Protection Services and Facebook data. To accomplish this goal the analysis initially leveraged data that included geolocation information. Many people share on Facebook traffic incidents and other traffic-related events which they find on the go. This information is very important as it can be used to identify traffic congestion and other traffic-related data, almost in real-time.

Singh et al. [26], Allouch et al. [27], and Bhoraskar et al. [28] present different solutions to detect the road surface conditions. The first one uses a smartphone-based sensing and crowdsourcing technique to detect the road surface conditions like potholes and bumps, based on the analysis of accelerometer readings. An Android application was developed to interact with the sensors of the smartphone to collect accelerometer and GPS data. Those smartphones were placed inside the vehicle at different positions (front dashboard or backseat), and when the vehicle experience a pothole or bumps the accelerometer sensor records these variations. RoadSense [27], based on The Pothole Patrol application [29] is a road condition monitoring framework based on smartphone built in sensors (accelerometer, gyroscope, and GPS) to analyze the quality of different road sections using machine learning techniques. By using this machine-learning approach, the application can identify potholes and other severe road surface anomalies. This framework employs unimodal accelerometer data, using a gyroscope sensor in conjunction with the accelerometer to derive more accurate road quality predictions. Wolverine [28] also use smartphone sensors (accelerometer, GPS, and magnetometer) for traffic and road conditions detection. This method was specifically designed to identify braking events, that frequently indicates congested traffic conditions, and bumps on the roads to characterize the type of road. It also applies machine learning techniques to classify the data to adapt to changing factors like the nature of the road and the type of vehicle.

Unlike the previously presented studies that use sensors to detect potholes, the proposed platform uses data retrieved from Facebook posts about potholes and other severe road surface anomalies. It also retrieves data from rockfalls and landslides, problems that extend to the whole island, especially in Winter. In Madeira Island, after the bad weather, it is normal that numerous sections of the regional roads are closed because of the rockfalls. The developed platform does not use any method to detect surface conditions, but in future it could be integrated in our solution. Our main goals for the application were to get the roads width (provided by Funchal's City Council), slope (retrieved from the MapQuest's Open Elevations API [30]), and to get information about traffic conditions (obtained through Madeira Civil Protection Services and from Facebook traffic-related pages).

Google Traffic and Waze are the most popular applications for real-time traffic conditions based on user contributions. Google Traffic is a feature on Google Maps that displays traffic conditions in real-time on major roads and highways. It works by analyzing the GPS-determined locations transmitted to Google by many mobile phone users. By calculating the speed of users along a length of road, Google can generate a live traffic map. Google processes the incoming raw data about mobile phone device locations and then excludes anomalies such as a postal vehicle that makes frequent stops. When a threshold of users in an area is noted, the overlay along roads and highways on the Google map changes color. In turn, Waze allows users to avoid traffic jams, police traps, and accidents. It is a community-driven GPS navigation application, providing turn-by-turn navigation information. It automatically reroutes around traffic as conditions change on the road and help users to find gas stations and the cheapest gas prices.

The applications mentioned above solved several traffic-related problems, also informing drivers about traffic conditions, and providing turn-by-turn navigation. But the existing applications do not work in a perfect manner for the Madeira Islands, and this was one of the motivations for the development of this study. The pros and cons of each application, namely Google Maps and Waze, will be better explained in the Problem Statement section.

3 Problem Statement

Smart Mobility, which is related to traffic conditions, is one of the key factors for the development of Smart Cities and is one of the biggest challenges of the 21st century. Traffic congestion, roads interrupted due to works, sports events or festive celebrations are some of the situations that influence the way drivers move through the cities. These unexpected situations require drivers to find fast solutions to reach their destinations on time.

With a focus on improving mobility and reducing daily stress, it provides a service for more efficient time management. In their daily lives, citizens frequently experience unexpected situations while driving, like suddenly finding interrupted roads due to works or another type of extraordinary events, happening in the city. When using the current GPS navigation systems, this problem can be minimized since they suggest alternative routes to the drivers. However, most people have probably experienced situations where GPS navigation systems have not been updated to accommodate the most recent changes in traffic, by not anticipating traffic congestions and traffic incidents, or that take drivers into extremely narrow streets, where a car barely fits, or into the middle of a forest. Moreover, current navigation systems do not consider the slope of the road, which could also be a problem, especially if drivers are taken to very steep roads. Therefore, it is so important to develop solutions to anticipate and alert users about these conditions.

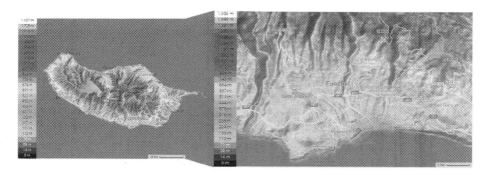

Fig. 1. Madeira island and Funchal city topographic maps

Madeira is a mountainous island (see Fig. 1), dominated by a vigorous volcanic landscape, with deep valleys steeped slopes and scarps. Only 16% of the island has a gradient of less than 30°. Flat terrain and sandy beaches are almost inexistent [31]. In Madeira, there is a rather peculiar and dangerous road called Estrada Regional 101 (ER101). It is one of the oldest and most beautiful roads of the island. Due to Madeira's dramatic coastline, the road has many curves, narrow passages, and steep climbs and descents, and is rugged, slow and old. Due to the many views on the coast and the Atlantic Ocean, this road is frequently taken by tourists. Even though passing close to the sea, it looks more like a mountain road, and from time to time the road gets very narrow, especially on the North coast of the Island. This road is considered one of the most dangerous roads in the world, as stated by dangerousroads.org [32] users.

Fig. 2. Areas of worst traffic congestion in Funchal

During the last decades, there has been massive construction in several areas of Madeira, particularly on the areas surrounding Funchal, and the network of paved roads and the construction of several tunnels expanded considerably leading to a higher mobility of people and goods throughout the island and the possibility to reach once inaccessible areas. But, Madeiran cities, such as other European cities, are still struggling with traffic congestion. In Funchal, the capital city of Madeira island, traffic congestion problem has grown to alarming proportions, and it is one of the most challenging issues. The causes of traffic congestion in Funchal are many. Its orography with narrow and steep roads does not let the traffic flow smoothly. There are many schools in Funchal center and traffic becomes chaotic when parents take and pick their children up from school. Also, as in other cities, people from other areas of the island come and get back to their home villages once they finish their day-to-day work, which only causes even more traffic. The heavy traffic entering and exiting the island's main road (VR1 – Via Rápida 1) typically leads to congestion on the entrance and exit ramps that give access to the Funchal's center (see Fig. 2).

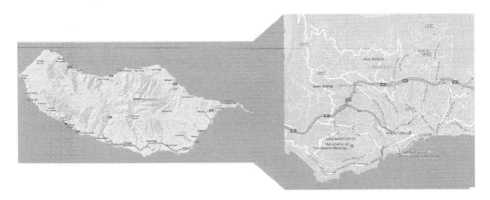

Fig. 3. Google traffic in Madeira Island

Another motivation to start this project was the lack of information about traffic conditions in Funchal. Google Traffic displays the traffic conditions in real-time, considering the users flow on a certain stretch of road, and takes advantage of the users' smartphones to calculate the vehicles speed along the road. However, for certain areas, it only has information about major roads. And when the project was started it was even worse, only showing information about one of the main roads of the island (see Fig. 3). Other problems found were that it does not display closed or conditioned roads, does not consider the road conditions (e.g., potholes) and it does not provide users additional information about the roads (e.g., roads width, pavement type, condition, etc.).

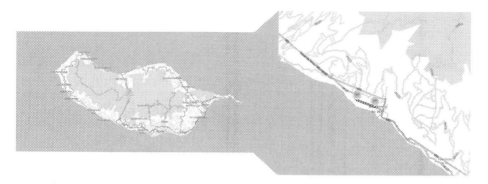

Fig. 4. Waze in Madeira Island

Other possible solution could be Waze, that allows sharing traffic information in real-time, being updated by users, by adding multiple traffic-related events, like accidents, or closed roads. But in Madeira island, there is a lack of users and contributions. Only one closed road is marked down on the island map by a contributor that probably went there on holidays (see Fig. 4). Besides that, the information becomes outdated as there are no contributions, and no one controls those contributions. Furthermore, there is imprecise information on the map (e.g., wrong road names, etc.). The applications mentioned above, when the project was started, they had the same problem, the lack of users, which meant that the applications had few information about the real traffic conditions.

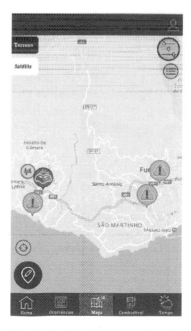

Fig. 5. ProCiv Madeira application

ProCiv Madeira [33] is an application developed for Madeira Civil Protection (see Fig. 5) that provides information about closed roads or accidents, that are shared by Madeiran municipalities and government websites. However, it does not provide traffic-related information in real-time.

Other issues found in the previously mentioned systems are:

- Driving users to steep roads. With winding mountain roads and vantage points that overlook the sea, driving in Madeira can be a challenge both for tourists and locals. A continuous maze of roads which take drivers up and down on close to 90 degrees steep (up and down) hills;
- Driving users to narrow roads. In the older urban zones, driving can be stressful. The road lanes are narrow, there are cars parked on the sides and there are many junctions with priorities difficult to understand;
- Especially tourists that are unfamiliar with the island or some part of the island, are often in need of help to take their rental cars from some roads;

Furthermore, in an island where from time to time there are rock falls, that lead to road closures, it is even more important to alert drivers before they get on the road to their destinations.

4 Proposed System

Based on the initial findings and identified challenges described in the previous section, a platform that uses mobile technologies were developed to support decision-making, improving users' mobility and helping citizens to optimize their time management, consequently reducing their daily stress. The proposed system automatically gathers roads traffic information from several sources and transmits it to the users' smart-phones. This collection of information focus on the events that are occurring inside the city, that could influence the traffic.

The application was developed for Android Operating System, showing information on a map about closed or conditioned roads, and integrating information about interrupted roads and changes in the direction of traffic. This mobile application allows sending notifications to the users about road conditions, based on the regular itineraries of the users.

Based on sensor data and information available on maps, the platform collects both geographic and orographic information, alerting the users about the existence of narrow or steep roads in a certain path.

The system architecture (see Fig. 6) is divided into three major modules: the server, the database and the Android application, all of which are explained in detail in the next three subsections.

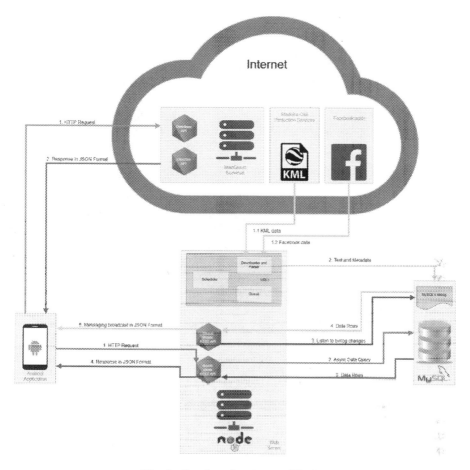

Fig. 6. Developed system architecture

4.1 Node.js Server

The server was built on Node.js because it is completely event driven and much of the code runs basing on callbacks, which helps the application not to pause or sleep, but to become available for other requests. Its main function is to parse HTML information about events, such as interrupted roads and changes in the direction of traffic, that is currently available on several websites. To not have this script always running on the server, the node-cron package was used that schedules the parsing of the web pages related with traffic, every day at the same hour. This is a way to run functions at specific times of the day, week, month or year. The Cheerio package was used to make the HTML parsing. It allows to parse, to manipulate, and to render the DOM data structure from the websites HTML documents. More precisely, it retrieves all the data available on the municipalities and government websites related with closed or interrupted roads, and then, sends it to the users' smartphones. It also saves the begin and the end GPS coordinates of the closed road sections, updating the mobile phones whenever a new event occurs.

The server gathers data from the devices that are accessing it to better give alerts to the user himself, and to the other users too. For that, it uses web sockets, more precisely Socket.io package that allows the server to communicate with the Android smartphones and enables real-time bidirectional event-based communication. It collects data from the smartphones using three identifiers, that together are unique: the smartphone brand, model, and serial number. This is a way to differentiate each access to the server.

It also collects real-time data about accidents, to inform the users about low traffic flow on the road and helping the drivers to choose another route to their destination.

4.2   Database

MySQL was the chosen database management system. It stores data about the width of the roads, as well as other road and traffic conditions. By using alerts, this data will help users to avoid roads where accidents have occurred, where there is a high traffic density or narrow or steep roads. If the users request a route on the application, it will send an HTTP request to the server to retrieve the width of each road. The data is retrieved in JSON, that is a lightweight data-interchange format.

The MySQL database is replicated using the binary log. This replication is important to achieve high availability and to record all changes made to the database along with additional information related to those changes such as time taken to for a statement to update date, etc. The binary log is not only used for replication but can be used for auditing and point in time recovery. By using bin log listeners like Zongji or LiveSQL, it's possible to capture every change made on the MySQL binary log. In this way, every time there is new data on the closed roads table, an alert is generated to the server and then the data is broadcast to all the application users.

4.3   Android Application

This application collects information about extraordinary events that take place in a city (works, sports events, celebrations, etc.) integrating information about these events, like interrupted roads and changes in the direction of traffic, that is currently spread across several websites where this information is usually published (municipality and government websites). This application also collects and provide useful information about interesting events taking place in the city.

The first problem found was about the dispersion of information found on the Internet about the condition of the roads and which ones are closed or conditioned. To solve it, the Android application shows on the map (see Fig. 7), the sections of closed or conditioned roads, sending notifications to the users about the roads that are in works or that are closed. Additionally, it sends notifications about events that will occur, to inform users which roads will be closed and when.

To determine the users' location, the smartphones GPS is used. This will help in the future to send personalized notifications to the users, considering their previous locations and routes. It is crucial to only send notifications to the users that are relevant for them. For example, if the user never goes to a certain location, probably he would not want to know if there is a closed road there.

Fig. 7. Closed road in Madeira Island

By determining if the Wi-Fi network that the user is accessing is one of the known networks (home, work, etc.), and because GPS and other sensors consume too much energy, when the user is connected to a known Wi-Fi network, all the sensors are off, decreasing the unnecessary usage of sensors indoors to reduce the energy consumption.

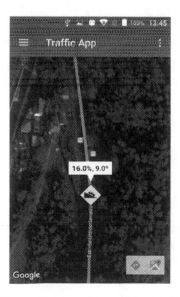

Fig. 8. Steep road in Madeira Island

To get the slope of the roads the Open Elevation API [30] was used. It provides elevation profile information such as elevation and distance given a latitude/longitude pair in JSON format. Having the elevation and distance between coordinates the slope of the road is calculated. Figure 8 shows an example of a steep road, and how the application indicates on the map the steep percentage and degrees.

To send notifications to the users in an adequate way, the Activity Recognition plugin developed by Aware Framework [34] was used. This plugin aims to accurately detect users' activity such as walking, running, driving, etc. Essentially, the app only needs to know if the user is driving or not. If he is, the smartphone reads the notification to the user, using the Text-to-Speech from Google and it does not disturb user's driving. If not, then the notification is sent as text, in a way that the user could read it anywhere and anytime. This plugin aims to reduce distractions on the road by sending audio notifications to the driver.

Fig. 9. Turn-by-turn navigation

The application also provides a turn-by-turn navigation (see Fig. 9), using the Mapquest Directions API [35], where the maneuvers for each interception are continuously presented to the user in the form of textual or audio instructions. This module requires GPS to be enabled as it needs to know the exact location of the user to provide the maneuvers to be performed.

5   Discussion

The implementation of the application was done using the AWARE Framework, and while the server collects and filters the data, the application shows the filtered data to the user. The application was tested to obtain information about local events, and if there were some real-time events occurring on the route to our destinations.

While the information from the Civil Protection website, is successfully obtained and shown to the user, by marking closed roads on the map and by notifying the user about these events in advance, the information obtained from the Facebook needs to be filtered. However, it is impossible to obtain only the relevant and accurate information, as it depends on what the users posted.

Although this solution can solve some of the issues related to traffic problems, it is still a prototype, and as solutions are found more new problems arrive. The future development will lead to a more robust solution, in order to help all of them who stress when they are on the road.

Currently, the application has only width data about the Funchal city. If we trace a route outside Funchal there will be no data, and then the width of the roads will not be shown in the application map. Another problem related to roads width that this solution cannot solve is when drivers park their cars on the road making it difficult for other drivers to pass on that road. By using IoT technologies it could be possible to know where a car is parked, or if there is no space for other vehicles to pass.

One problem, that is difficult to solve, and happened during the application development, is related to HTML parsers. While server is parsing to get the data, if the owner of the website decides to change the DOM of the webpage document (a cross-platform and language-independent application programming interface that treats an HTML, XHTML, or XML document as a tree structure wherein each node is an object representing a part of the document), then the script to read that webpage must be redone. One possible solution could be to suggest to the website owners the uni-formization or the best distribution of the data, for example by using web services.

Currently, our platform collects data only for Madeira Island, but it can be expanded to integrate other data sources related to other locations traffic and road conditions.

The application was only tested with three smartphones: ONN V9 Only with Android KitKat, Samsung Galaxy S6 Edge with Android Nougat and Alcatel PIXI 4 with Android Marshmallow. Another problem related with Android versions and the innumerous smartphones available, and because it will be impossible to test the application in each different mobile device, is that our application could not work on some smartphone's brands and/or Android versions. Regarding the Operating System (OS), the application is restricted to Android smartphones and future studies could implement software for another OS.

As the development of the application started with previous versions of Android, the battery-saving features were not a problem. Android Marshmallow introduced a pair of new battery-saving features called Doze and App Standby, that used to kill some background processes that were consuming more battery than normal. One of the features used was Socket.io that uses web sockets, and because it maintains a communication tunnel open, Doze tends to shut down the process that is using this feature, causing the app to crash.

Current studies and applications solve a range of traffic-related problems. But there are specific problems, for certain areas of the world, where those applications are almost useless. This force researchers to create specific solutions for certain areas of the world. Madeira island, with its orography, narrow and steep roads, is a very peculiar scenario for this kind of apps and more generic solutions are not adequate. Nevertheless, we based our development on these apps, and it was much better than having to start from scratch.

One of the challenges of this type of studies is to get out and test the application while driving on the road. Each time a bug appears, it needs to be solved by returning to the computer. It could be easier for developers to change their own scripts directly on the mobile device.

Another challenge was to collect the data from the websites and to extract only the relevant information. Some websites have all the information well-organized, but for others, it must be done manually.

6   Conclusion

Smart Cities depend on solutions that can reduce and optimize the traffic on their streets. The implementation of smart solutions that integrate mobile phone sensors with environment sensors, can transform the way drivers see the traffic, avoiding certain problems that only increase the stress of whoever is on the road. Knowing these situations in advance will give drivers some more time and comfort.

The design and implementation of an Android application to help users to avoid certain types of roads and events, using data retrieved from the Internet were presented. The application was created to a point where all the functionalities for using the information from the closed and conditioned roads were completed. Other functionalities include displaying the location of the narrow or steep roads.

For future work, the next steps will focus on taking advantage of additional data sources of real-time data about traffic density, potholes, and free parking spaces. Other objectives will be to use the data collected by the smartphone sensors to know the user habits (routes used, frequently visited places and so on) to issue only relevant notifications for each user. Lastly, it will be important to ask users their opinion about each route. In this way, it will be possible to identify road problems that were difficult to detect through the sensors (e.g. potholes).

Other future implementations will include options to know the preferences of the drivers while parking their cars (e.g., the closest parking lot to their destination or the cheapest) and give information to the users about where they can park their cars (sometimes users do not know about some parking lots that can be closer to their destinations or cheaper than the ones where they are actually parking).

Acknowledgments. This research has been supported by FCT – Fundação para a Ciência e Tecnologia, within the Project Scope: UID/EEA/500009/2013.

References

1. United Nations: Department of Economic and Social Affairs: World Urbanization Prospects, the 2014 Revision: Highlights (2014)
2. Jerzy, K., Anna, N.K.: Rise of Megacities, The: Challenges, Opportunities and Unique Characteristic. World Scientific, Singapore (2018)
3. van der Ploeg, F., Poelhekke, S.: Globalization and the rise of mega-cities in the developing world. Camb. J. Reg. Econ. Soc. **1**, 477–501 (2008)
4. Pelton, J.N., Singh, I.B.: Smart Cities of Today and Tomorrow: Better Technology, Infrastructure and Security. Springer, Cham (2019). https://doi.org/10.1007/978-3-319-95822-4
5. Ramaprasad, A., Sánchez-Ortiz, A., Syn, T.: A unified definition of a smart city. In: Janssen, M., et al. (eds.) EGOV 2017. LNCS, vol. 10428, pp. 13–24. Springer, Cham (2017). https://doi.org/10.1007/978-3-319-64677-0_2
6. Zubizarreta, I., Seravalli, A., Arrizabalaga, S.: Smart city concept: what it is and what it should be. J. Urban Plann. Dev. **142**, 04015005 (2016)
7. Khanna, P.: Urbanisation, technology, and the growth of smart cities, pp. 52–59. Asian Management Insights (2015)
8. Pati, B., Panigrahi, C.R., Misra, S., Pujari, A.K., Bakshi, S. (eds.): Progress in Advanced Computing and Intelligent Engineering. AISC, vol. 713. Springer, Singapore (2019). https://doi.org/10.1007/978-981-13-1708-8
9. Rodrigue, J.P., Comtois, C., Slack, B.: The Geography of Transport Systems. Routledge, Abingdon (2006)
10. Neckermann, L.: Smart Cities, Smart Mobility: Transforming the Way We Live and Work. Troubador Publishing Ltd., Leicester (2017)
11. Aletà, N.B.: Smart mobility in smart cities. In: Libro de Actas CIT2016. XII Congreso de Ingeniería del Transporte. Universitat Politècnica València (2016)
12. Bazzan, A.L.C., Klügl, F.: Introduction to Intelligent Systems in Traffic and Transportation. Morgan & Claypool Publishers, San Rafael (2014)
13. Koch, F., Meneguzzi, F., Lakkaraju, K.: Agent Technology for Intelligent Mobile Services and Smart Societies. Springer, Heidelberg (2015). https://doi.org/10.1007/978-3-662-46241-6
14. Benevolo, C., Dameri, R.P., D'Auria, B.: Smart mobility in smart city. In: Torre, T., Braccini, A.M., Spinelli, R. (eds.) Empowering Organizations. LNISO, vol. 11, pp. 13–28. Springer, Cham (2016). https://doi.org/10.1007/978-3-319-23784-8_2
15. Golub, A.: Community-Based Assessment of Smart Transportation Needs in the City of Portland. Transportation Research and Education Center. Portland State University (2018)
16. Flügge, B.: Smart Mobility – Connecting Everyone: Trends, Concepts and Best Practices. Springer, Cham (2017). https://doi.org/10.1007/978-3-658-15622-0
17. Amoretti, M., Belli, L., Zanichelli, F.: UTravel: smart mobility with a novel user profiling and recommendation approach. Pervasive Mob. Comput. **38**, 474–489 (2017)
18. Gebresselassie, M., Sanchez, T.: Smart tools for socially sustainable transport: a review of mobility apps. Urban Sci. **2**, 45 (2018)
19. Hernandez, J., McDuff, D., Benavides, X., Amores, J., Maes, P., Picard, R.: AutoEmotive: bringing empathy to the driving experience to manage stress. In: Proceedings of the 2014 Companion Publication on Designing Interactive Systems - DIS Companion 2014, pp. 53–56. ACM Press, Vancouver (2014)
20. Berlitz: Berlitz: Madeira Pocket Guide. Apa Publications (UK) Limited (2014)
21. Home - Serviço Regional de Proteção Civil – Madeira. https://www.procivmadeira.pt/pt/
22. Ocorrências na Madeira. https://www.facebook.com/groups/ocorrencias.madeira/?fref=nf

23. Khatri, C.: Real-time road traffic information detection through social media. arXiv:1801. 05088 [cs] (2018)
24. Chatterjee, S., Mridha, S.K., Bhattacharyya, S., Shakhari, S., Bhattacharyya, M.: Dynamic congestion analysis for better traffic management using social media. In: Satapathy, S.C., Das, S. (eds.) Proceedings of First International Conference on Information and Communication Technology for Intelligent Systems: Volume 2. SIST, vol. 51, pp. 85–95. Springer, Cham (2016). https://doi.org/10.1007/978-3-319-30927-9_9
25. Zhang, Z., Ni, M., He, Q., Gao, J.: Mining transportation information from social media for planned and unplanned events (2016)
26. Singh, G., Bansal, D., Sofat, S., Aggarwal, N.: Smart patrolling: an efficient road surface monitoring using smartphone sensors and crowdsourcing. Pervasive Mob. Comput. **40**, 71–88 (2017)
27. Allouch, A., Koubaa, A., Abbes, T., Ammar, A.: RoadSense: smartphone application to estimate road conditions using accelerometer and gyroscope. IEEE Sens. J. **17**, 4231–4238 (2017)
28. Bhoraskar, R., Vankadhara, N., Raman, B., Kulkarni, P.: Wolverine: traffic and road condition estimation using smartphone sensors. In: 2012 Fourth International Conference on Communication Systems and Networks (COMSNETS 2012), pp. 1–6. IEEE, Bangalore (2012)
29. Eriksson, J., Girod, L., Hull, B., Newton, R., Madden, S., Balakrishnan, H.: The pothole patrol: using a mobile sensor network for road surface monitoring. In: Proceeding of the 6th International Conference on Mobile Systems, Applications, and Services - MobiSys 2008, p. 29. ACM Press, Breckenridge (2008)
30. Open Elevation API – Overview. https://developer.mapquest.com/documentation/open/elevation-api/
31. View of Modelling Tourism Demand in Madeira Since 1946: and Historical Overview Based on A Time Series Approach. https://www.jsod-cieo.net/journal/index.php/jsod/article/view/68/66
32. ER101 Antiga. https://www.dangerousroads.org/europe/portugal/115-er101-antigua-portugal.html
33. ProCiv Madeira – Apps on Google Play. https://play.google.com/store/apps/details?id=com.dobsware.procivmadeira&hl=en
34. AWARE – Open-source Context Instrumentation Framework for Everyone. http://www.awareframework.com/
35. Open Directions API – Overview. https://developer.mapquest.com/documentation/open/directions-api/

Prediction of Journey Destination for Travelers of Urban Public Transport: A Comparison Model Study

Vera Costa[1,2(✉)], Tânia Fontes[1], José Luís Borges[1,2],
and Teresa Galvão Dias[1,2]

[1] INESC TEC - INESC Technology and Science, Porto, Portugal
veracosta@fe.up.pt
[2] FEUP - Faculty of Engineering, University of Porto, Porto, Portugal

Abstract. In public transport, smart card-based ticketing system allows to redesign the UPT network, by providing customized transport services, or incentivize travelers to change specific patterns. However, in open systems, to develop personalized connections the journey destination must be known before the end of the travel. Thus, to obtain that knowledge, in this study three models (Top-K, NB, and J48) were applied using different groups of travelers of an urban public transport network located in a medium-sized European metropolitan area (Porto, Portugal). Typical travelers were selected from the segmentation of transportation card signatures, and groups were defined based on the traveler age or economic conditions. The results show that is possible to predict the journey's destination based on the past with an accuracy rate that varies, on average, from 20% in the worst scenarios to 65% in the best.

Keywords: Urban public transportation · Travel patterns ·
Journey destination · Prediction models

1 Introduction

Enlargement of urban public transport (UPT) is essential to promote sustainable development of cities [1]. Nevertheless, the use of such systems by its users is not always easy, due its complexity and inflexibility [2]. To improve the efficiency of existing transportation networks, in recent years, UPT systems have adopted sophisticated Information and Communication Technologies (ICT). The use of such technologies allows the possibility to provide information to travelers using innovative ways [3] rather than expanding infrastructures [4]. Two main factors have contributed to this: (i) the adoption of smart cards in UPT; and (ii) the significant increase in the usage of mobile devices.

Adoption of smart cards has provided several benefits to the UPT management. To monitoring the network, surveys and other less reliable methods were replaced by these cards [5]. Therefore, UPT systems can provide real-time access to public transport data, which could be used for estimating the arrival times of buses, incidents, or delays [6]. Data provided by smart cards enable access to detailed information on the use, travel

J. C. Ferreira et al. (Eds.): INTSYS 2018, LNICST 267, pp. 113–132, 2019.
https://doi.org/10.1007/978-3-030-14757-0_9

patterns and demand. Also, the exploration of this data allows deriving useful information about transit passenger behavior, such as travel purpose or activity [7].

Availability of descriptive data about service usage will allow UPT providers to optimize the transport network and manage their resources more efficiently [8]. To do this, some information, as the main factors that influence travel's occurrence, should be well known. Having this knowledge, it is possible to define measures at two levels: (i) redesign the network, for example, by providing customized transport systems (e.g., DRT); or (ii) creating incentives to change certain travel patterns. Incentives may be, for example, pricing policies to restrict travels to some specific locations (e.g., access to monuments, cable cars), information management policies during the occurrence of critical events (e.g., floods, popular manifestations), or commercial policies to influence consumers to explore/visit other locations or at different times of the day (e.g., through the attribution of offers or discount vouchers). Taking in mind the development of efficient tools to implement these and other possible measures, the knowledge of journey destination when the user validates his ticket at the entrance of public transport, is of great importance. Thus, the central questions of this research are:

- How to predict the journey destination of a traveler from a UPT system? How can past data be efficiently used to improve such prediction?
- Are there any significant differences between the predictions of journey destinations for different traveler's groups? What are those differences and main reasons for this occurs?
- Is there any significant difference in the prediction of a journey destination for different time periods? How model these periods to improve such predictions?

To answer these questions, data from travel validations of a multimodal network of a UPT system, collected over a year, was explored. Two factors that may influence the travel purpose were considered: travel day and traveler type.

The paper is structured as follows: Sect. 2 presents the related work. Section 3 describes the methodology used while the presentation and discussion of the most significant results are present in Sect. 4. Some policy implications are presented in Sect. 5. Finally, the conclusions and answers to the previous questions are given in Sect. 6.

2   Related Work

The implementation of smart card-based ticketing occurred in many public transport systems around the world with different characteristics. Closed gate system allows an explicit recognition of patterns of mobility. It is possible to identify the origin and destination, time and duration travel, but there no transshipments information when multiple alternatives are provided. To avoid alighting delays, several bus services around the world use open gate systems. This system collects the origin of each journey without identifying the exact destination [9] and uses flat fare structures. However, some public transport providers are driven to adjust the price, based on the travel distance [10]. In this context, an algorithm of destination's inference based on the past usage of travelers is crucial.

Journey prediction is a central component that supports the development and delivery of personalized information services in UPT. Destination's inference provides relevant information to UPT providers, identifying behavior patterns, namely the traveler entrances and exits. The trend towards personalized Traveler Information Systems (TIS) supports the development of services capable of assessing and delivering contextually relevant information. The vast amount of data requires efficient processing and storage methods.

The latest developments in ICT have paved the way for the emergence of ubiquitous environments and ambient intelligence in UPT, mostly supported by miniaturized computer devices and pervasive communication networks. Such environments have been simplifying the collection and distribution of detailed real-time data, allowing the access to a rich information and support the development of next-generation TIS [11]. Some research has used these technologies to produce large matrices of origin-destination from smart card data [12]. These approaches focus on the destination's inference after the trip ended, allowing the identification of behavior patterns [13, 14], traveler segmentation [15, 16] and provision of information services [17]. Another group of studies was developed to understand travel patterns. Table 1 shows a summary of some studies formulated the last years.

Several authors studied urban traffic in different cities [18–21]. In these studies, some places in the city were identified as more popular. The conclusions allowed optimizing the public transport demand. On the other hand, the knowledge about travel time distribution along weekdays seemed to be another critical factor to optimize the system. Additionally, improving the knowledge of demand for public transport and identify travel peaks can allow transport providers to adjust the availability of vehicles [22].

The occurrence of individual travel and their primary purpose (work, school, for example) was also predicted [7, 23–25]. Thus, travelers with different mobility patterns were found. The acknowledging of their main patterns was one of the goals of a vast number of transport providers. In that way, two conditions are analyzed: if regular transit travelers tend to maintain their patterns and if it is easier to predict the future travels [26–28].

Although the analyzed studies focused on understanding the usage of public transportation and in the optimization of their network, a lack of knowledge about the best way of how a model can predict mobility patterns can be highlighted. Only a restrict number of works studied the prediction of journeys of travelers from public transport [23, 26]. In these studies, some of them distinguished travel patterns between different groups of passengers (with fixed routines and almost random routines) [20], which does not allow to understand if some models can be more suitable for specific traveler groups. Last, to our best knowledge an inter-comparison study to analyze different models and data configurations to predict the journey destination using UPT is missing, particular by exploring the potential of an extensive dataset.

Table 1. Summary of studies developed in the last years to know travel patterns using of urban public transport.

Author	City (Country)	Input variables	Methods or analysis	Period	Number of trips or users	Main conclusions
[18]	London (UK)	Origin, destination, individual trajectories without their history	Clustering (stations)	7 days	11.22 million trips	Heterogeneous patterns of intra-urban movement. Large flows around a limited number of activity centers
[13]	Beijing (China)	Distance between stops, card ID, route number, driver ID, transaction time, remaining balance, transaction amount	Markov chain (prediction of origin)	1 day	36,246 validations	The method is effective in extracting transit passengers' origin information from transactions with relatively high accuracy (90%)
[22]	Shenzhen (China)	Card ID, action type, station ID, time of the action, check-in and check-out records	Spatial/temporal analysis (day's peak)	6 days	2.5 million trips	The intra-urban trips: - have two significant peak hours over a day - are different between weekday and weekend - have significant periodicity
[19]	London (UK)	Boarding the bus, entering into or exiting	Probabilities (visited locations)	3 months	626 users	Two most frequent locations can be modelled with fixed probabilities. Other destinations (not the two most visited) are popular places in the city
[7]	Minneapolis/St. Paul (USA)	Date/time, route number, card type, is initial boarding or transfer, GPS location	Inference of trip purpose (work or school)	1 week	3,687 validations	Different groups of users have different routines. The return trip time in the Post Meridiem (PM) peak is the primary determining factor of whether an activity is work-related
[26]	Beijing (China)	Card ID, route number, driver ID, transaction time, remaining balance, transaction amount, boarding and alighting stop	Clustering (mobility patterns)	5 days	3.8 million users	Most regular transit riders are commuters who do not own private cars and thus tend to be very sensitive to service reliability
[23]	Lisbon (Portugal)	Card ID, bus boarding time	Prediction of travel (travel occurs/not occurs)	61 days	24 million trips	Longitudinal data from automated fare collection (AFC) systems can be mined to uncover characteristic patterns of temporal regularities in accessing transport system

(*continued*)

Table 1. (*continued*)

Author	City (Country)	Input variables	Methods or analysis	Period	Number of trips or users	Main conclusions
[20]	Brisbane (Australia)	Boarding and alighting stop, boarding and alighting times, route ID, direction, card ID, card type, trip ID	GIS techniques (travel patterns)	1 day	5 million trips	Identification of traffic/users in the city's zones for different groups of people
[21]	Beijing (China)	Deal time and status, entry time, line and station, exit line and station	Analysis of spatial relationships (location, times)	1 day	8.7 million users	The urban development is increasingly concentrated near subway lines and transit stations The people flow in the morning peak shows that the construction of the new cities in Beijing's surrounding area is reinforced
[24]	Lisbon (Portugal)	Bus stops, geographic locations, bus line id, direction, stops on the route, card ID, time of bus boarding, id of the bus boarded	Personal+, Network+, (mobility patterns of urban bus riders)	61 days	24 million trips	Prior knowledge of the user's behaviour can improve the prediction For active users, the rider's own history covers a large portion of the future stop usage. For low demand riders, there is a high degree of uncertainty involved resulting in inaccurate prediction
[25]	All country (Netherlands)	Card ID, date, check-in time and location, check-out time and location	Route deduction	5 days	500,000 journeys	Found the route deduction to perform an accuracy of over 90% for the best selection rule, STA (Selected Least Transfers Last Arrival)
[27]	Oporto (Portugal)	Origin, destination (inferred), date, card ID, line, direction	Probabilities (destination)	2 months	5,000 journeys	Depending the probability stabilizes around two months of data (about 120 travels) or near three months of data (around 351–400 travels)
[28]	Oporto (Portugal)	Origin, destination (inferred), date, card ID, line, direction	Top-K, NB, J48 (destination)	2 months	800 users	The performance of journey predictions seems to be directly related to the mobility patterns
[9]	Oporto (Portugal)	Origin, destination (inferred), date, card ID, line, direction	Top-K, J48 (destination)	2 months	803,892 trips	Similar accuracy in the two methods. The Top-K is several orders of magnitude less memory demanding and much faster, showing great promise for large-scale systems

3   Materials and Methods

To predict the journey destination of a traveler using urban public transport three main steps were considered: (i) firstly, travel data was collected from different travel providers (first subsection); (ii) secondly, journey destination's inference was performed (second subsection); and (iii) last, journey destination's prediction was made (third subsection). Such methodology was applied to a European medium size Metropolitan Area. Figure 1 presents an overview of the methodology followed.

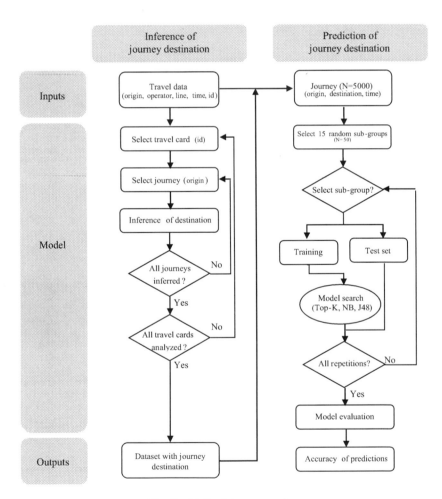

Fig. 1. Methodology overview.

3.1   Data Collection

One year of travel data obtained from the UPT of the Metropolitan Area of Oporto was collected (January 2013 to December 2013). Such network covers an area of 1,575 km^2

and serves 1.75 million of inhabitants. It is composed of 126 buses lines (urban and regional), six metro lines, one cable line, three tram lines and three train lines. This system is operated by 11 transport providers, which Metro do Porto (metro system) and STCP (bus system) are the largest [29].

Oporto network is based on an open and intermodal zonal system. The payment uses a rechargeable intermodal smart card called Andante. There are two types of Andante transport tickets: Signature Titles and Occasional Titles. Signature Titles have different groups of users where the charge depends, besides the journey length, also on the traveler age or economic conditions. While signatures cards can only be used to the cardholder, Occasional Titles can be used by different travelers (it has no personal information). Both cards are valid for a set of adjacent areas previously chosen by the passenger. Signature Titles are valid for the charged month while Occasional Titles are valid within the limit ring acquired during a particular period, currently 1 h for the minimum 2-zone ticket and longer as the number of valid zones increases. Thus, one journey may have one or more stages (validations), depending on the journey's period and the number of zones included in that journey.

For each traveler (i.e., for each Andante smart card), the information related to the boarding time (first boarding on the route), the line (or lines for each journey) and the stop (or stops for each journey) is available. Table 2 shows an extracted trip chain information for an individual traveler during a week of January 2013. The first row shows a journey with two stages. First, the traveler uses stop 2716 and line 303 at 9:14 a.m. followed the stop 3175 and line 302. The second row shows a journey with only one stage.

Table 2. Extracted trip chain information for a traveler during a week of January 2013.

Journey ID	Date	First boarding time of the route	Route sequence (Line ID)	Stop sequence (Stop ID)
1036866	02/01/2013	09:14 a.m.	303 → 302	2716 → 3175
1036867	02/01/2013	06:27 p.m.	203	1822
1036868	03/01/2013	11:24 p.m.	200	1035
1036869	04/01/2013	09:02 a.m.	402	2632
1036870	04/01/2013	10:29 p.m.	400 → 400	1675 → 1689
1036871	05/01/2013	09:09 a.m.	402	2632
1036872	05/01/2013	07:11 p.m.	206	1338
1036873	06/01/2013	08:45 a.m.	302 → 500	2632 → 1390
1036874	06/01/2013	10:11 p.m.	303	1338

To model urban travel patterns, this study used data from the two most significant urban public transport providers operating in Oporto's city: STCP and Metro do Porto, which corresponds to 135 million of annual validations distributed by different types of cards. Traveler routines were identified for different traveler profiles using Andante signature. Andante cards represent 67% of the total number of validations. In this work, six datasets of typical travelers were selected from the segmentation of Andante signatures based on the traveler age or economic conditions, as follow:

- G1 (4–12 students): includes students from 4 to 12 years old;
- G2 (13–18 students): includes students from 13 to 18 years old;
- G3 (sub23-superior students): contains students of higher education, public or private, with less than 23 years;
- G4 (normal): in general, this group is composed of regular workers. Any discount is provided for this group;
- G5 (social): includes people with a low monthly income (gross monthly income per household member smaller than 1.2 times of IAS - Social Support Index);
- G6 (seniors): includes retired people or people with 65 years old or more.

3.2 Inference of Journey Destination

UPT of the Metropolitan Area of Oporto is an open system which means there is tickets validation at the entrance only to each stage/journey. Thus, to know each traveler's destination, the application of an inference algorithm is required [30].

For this purpose, an updated version of an algorithm proposed by [10] was used in this work. Such algorithm is supported by the following assumptions:

1. "The most likely destination of a journey stage is the route stop located downstream from its own origin that is nearest to the origin of the next journey stage from that passenger";
2. "The most likely destination of the last journey stage of a day is the route stop located downstream from its own origin that is nearest to the origin of the first journey of the day from that passenger."

After setting candidate destinations, spatial validation rules were used to ascertain whether these assumptions are likely to hold for each transaction record. Some additional spatial validation rules were included in the proposed algorithm [10]. The rules are:

1. Origin and candidate destination of a journey stage are the same;
2. Candidate destination of a journey stage is beyond a set Euclidean distance from the next journey origin (or from daily origin if the stage is last) for the passenger;
3. Number of travel zones is exceeded for the passenger to reach the candidate destination.

Before applying this algorithm, the data was first pre-processed namely to remove: (i) validation records with missing data; and (ii) repeated validation records (or spaced by seconds or few minutes, but insufficient time for to go, to return and to go again). Also, a maximum walkable distance of 640 m was considered which corresponds to 8 min on foot at 4.8 km h^{-1}. This distance is recognized as the maximum walking distance for bus stops in Great London (TfL, 2010).

The algorithm used in this work inferred 85.9% of journey destinations. The destinations' percentage not inferred in the presented work could be related to the use of only 2 of the 11 transport providers operating in the network. Still, such result not affect the further development of the work since traveler samples will be used to evaluate the capability of a model to predict the journey destination. Other values were obtained in similar studies: 71% in estimating alighting stations for rail boarding [31], 66% using a bus-only system [30]; and 80% in a multimodal public transport system [32].

3.3   Models of Prediction of Journey Destination

In this section, it is described models, models' optimization and results' evaluation used. All implementations and computations were performed using R software.

Models

To estimate the traveler destination, three models were applied: Top-K, Naïve Bayes (NB) and Decision Trees (J48).

Top-K. Top-K model is focused on the demand for more numerous elements (or item sets) based on an increment counter [33]. Two different techniques of Top-K are available: (i) Counter-based techniques, that keep an individual counter for a subset of the elements in the dataset, guaranteeing their frequency; and (ii) Sketch-based techniques, that provide an estimation of all elements, with a less stringent guarantee of frequency.

To optimize the performance and efficiency of predictions, required in the context of UPT, an update of Top-K model based in the Space-Saving technique that targets performance and efficiency for large-scale datasets was used in this work [33, 34]. The Space-Saving maintains partial information of interest, with accurate estimates of significant elements supported by a lightweight data structure, resulting in memory saving and efficient processing.

In this work, Top-K Space-Saving model was updated to account for the specificities of transportation networks, where a journey is considered to be an edge, i.e., a connection between any node A and B. This method showed to be several orders of magnitude less memory demanding and much faster [9]. Therefore, to identify the journey destination, only the origin of the journey (O) and the past origins of that traveler (OP) were considered in Top-K.

Top-K model applied for the first three days of the test set is shown in Fig. 2. Note that on day 1, all journeys would be correctly predicted based on origin, except for journey AC. In this case, journey AB is more frequent. However, on day 2, all counters are incremented based on the previous day, and journey CA would become increasingly relevant. Also, the new journey CD is added to the list. On day 2, the traveler always starts on C stop. As CA is the most frequent journey, the predicted destination failed for the three journeys (stop G, stop G and stop I). Finally, on day 3, no new journeys occur, but the counters are updated accordingly.

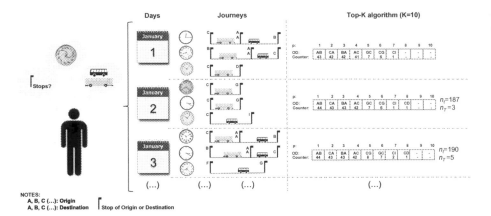

Fig. 2. Application of the Top-K model for the first three days of the test set.

Naïve Bayes. Naïve Bayes model is one of the most well-known classification techniques. This technique is based on statistical data and uses Bayes' Theorem proposed by Thomas Bayes to compute unknown conditional probabilities [35], assuming all attributes are independent given the class value, that is,

$$P(X|C) = \prod_{i=1}^{n} P(X_i|C) \tag{1}$$

where $X_i = (X_1, \ldots, X_n)$ is the feature vector and C is a class. A feature's probability in data appears as a member of the probabilities' set and is calculated by the frequency of each feature value within a class of a training dataset. Training dataset is a subset, used to train a classifier algorithm by using known values to predict unknown values [36].

Naïve Bayes is a very efficient model which have simplicity and unrealistic independence assumption. However, the Naïve Bayes classifier's performance is remarkably successful in practice [37].

Naïve Bayes classifier is also well known as very sensitive to the presence of redundant and/or irrelevant attributes. Redundant (highly correlated) attributes can bias the decision taken by this classifier [38]. Thus, only relevant attributes should be considered in this model.

In this work, the e1071's package of R software was used.

Decision Tree. Decision Tree model is one of the most widely used techniques for text-based automatic classification [39]. It is a tree-based knowledge representation methodology, which is used to represent classification rules in a simple structure. Tree' non-terminal nodes represent tests on one or more attributes, and terminal nodes reflect decision outcomes [40].

Decision Tree has several advantages over traditional supervised classification algorithms [41]. In particular, it is strictly nonparametric and does not require assumptions regarding input data distributions. Also, for missing values, it accepts nonlinear relations between features and classes and can receive both numeric and categorical inputs naturally [42].

To generate a decision tree model to classify the destination based on available training data's attribute values, J48 was performed. J48 is an open source Java implementation of the C4.5 algorithm in the Weka data-mining tool.

In this work, RWeka's package of R software was used.

Model Search

To obtain a traveler's behavior representative sample throughout a year, they were selected 5,000 travelers with at least 300 validations inferred with success for each traveler group previously defined in Sect. 3.1 (G1–6). Student's groups (G1, G2 and, G3) do not have enough travelers in these conditions. So, in these cases, a reduced number of travelers were used (NG1 = 870, NG2 = 4,337 and NG3 = 3,707).

For each traveler group (G1–6) and model (Top-K, NB, and J48) 15 repetitions were computed. Each repetition included 50 travelers randomly selected. Predictions started on the 2nd day (January 2nd) by using the 1st day (January 1st) as a training set. Also, the training set was updated with previous journeys for each iteration. Consequently, for each traveler on an nth day, the model was trained with the corresponding training set, up to the $(n - 1)^{th}$ day, and predicted the journeys' destination for the nth day. After performing predictions, all journeys are added to the training set, and the iteration moves on $(n + 1)^{th}$ day. Thus, the test set is always composed of journeys of one day while training set continuously grows.

For each simulation, two different approaches were considered. Firstly, a simulation was applied to all days of the week (Sunday to Saturday), i.e., not distinguish different patterns of weekdays and weekends. Then, to consider such differences, two another simulation was performed, one for weekdays (Monday to Friday) and another for weekend days (Saturday and Sunday).

Model Evaluation

Accuracy measure (2) was applied to evaluate the algorithm's performance. This measure uses the confusion matrix, a two-way table, which summarizes the classifier's performance to represents the proportion of correctly identified results. Considering one class as positive (P) class and other as negative (N) class, four quantities may be defined: true positives (TP), true negatives (TN), false positives (FP) and false negatives (FN). So, the accuracy (A) is given by:

$$A = \frac{TP + TN}{TP + TN + FP + FN} \tag{2}$$

4   Results

Results are represented in two main sections. Firstly, a sensibility analysis of Top-K model is presented. Here, it is discussed the average accuracy variability for different K values (1st section). Secondly, the accuracy of the destination's prediction is analyzed taking into account the various traveler group routines (G1–6), the influence of different periods (weekdays and weekends) and the models' sensibility (Top-K, NB, J48). In this study, frequency and the average number of daily travels are analyzed (2nd section).

4.1   Sensibility Analysis

Figure 3 shows the annual average accuracy on weekdays and weekends for different K values (2–16) and traveler groups (G1–6). As it can be observed, the highest values are always obtained for travelers from group G4, both on weekdays and on weekends (65% and 45%, respectively). Travelers from group G6 and G2 has, respectively, the lowest average annual accuracy on weekdays (48%) and weekends (28%). Nonetheless, as it is possible to observe when K value is higher than ten, the accuracy keeps approximately a constant value for all traveler groups. Thus, a K value of 10 was adopted to retain more information.

4.2   Prediction Analysis

Figure 4 shows the monthly accuracy of destination's prediction for each traveler group (G1–6) on different time periods (weekdays and weekends) using three different models (Top-K, NB, J48). The variation represents the standard deviation using 15 repetitions.

In general, the maximum levels of accuracy to predict the destination of a traveler using UPT are reached after the model learn two months of travel patterns. For travelers from groups with high variance of daily travel patterns, such optimal is only achieved three to four months after the model starts the learning process. This usually happens, for example, for elderly and retired people (G6), since these travelers tend to frequent a big list of different places. Thus, a long-time period is required to identify all locations used by these travelers. This suggests the model's efficiency is directly affected by the number of different destinations used by a traveler and historical data available.

An in-depth analysis of average monthly accuracy variability shows different levels between different traveler groups, which is in line with the above findings. G4 and G5 are the groups with highest average accuracy. During weekdays, values are around 65% and 55%, respectively, for almost every month. Standard deviation has also lower than the remaining analyzed groups which suggest a higher confidence level.

In fact, G4 and G5 are mostly workers. Travelers from these groups have no fixed period for vacations. However, many of them keep routines in summer which may explain the higher accuracy values obtained. As opposite, particular groups of students (G1 and G2) need to restart frequently the learning process due holiday or exam periods, which affect the average capability of models to predict destination of these travelers. In these cases, the average accuracy range, during weekdays, between 25% and 55%. Lower accuracy values are obtained during periods of routine change.

For each traveler group, similar model performances were achieved for each analyzed model (Top-K, NB, J48). Accuracy monthly differences between each model are constant ranging between 1% and 5% (Fig. 4). A daily analysis of this accuracy shows higher differences.

Figure 5 shows an example for traveler group G4 distinguishing (i) weekdays and (ii) weekends. Note, however, in both graphs of Fig. 5. There is an evident similarity between the results from different models (Top-K, NB, and J48). This suggests, regarding accuracy, all models can be used equivalently.

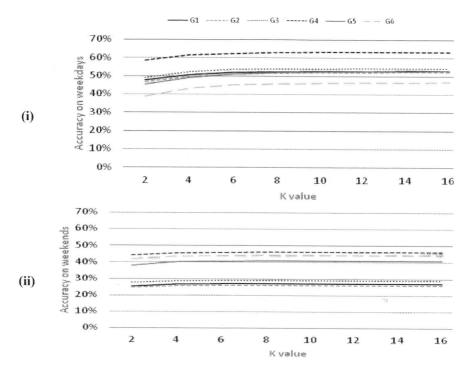

Fig. 3. Annual average accuracy of the prediction of journey destination for (i) weekdays and (ii) weekends of 2013. Predictions were made for different K values (2 to 16) and traveler groups (G1–6).

Although no variations of ranking accuracy performance between the models are observed, differences between weekdays and weekends can be identified. During weekdays J48 presents the highest values of accuracy (AG1 = 49.4%, AG2 = 47.3%, AG3 = 51.4%, AG4 = 63.2%, AG5 = 53.8% and AG6 = 47.2%), while during weekends the best model is NB (AG1 = 29.9%, AG2 = 29.0%, AG3 = 33.5%, AG4 = 48.9%, AG5 = 43.3% and AG6 = 46.5%). Additionally, besides accuracy other factors as the computing time must be considered by decision makers to select the most efficient model.

Analysis of accuracy's performance in predict a journey destination by traveler group allow to conclude the model ranking is not affected by short routines interruption. Short routines could be public holidays with one or two days, medium routines interruptions (as occurred during public holidays Easter and Christmas with one or two weeks), or even long routines interruption as summer vacations (July and August). Still, especially during long break travel patterns, the average capability of models to predict the journey destination decreases (Figs. 4 and 5). Such changes are not usually observed for short and medium interruptions. An exception to these patterns is the perceived for elderly and retired people (G6). For this traveler group, no significant variations of accuracy are observed across the year. This happens for this group because travel patterns seem not change significantly over the year. For long interruption periods, a high variance of the standard deviation is also observed.

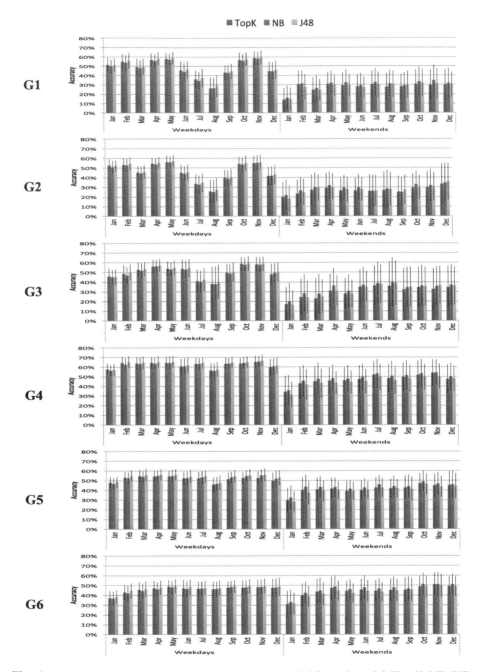

Fig. 4. Monthly accuracy of destination's prediction recorded for each model (Top-K, NB, J48), traveler group (G1–6) and time period (weekdays and weekends).

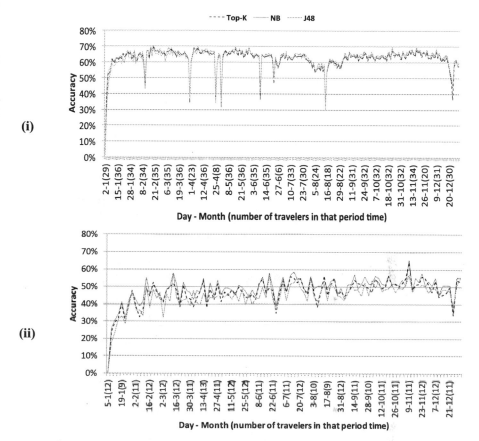

Fig. 5. Daily accuracy of the prediction of journey destination recorded during the (i) weekdays and (ii) weekends of 2013 for the traveler group G4 and applying different models (Top-K, NB and J48).

Since all models have similar values of average monthly accuracy for prediction of journey destination, Fig. 6 shows the daily accuracy (grey line) and the average number of daily travels (black line) for G4 using Top-K algorithm. The variation represents the standard deviation using 15 repetitions.

The average number of daily travels displayed in Fig. 6 was obtained by dividing the number of journeys in each group by the number of signature cards used. During weekdays and weekend days, the average number of trips is approximately constant along the year. The main exceptions are observed during strikes (February 1st, March 5th, June 27th, November 7th, November 26th) or public holidays (January 1st, February 12th, March 29th, April 25th, May 1st, June 10th, June 24th, August 15th, December 25th). During these periods, both on weekdays and weekends, a smaller number of signature travel cards are recorded (approximately 20%).

The average number of daily travels for G4 individuals are around 2.2 travels daily, which suggest that, on weekdays, journeys are mostly home-to-work and work-to-

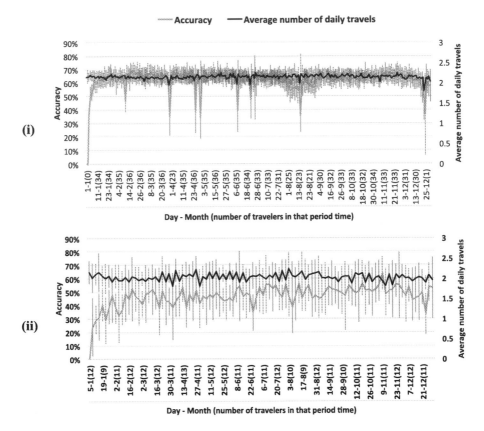

Fig. 6. Daily accuracy of destination's prediction (grey line) and average number of daily travels (black line), recorded during (i) weekdays and (ii) weekend days of 2013, for the traveler group G4 using the Top-K algorithm.

home. On weekends, this average has approximately the same values, which indicate the travelers go to a place and return.

Regarding the accuracy of destination's prediction, differences between weekdays and weekends were obtained. On weekdays, the average accuracy of travelers is around 65%. If holidays and strikes are excluded, it is possible to verify the very regular patterns for travelers from group G4, throughout the year, either during weekdays either weekend. In this group, deviations are lower and the accuracy only down about 10% in the summer months. In summer, the excellent weather usually invites travelers to visit different places in the city.

5 Policy Implications

Personalized information provision to travelers is a new research topic. While in closed urban networks the prediction of traveler destination is irrelevant, the opposite not happens with an open system as the implemented in Metropolitan Area of Oporto.

As explained previously in Sect. 1, such personalized information can be used to redesign the UPT network, by providing customized transport services, or incentivize travelers to change specific patterns. The redesign of UPT network can bring several benefits for travelers, namely: (i) to optimize travelers waiting time; (ii) allow to use public transport by a lower price by choosing a different transport route or time; (iii) benefit from offers or discount vouchers; and (iv) explore unknown parts of the city for travels with similar purpose (e.g. shopping, leisure). For transport providers, such redesign may: (i) improve levels of service appraisal; (ii) optimize the efficiency of services provided; and (iii) develop innovative and competitive services.

In this work, we obtained a maximum average accuracy of models evaluated ranging between 55% and 65%. Although these values are quite low, the results' deep analysis suggests the acceptance of many wrong predictions as correct by travelers. It happens because in Oporto's city the density of UPT stops is very high: 3,959 stops distributed by 1,575 km^2. Thus, for time-saving, travelers often use close stops to their primary destination.

Such happens especially during journeys affected by traffic congestion (e.g., accidents) or trips with double purpose (e.g., take a cafe before work).

For some traveler groups (e.g., G1 and G2) and particular days (e.g., weekend and public holidays) low levels of accuracy in journey destination's prediction are achieved. In these cases, personalized information cannot be provided with confidence. It seems not be critical to the overall system since during days with higher congestion (mostly weekdays) an acceptable level of confidence was achieved to the majority of travelers' population (G4 = 47.6%, G5 = 19.8% and G6 = 23.9% of total travelers using Andante).

6   Conclusions

Three models (Top-K, NB, and J48) were used to predict journeys destination for travelers of urban public transport of Oporto (Portugal). More than 90 million of trips recorded from signatures cards in two main transport providers of the city along one year were considered. Travelers were targeted in different groups, and different periods were analyzed. The results obtained show no differences statistically significant between the three prediction methods studied. Also, they provide answers to the initial questions:

- It is possible to predict the journey destination based on traveler's past. Such predictions are improved when past travel data are used. Additionally, some differences in accuracy in prediction of journey destination are observed between weekdays and weekends. While on weekdays, the higher average accuracy is reached between the second (February) and the fourth (April) months, on weekends, although little pronounced, the accuracy continuously grows over the year;
- Several differences were found between the predictions of journey destination for different traveler groups. The degree of success is widely affected by travel patterns. Since group G4 (normal) is the most regular, the high accuracy is found for this group. On the opposite, the worst values are found for students (G1, G2, and G3), the most irregular. In general, groups with stable work (G4) have established

routines while groups without work (G1–3 and G6) are very flexible regarding journey destinations;

- Significant differences in predictions of journey destination were found between (i) weekdays and weekends, and (ii) regular and irregular days. On weekends, the average accuracy is 20% to 30% lower than weekdays for all travelers. When a model is applied to all days of the week (i.e., without distinction between weekdays and weekend) 10% lower accuracy is obtained during weekends, which highlights the importance to predict weekdays and weekends separately. The learning process is also affected by the interruption of routines during irregular days (strikes, public holidays or school holidays). During these periods accuracy decreases 20–30%.

All this knowledge allows transport providers to detailed know their customers and to adjust the network or service. Future work expects to study the variation of travel patterns during irregular days, the model sensibility to sample size and to the use of past data. To improve the results for weekends and irregular days, an analysis of more efficient models using these datasets must be explored. Other types of travelers (as tourists) must also be investigated. Additionally, since the high density of stops in Oporto's city may be a reason for the low accuracy values, prediction of the user destination within a certain radius should be analyzed.

Acknowledgments. The Portuguese Science and Technology Foundation (FCT) funded the Doctoral scholarship of V. Costa (Ref. PD/BD/128065/2016) and the Post-Doctoral scholarship of T. Fontes (Ref. SFRH/BPD/109426/2015). The authors also acknowledge to the transport providers of Oporto, TIP, STCP, Metro do Porto and Transdev which provide travel data for the project, and also to our partner in the project, OPT company.

References

1. Foell, S., Phithakkitnukoon, S., Kortuem, G., Veloso, M., Bento, C.: Predictability of public transport usage: a study of bus rides in Lisbon, Portugal. IEEE Trans. Intell. Transp. Syst. **16**, 2955–2960 (2015)
2. Gardner, B., Abraham, C.: What drives car use? A grounded theory analysis of commuters' reasons for driving. Transp. Res. Part F Traffic Psychol. Behav. **10**, 187–200 (2007)
3. Zimmerman, J., et al.: Field trial of Tiramisu: crowd-sourcing bus arrival times to spur co-design. In: Proceedings of 2011 Annual Conference Human Factors Computing System - CHI 2011, pp. 1677–1686 (2011)
4. Caragliu, A., del Bo, C., Nijkamp, P.: Smart cities in Europe. J. Urban Technol. **18**, 65–82 (2011)
5. Gordon, J.J., Koutsopoulos, H., Wilson, N., Attanucci, J.: Automated inference of linked transit journeys in London using fare-transaction and vehicle location data. Transp. Res. Rec. J. Transp. Res. Board. **2343**, 17–24 (2013)
6. Weigang, L., Koendjbiharie, M.W., De Jucá, R.C.M., Yamasiiita, Y., Maciver, A.: Algorithms for estimating bus arrival times using GPS data. In: IEEE Conference on Intelligent Transportation Systems Proceedings, ITSC, pp. 868–873 (2002)
7. Lee, S.G., Hickman, M.: Trip purpose inference using automated fare collection data. Publ. Transp. **6**, 1–20 (2014)

8. Giannopoulos, G.A.: The application of information and communication technologies in transport. Eur. J. Oper. Res. **152**, 302–320 (2004)
9. Costa, V., Fontes, T., Costa, P.M., Galvao, T.: How to predict journey destination for supporting contextual intelligent information services? IEEE Conference on Intelligent Transportation Systems Proceedings, ITSC, pp. 2959–2964 (2015)
10. Nunes, A.A., Dias, T.G., Cunha, J.F.: Passenger journey destination estimation from automated fare collection system data using spatial validation. IEEE Trans. Intell. Transp. **17**, 133–142 (2016)
11. Patterson, D.J., et al.: Opportunity knocks: a system to provide cognitive assistance with transportation services. International Conference on Ubiquitous Computing (UbiComp), pp. 433–450 (2004)
12. Bera, S., Rao, K.V.K.: Estimation of origin-destination matrix from traffic counts: the state of the art. Eur. Transp. - Trasp. Eur. **49**, 3–23 (2011)
13. Ma, X., Wang, Y., Chen, F., Liu, J.: Transit smart card data mining for passenger origin information extraction. J. Zhejiang Univ. Sci. C. **13**, 750–760 (2012)
14. Kusakabe, T., Asakura, Y.: Behavioural data mining of transit smart card data: a data fusion approach. Transp. Res. Part C Emerg. Technol. **46**, 179–191 (2014)
15. Krizek, K., El-Geneidy, A.: Segmenting preferences and habits of transit users and non-users. J. Publ. Transp. **10**, 71–94 (2007)
16. Kieu, L.M., Bhaskar, A., Chung, E.: Transit passenger segmentation using travel regularity mined from smart card transactions data. In: Transportation Research Board, 93rd Annual Meeting Washington, D.C. (2014)
17. Foth, M., Schroeter, R., Ti, J.: Opportunities of public transport experience enhancements with mobile services and urban screens. Int. J. Ambient Comput. Intell. **5**, 1–18 (2013)
18. Roth, C., Kang, S.M., Batty, M., Barthélemy, M.: Structure of urban movements: polycentric activity and entangled hierarchical flows. PLoS ONE **6**, e15923 (2011)
19. Hasan, S., Schneider, C.M., Ukkusuri, S.V., González, M.C.: Spatiotemporal patterns of urban human mobility. J. Stat. Phys. **151**, 304–318 (2013)
20. Tao, S., Rohde, D., Corcoran, J.: Examining the spatial-temporal dynamics of bus passenger travel behaviour using smart card data and the flow-comap. J. Transp. Geogr. **41**, 21–36 (2014)
21. Yu, W., Mao, M., Wang, B., Liu, X.: Implementation evaluation of Beijing urban master plan based on subway transit smart card data. In: Proceedings of 2014 22nd International Conference on Geoinformatics, Geoinformatics 2014, pp. 1–6 (2014)
22. Gong, Y., Liu, Y., Lin, Y., Yang, J., Duan, Z., Li, G.: Exploring spatiotemporal characteristics of intra-urban trips using metro smartcard records. In: Proceedings of 2012 20th International Conference on Geoinformatics, Geoinformatics 2012, pp. 1–7 (2012)
23. Foell, S., Kortuem, G., Rawassizadeh, R., Phithakkitnukoon, S., Veloso, M., Bento, C.: Mining temporal patterns of transport behaviour for predicting future transport usage conference item mining temporal patterns of transport behaviour for predicting future transport usage. In: ACM Conference on Pervasive Ubiquitous Computing Adjunct Publication, pp. 1239–1248 (2013)
24. Foell, S., Phithakkitnukoon, S., Kortuem, G., Veloso, M., Bento, C.: Catch me if you can: predicting mobility patterns of public transport users conference item predicting mobility patterns of public transport users. In: IEEE 17th International Conference. Intelligent Transportation Systems, pp. 1995–2002 (2014)
25. Van Der Hurk, E., Kroon, L., Maróti, G., Vervest, P.: Deduction of passengers' route choices from smart card data. IEEE Trans. Intell. Transp. Syst. **16**, 430–440 (2015)
26. Ma, X., Wu, Y.J., Wang, Y., Chen, F., Liu, J.: Mining smart card data for transit riders' travel patterns. Transp. Res. Part C Emerg. Technol. **36**, 1–12 (2013)

27. Fontes, T., Costa, V., Costa, P.M., Dias, T.G.: Analysis of urban mobility patterns using data from public transport ticketing system: implications for developing autonomic systems. In: Autonomous Road Transport Support Systems Early Career Research Conference, Greece, pp. 1–6 (2015)
28. Costa, V., Fontes, T., Costa, P.M., Dias, T.G.: Prediction of journey destination in urban public transport. In: Progress in Artificial Intelligence: 17th Portuguese Conference on Artificial Intelligence, pp. 169–180 (2015)
29. TIP: Relatório e Contas. Transportes Intermodais do Porto (2014)
30. Trépanier, M., Tranchant, N., Chapleau, R.: Individual trip destination estimation in a transit smart card automated fare collection system. J. Intell. Transp. Syst. Technol. Plann. Oper. **11**, 1–14 (2007)
31. Zhao, J., Rahbee, A., Wilson, N.H.M.: Estimating a rail passenger trip origin-destination matrix using automatic data collection systems. Comput. Civ. Infrastruct. Eng. **22**, 376–387 (2007)
32. Munizaga, M.A., Palma, C.: Estimation of a disaggregate multimodal public transport origin-destination matrix from passive smartcard data from Santiago, Chile. Transp. Res. Part C Emerg. Technol. **24**, 9–18 (2012)
33. Metwally, A., Agrawal, D., El Abbadi, A.: Efficient computation of frequent and top-k elements in data streams. In: Eiter, T., Libkin, L. (eds.) ICDT 2005. LNCS, vol. 3363, pp. 398–412. Springer, Heidelberg (2004). https://doi.org/10.1007/978-3-540-30570-5_27
34. Sarmento, R., Cordeiro, M., Gama, J.: Streaming networks sampling using top-K networks. In: ICEIS 2015 - 17th International Conference on Enterprise Information Systems Proceedings, vol. 1, pp. 228–234 (2015)
35. Yildirim, P., Birant, D.: Naive Bayes classifier for continuous variables using novel method (NBC4D) and distributions. In: 2014 IEEE International Symposium Innovations in Intelligent Systems and Applications Proceedings, pp. 110–115 (2014)
36. Patil, T.R.: Performance analysis of Naive Bayes and J48 classification algorithm for data classification. Int. J. Comput. Sci. Appl. **6**, 256–261 (2013). ISSN 0974–1011
37. Hand, D.J., Yu, K.: Idiot's Bayes-not so stupid after all? Int. Stat. Rev. **69**, 385–398 (2001)
38. Inza, I., Larrañaga, P., Etxeberria, R., Sierra, B.: Feature subset selection by Bayesian networks based optimization. Artif. Intell. **123**, 157–184 (2000)
39. Peng, Y., Ye, Y., Yin, J.: Decision tree construction algorithm based on association rules. In: Proceedings 2nd International Conference on Computer Science and Application System Model, pp. 754–756 (2012)
40. Mohamed, W.N.H.W., Salleh, M.N.M., Omar, A.H.: A comparative study of reduced error pruning method in decision tree algorithms. In: Proceedings 2012 IEEE International Conference on Control System Computing and Engineering, ICCSCE 2012, pp. 392–397 (2012)
41. Friedl, M.A., Brodley, C.E.: Decision tree classification of land cover from remotely sensed data. Remote Sens. Environ. **61**, 399–409 (1997)
42. Fayyad, M.U., Irani, K.B.: The attribute selection problem in decision tree generation. In: Proceeding of AAAI 1992 Proceedings of tenth National Conference on Artificial intelligence, pp. 104–110 (1992)

With Whom Transport Operators Should Partner? An Urban Mobility and Services Geolocation Data Analysis

Marta Campos Ferreira[1,2(✉)], Teresa Galvão Dias[1,2],
and João Falcão e Cunha[1,2]

[1] Faculty of Engineering, University of Porto, Rua Dr. Roberto Frias,
4200-465 Porto, Portugal
{mferreira, tgalvao, jfcunha}@fe.up.pt
[2] INESC-TEC, Faculty of Engineering, University of Porto,
Rua Dr. Roberto Frias, 4200-465 Porto, Portugal

Abstract. Automated Fare Collection (AFC) systems produce a large amount of very detailed data, which analysis may be very useful to authorities and transport planners to define future service delivery strategies. Such analysis can be further improved by relating to other data sources, such as points-of-interest (POI) data. As a result public transport operators are able to identify the city service providers with whom it would be more interesting to establish partnerships and propose joint value propositions benefiting both service providers. The objective of such partnerships is to attract new customers and retain those that already exist by providing combined offers, discounts or loyalty schemes. The potential of such analysis is demonstrated by using data related to the city of Porto, Portugal. This study relies on two different data sources: AFC system data and points-of interest data. Urban mobility data is used to identify mobility patterns of different segments of passengers and points-of-interest data is used to analyse the type of services that are likely to concentrate around public transport stations. The results allowed to identify the potential city services to establish partnerships according to the mobility profiles of passengers and the concentration levels of services around public transport stations.

Keywords: Public transport · AFC systems · Points-of-Interest

1 Introduction

The pervasive adoption of Automated Fare Collection (AFC) systems by transport operators worldwide broadens the range of new possibilities beyond fare collection. Such systems produce a large amount of very detailed data regarding on-board transactions, which have been the subject of several research studies. Examples of such studies include: estimation of the origin-destination matrix of the passenger trips [1]; analysis of individual characteristics of travel behaviour to develop user-tailored travel time estimates [2]; validation of estimated travel behaviour [3]; understanding the travel patterns of regular public transport users [4]; and refining public transport

J. C. Ferreira et al. (Eds.): INTSYS 2018, LNICST 267, pp. 133–143, 2019.
https://doi.org/10.1007/978-3-030-14757-0_10

operations, planning, and strategic decisions [5]. Analysis of AFC systems data to investigate other services than mobility related has not been much explored.

As the number and size of cities grow, cities are increasingly facing challenges to develop sustainable modes of transport such as public transport. Several initiates have been carried on to attract more people to public transport and move towards more sustainable mobility. Private car license purchase to access metropolitan areas during peak hours in Singapore [6], vehicle restrictions through congestion pricing in Latin American cities [7] and cities organizing days without cars on the streets are examples of such initiatives. However, these initiatives are not enough and some even proved to cause negative externalities such as excessive mileage accumulation, resource depletion and losses in time and productivity [8].

Therefore, public transport has to be more appealing. The use of mass media to convey the benefits of public transport has proved to have a positive impact on people's attitude to the use of public transport [9]. Another study [10] revealed that newsletter marketing campaigns and sending free bus tickets to households had a positive impact in bus use after the campaign period. Price changes have a significant impact on the number of people that choose the public transport for leisure activities, but do not have much influence on work trips [11]. Therefore, one of the main challenges of public transport is how to address an audience so different and with distinctive characteristics. The composition of public transport customers is extremely varied, including different ages, behaviours, routines, and needs and also different motives for travelling (work, school, leisure, shopping). Thus, we propose a holistic view of the public transport ecosystem, which is composed by several stakeholders such as transport operators, travellers and city services (e.g. hospitals, schools, stores, restaurants, theatres, and gyms).

A multiservice approach is proposed to encourage the use of public transport services, consisting of partnerships between transport operators and city service providers [12]. Such partnerships may include marketing campaigns, combined packages and discounts, offered exclusively to public transport customers. Some cities, like Berlin[1] and Hamburg[2], have already implemented these type of initiatives, but very oriented towards tourists. They offer combined packages of free public transport and discounts at partners. Most of these partners include museums, art-galleries and city tours and very few partnerships are established with restaurants, shopping and stores. The question is: are these the most interesting partners that transport operators should cooperate with? Are these partners also interesting to locals living in the city?

Research work related to this topic are scarce. [13] introduce a case of a service (chain of electronic stores) exposure to different demographic segments during week days and weekends, using data from Porto, Portugal. Another study [14] based on data from the city of Montreal, Canada, explores possible commercial partnerships that might benefit from the characteristics of smartcards. However, this study only consider few services of the city and does not complement the analysis with smartcard data.

---

[1] www.visitberlin.de/en/berlin-welcome-card.

[2] www.hvv.de/en/tickets/single-day-tickets/hamburg-card/.

To explore partnerships between city services and transport operators it is vital to identify the city service providers with whom it would be more interesting to establish partnerships and propose joint value propositions benefiting both service providers. This study explores two data sources from the city of Porto, Portugal: AFC system and points-of-interest (POI) data. Urban mobility data is used to identify mobility patterns of different segments of passengers and POI data is used to analyse the type of services that are likely to concentrate nearby public transport stations. Results allow us to identify potential city services to establish partnerships with, according to mobility profiles of passengers and concentration levels of services around public transport stations. The service exposure of a selected mobility profile is also presented.

The paper is organized as follows: next section describes the datasets that were analysed. Section 3 describes the methodology followed. Section 4 details the main results and Sect. 5 presents the main conclusions and future work.

2 Data

In order to understand the services that are interesting to establish partnerships with, it is important to analyse the demand of each station and the services that are likely to concentrate near stations. To perform the analysis two data sources, from the city of Porto, are used as an illustrative example: AFC system and POI data.

2.1 Metropolitan Area of Porto Public Transport

The public transport network of the Metropolitan Area of Porto (MAP) is composed by an area of 1,575 km2, serving 1.75 million of dwellers. The network is consists of 3.959 stops and 11 operators: 128 bus lines (72 public and 56 private), 81 metro stations and 19 train stations. The electronic ticketing system is an open (ungated) system, composed by ticket readers along the platforms at each metro/train station and at each bus vehicle, and handheld devices for inspectors. The fare media consists of contactless cards, called Andante, which are accepted by all 11 operators. During the year of 2013, a total of 136.32 million journeys were performed [15].

Andante is an entry-only AFC system and the fares are defined according to a zonal structure. The MAP network is divided into 48 geographic travel zones as represented in Fig. 1(a)) and the price to pay for the journey depends on the number of zones crossed from its origin and final destination. The Andante travel cards can be one of the two types: occasional tickets (OT) and monthly subscription (MS). Passengers charge the OT cards with the number of zones they want to cross during a certain journey. In the case of MS it can be used to travel in a set of adjacent zones that were previously chosen by the passenger. Usually, MS are used by locals living in the city who use public transport on a regular basis. OT are mostly used by occasional passengers and tourists. Andante is also a system based on time, allowing passengers to travel for a certain period of time, which increases with the number of zones included in the ticket. To start a journey, passengers tap the Andante card on a ticket reader. Passengers must validate the travel card in the beginning of the journey and whenever changing vehicles during the journey. Therefore, a journey can be composed of more than one journey stage performed in different routes and/or vehicles.

2.2   AFC Data

The Andante system records a validation every time a passenger taps the travel card on the ticket reader. This happens at the beginning of each journey stage, and whenever passengers change vehicles during the journey. Concerning each validation several attributes are recorded, of which are used in this analysis: travel card id, metro station or bus stop where the validation occurred, zone and corresponding coordinates, operator (public bus operator (STCP) or metro operator (MP)), and type of travel card (OT or MS). The data used as an illustrative example of the multiservice approach are the validations recorded in 2013. In this year, 133.979.203 validations were recorded and were performed by 3.017.357 different travel cards, with 45 average validations per card, and in 3.042 different stops. Table 1 shows the number of validations that were recorded, per month, during the year of 2013. Despite the richness of data the researchers had access to, the customer cannot be identified, which is desirable from a privacy perspective. It is not possible to link the travel id card to the customers' name, address, phone number or any other private information.

Table 1. Number of validations during 2013 per month

Month	Nr of validations (millions)	Month	Nr of validations (millions)
January	11.733	July	11.193
February	10.524	August	8.389
March	10.922	September	11.518
April	11.532	October	13.092
May	13.107	November	11.231
June	10.796	December	9.938

2.3   POI Data

The second dataset used in this analysis was extracted from Google Places API. This database has very detailed information regarding the location and types of POI. Google Places API allows to scan the centre point and range of an area, but it is limited to 20 results at a time. To cover the areas of the city with the highest concentration of POI, an area of about 400 km^2 was manually estimated, represented by the green line in Fig. 1 (a). This area was then divided into a matrix, resulting in 69.696 scan areas, with each cell having 75 m side. The POI scan was performed after calculating the centre point of each cell. A total of 33.330 POI were retrieved, after filtering duplicate results at each cell scan.

The Google Places API returned the POI categorised according to 97 categories. These were then manually grouped in 11 high-level categories. Of the attributes provided by the Google Places API, the following were selected to perform the analysis: name (the place's name), type (the place's category) and geographic coordinates.

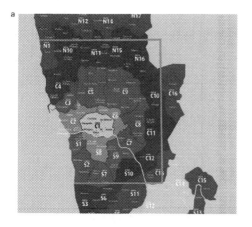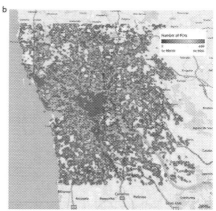

Fig. 1. (a) All public bus stops and metro stations of MAP divided by zones; (b) Heat map of POI distribution

The POI were classified taking into consideration the following high-level categories (number of establishments): Shopping (11.855), Eat and drink (8.513), Service (5.650), Healthcare (3.028), Lodging (1.011), Lifestyle and beauty (997), Education (773), Religion (595), Leisure and culture (440), Government (274), Transportation (194). Comparing Fig. 1 (a) and (b) it is possible to observe that zones C1, C3, C4, C2 and S8 are those with the highest number of POI per unit area.

Shopping high-level category includes places categorized as stores, clothing stores, grocery or supermarket, electronics store, jewelry and shoe store, shopping mall, book and liquor stores. Eat and drink includes restaurants, cafes, bakeries and bars. Service category comprise services such as finance, accounting, car repair, travel agencies, banks, laundries, florists, and insurance agencies. Healthcare includes doctors, dentists, pharmacies and hospitals. Lodging refers to places categorized as lodging. Lifestyle and beauty includes hair care, beauty salons, gyms and spas. Education refers to schools and universities. Religion includes churches, cemeteries and places of worship. Leisure and culture category includes parks, museums, art galleries, movie theatres, libraries and stadiums. Government category comprises city hall, courthouses, police and fire stations. Finally, transport includes some transit stations, subway and train stations.

3   Methodology

The flowchart of the proposed research method in this study is presented on Fig. 2. First, boarding stops/stations of each journey stage can be extracted from AFC system data. The boarding stop/station is sufficient for the analysis, since at a certain time of the day it will be the alight stop/station [1]. Second, the type of POI located around each stop/station can be retrieved from the POI dataset. The distance between the POIs and the stops/stations is calculated a posteriori. Third, the passenger mobility profile is analyzed taking into account the nearest POIs from the travelled stops/stations.

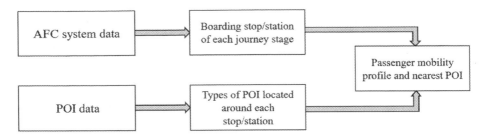

Fig. 2. Flowchart of the research method

The analysis of both datasets followed a granular model, from superior granularity analysis to inferior granularity. The choice criterion to narrow the sample was to choose the sub-samples with the highest number of validations comparing to the others. First we analyzed the full AFC dataset of the year of 2013. Then the month of October was selected and all travel zones were analyzed. During this month 13.570.975 validations were recorded, representing the highest number of validations when compared to other months (see Table 1). The validations were performed with 714.836 different travel cards, in 2.465 different stops and 76 lines. Then we analyzed the zone C1 (shown in yellow in Fig. 1(a)), which accounts for the highest number of validations (48%) during the month of October when compared to the other zones. Zone C1 encompasses the center of the city, being very frequented by tourists and locals. From this we further narrowed the sample and selected the station with the highest number of validations of zone C1 during October – Trindade. Finally we analyzed an individual mobility profile as a case of service exposure. When narrowing the sample, we could observe that despite the number of OT cards is much higher than the number of MS cards, they account for very few number of validations. Therefore, we calculated a validations per card (VPC) ratio, given by:

$$VPC\ ratio = \frac{\sum validations}{\sum travelcards} \qquad (1)$$

To measure the agglomeration of POIs around public transport stations, we calculated the distance between POIs and stations using a max radial geodistance of 600 m for each station. This parameter value was based on the Public Transport Accessibility Levels methodology, which assumes an area of 8 min. at 4.8 km/h as the longest distance a person would normally walk to access a bus service [16]. In this work, to perform the analysis, we used the MongoDB, which comes with Node.js, and used Microsoft Excel Power Map to produce the visualization elements.

4 Results

This section presents the main results regarding the analysis of the AFC and POI datasets and present an example of service exposure of a selected mobility profile.

4.1   Analysis of AFC Data

During the year of 2013, 133.979.203 of validations were performed with 2.516.476 different OT travel cards and 500.881 MS travel cards (see Table 2). Despite the high number of OT cards, they only account for 26,1% of the total validations, which corresponds to an average of 14 annual validations per OT card against 198 annual validations per MS card. The same rationale applies to the month of October, zone C1 and Trindade station.

Table 2. Number of validations, travel cards and VPC ratio

	2013 (year)	October (month)	C1 zone October	Trindade station (October)
Nr of validations (% of validations)	133.979.203 (100%)	13.570.975 (100%)	6.513.385 (100%)	1.163.976 (100%)
MS card	99.010.631 (73,9%)	10.418.602 (76,8%)	5.008.001 (76,9%)	787.462 (67,7%)
OT card	34.968.571 (26,1%)	3.152.373 (23,2%)	1.505.384 (23,1%)	376.514 (32,3%)
Nr of cards (% of cards)	3.017.357 (100%)	714.836 (100%)	542.764 (100%)	231.104 (100%)
MS card	500.881 (16,6%)	164.149 (23,0%)	134.102 (24,7%)	68.466 (29,6%)
OT card	2.516.476 (83,4%)	571.183 (79,9%)	408.662 (75,3%)	162.638 (70,4%)
VPC ratio	44	19	12	5
MS card	198	63	37	12
OT card	14	6	4	2

During October 13.570.975 of validations were recorded, from which 76,8% were performed with MS cards and 23,2% with OT cards. Usually, MS cards are used by locals living in the city who use public transport on a regular basis, while OT cards are mostly used by occasional passengers and tourists. Therefore, the main users of the public transport service are people who live in the city and use the public transport regularly.

4.2   Analysis of POI Data

Each stop of zone C1 was measured with each POI considering a max radial geodistance of 600 m, and those above that geodistance were discarded, which resulted on a 7.138 POI sample (see Table 3). The same was done for Trindade station, resulting on 988 POI located around it. This station is located in the city centre, in zone C1, and is the most important one where all metro lines pass by, and passengers change line or vehicle. Additional calculations were made for POIs located between 200 m and 300 m, and 0 m and 100 m around this station.

Analysis of Table 3 shows that eat and drink, shopping, and services are the kind of services that tend to concentrate around public transport stations located in C1 at a maximum distance of 600 m. These are followed by healthcare services and lodging. Education, lifestyle and beauty, religion and leisure and culture show lower levels of concentration around stations. At a distance of 300 m to Trindade station shopping and service are the categories with more services near the station, followed by healthcare, lodging and eat and drink. For a distance of 100 m eat and drink and healthcare are the categories with more services near the station. The overall analysis shows that regardless of analyzing a zone (composed of several stations), a particular station or different distances, the type of services that tend to concentrate around the stations is practically the same.

Table 3. Number and percentage of POI

Category	Nr of POI total sample (%)	Nr of POI C1 zone (0 m–600 m) (%)	Nr of POI Trindade st (0 m–600 m) (%)	Nr of POI Trindade st (200 m–300 m) (%)	Nr of POI Trindade st (0 m–100 m) (%)
Shopping	11.855 (35,6%)	1.821 (25,5%)	284 (28,7%)	32 (22,5%)	5 (17,9%)
Eat and drink	8.513 (25,5%)	1.516 (21,2%)	187 (18,9%)	18 (12,7%)	8 (28,6%)
Service	5.650 (17,0%)	1.446 (20,3%)	172 (17,4%)	36 (25,4%)	2 (7,1%)
Healthcare	3.028 (9,1%)	692 (9,7%)	93 (9,4%)	21 (14,8%)	7 (25,0%)
Lodging	1.011 (3,0%)	733 (10,3%)	159 (16,1%)	21 (14,8%)	1 (3,6%)
Lifestyle and beauty	997 (3,0%)	252 (3,5%)	27 (2,7%)	2 (1,4%)	2 (7,1%)
Education	773 (2,3%)	245 (3,4%)	23 (2,3%)	2 (1,4%)	0 (0%)
Religion	595 (1,8%)	125 (1,8%)	8 (0,8%)	2 (1,4%)	1 (3,6%)
Leisure and culture	440 (1,3%)	189 (2,6%)	19 (1,9%)	4 (2,8%)	0 (0%)
Government	274 (0,8%)	78 (1,1%)	10 (1,0%)	4 (2,8%)	0 (0%)
Transport	194 (0,6%)	41 (0,6%)	6 (0,6%)	0 (0%)	2 (7,1%)
Total	33.330 (100%)	7.138 (100%)	988 (100%)	142 00%)	28 100%)

4.3 Case of Service Exposure

Performing an individual analysis allows to understand the value of the proposed study. To perform the analysis, an individual mobility profile was selected from the AFC dataset. The selection of this profile followed the following criteria: travel card with validations at Trindade station and with an average of 4 validations per day (2 journeys with 2 stages each). Considering 22 working days per month and 4 validations per day, we selected travel cards with 88 validations. This resulted on a 432 MS travel cards sample, from which an individual mobility profile was randomly selected. The most frequent locations of the travel card is calculated by the ratio between the number of validations in each station/stop and the total number of validations of the travel card, paired with stations/stops' geolocations.

The selected mobility profile is represented in Fig. 3(a). The circles indicate the stations where the travel card was validated. The larger the circles, the more validations were performed at the station. Analysis of the AFC data shows that the user travels daily south-north-south, being Trindade the main cross point with a quarter of all its validations. The services that are located around the stations travelled by user, up to a distance of 100 m, were calculated. This resulted in 281 services, represented in Fig. 3 (b). Once again, the services that tend to concentrate around the stations are shopping (27,8%), eat and drink (22,1%), services (18,1%), healthcare (13,5%), lodging (6,4%) and lifestyle and beauty (4,6%). Therefore, customized services offerings could be targeted to this person in order to meet his/her mobility profile and the type of services located near the places frequented by the user. From this analyses it is possible to know exactly the restaurants, stores and services that are near the stations travelled by this person and discounts or deals of his/her interest could be sent.

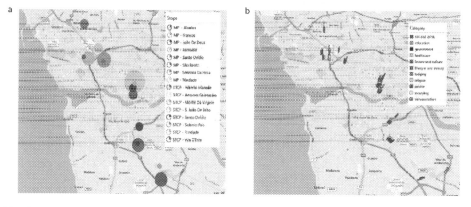

Fig. 3. (a) Mobility profile of a selected user; (b) Number of POI per category, at 100 m, matched with the mobility profile

5 Conclusions and Future Work

Cities all over the world are increasingly facing challenges to develop sustainable modes of transport such as public transport. Taking into consideration that every journey has a motive, such as school, work, leisure, entertainment, we advocate for a multiservice approach to attract new customers to the public transport and retain the ones that already exist. It involves creating partnerships between public transport operators and city service providers, such as service packages, discounts, loyalty schemes, and marketing campaigns. It is expected that these initiatives will make public transport more attractive by offering benefits and service packages exclusively to its customers.

To explore these partnerships it is vital to understand the public transport usage and identify the city service providers with whom it would be more interesting to establish partnerships and propose joint value propositions benefiting both service providers. Two data sources from the city of Porto, Portugal, are used as an demonstrative example: AFC system and points-of-interest data.

The overall analysis performed showed that the majority of customers using the public transport network are locals living in the city, who use the public transport on a regular basis. Regarding the agglomeration of services nearby public transport stations, shopping, eat and drink and services like accounting, travel agencies, banks, laundries and florists are the services that tend to concentrate around public transport stations. These are followed by healthcare service providers such as doctors, dentists and pharmacies and by lodging services. Education, religion, leisure and culture, government and transport are the services that display lower concentration levels around public transport stations. The methodology followed in this paper can be replicated with other datasets (different cities or countries) and results may be compared.

From a managerial perspective, most of the partnerships that already exist, in some cities, are very oriented towards tourists and consist of discounts and combined packages of public transport and leisure and culture services such as museums, art galleries and touristic attractions. However, the analysis performed revealed that these are not the services that are likely to concentrate nearby public transport stations. Partnerships with service providers that tend to concentrate nearby stations, such as stores, shopping and restaurants are not being exploited to its full potential. Moreover, combined service offerings geared to locals living in city is missing. It is expected that these initiatives make public transport more attractive by providing benefits and services exclusively accessible for passengers.

This study allowed to comprehend the complexity and dynamic of a city and to identify interesting topics to be addressed in future research. Further and richer datasets could be added to the analysis, such as datasets with information about service providers like ratings, satisfaction index and influx hours. The users' interests and preferences could also be added to the mobility profiles in order to define and target effective service offerings. Such analysis can be the basis to the design and development of recommender systems that promote the use of public transport services. Moreover, its offer may be adjusted by taking into account the location of POIs that are not being served by public transport.

Acknowledgements. The authors thank Transportes Intermodais do Porto for providing the AFC system data necessary for this work.

References

1. Nunes, A.A., Dias, T.G., e Cunha, J.F.: Passenger journey destination estimation from automated fare collection system data using spatial validation. IEEE Trans. Intell. Transp. Syst. **17**(1), 133–142 (2016)
2. Lathia, N., Smith, C., Froehlich, J., Capra, L.: Individuals among commuters: building personalised transport information services from fare collection systems. Pervasive Mob. Comput. **9**(5), 643–664 (2013)
3. Munizaga, M., Devillaine, F., Navarrete, C., Silva, D.: Validating travel behavior estimated from smartcard data. Transp. Res. Part C Emerg. Technol. **44**, 70–79 (2014)
4. Lee, S.G., Hickman, M.: Travel pattern analysis using smart card data of regular users. In: 90th Annual Meeting of the Transportation Research Board, no. 520 (2011)
5. Van Oort, N., Cats, O.: Improving public transport decision making, planning and operations by using big data: cases from Sweden and the Netherlands. In: Proceedings of IEEE Conference on Intelligent Transportation Systems, ITSC, vol. 2015–Octob, pp. 19–24 (2015)
6. Seik, F.T.: A unique demand management instrument in urban transport: the vehicle quota system in Singapore. Cities **15**(1), 27–39 (1998)
7. Mahendra, A.: Vehicle restrictions in four latin American cities: is congestion pricing possible? Transp. Rev. **28**(1), 105–133 (2008)
8. Chu, S.: Car restraint policies and mileage in Singapore. Transp. Res. Part A Policy Pract. **77**, 404–412 (2015)
9. Beale, J.R., Bonsall, P.W.: Marketing in the bus industry: a psychological interpretation of some attitudinal and behavioural outcomes. Transp. Res. Part F Traffic Psychol. Behav. **10**(4), 271–287 (2007)
10. Taniguchi, A., Fujii, S.: Promoting public transport using marketing techniques in mobility management and verifying their quantitative effects. Transp. (AMST) **34**(1), 37–49 (2007)
11. Ibraeva, A., de Sousa, J.F.: Marketing of public transport and public transport information provision. Procedia - Soc. Behav. Sci. **162**(Panam), 121–128 (2014)
12. Campos Ferreira, M., Galvão Dias, T.: How to encourage the use of public transport? A multiservice approach based on mobile technologies. Lect. Notes Bus. Inf. Process. **201**, 314–325 (2015)
13. Campos Ferreira, M., Costa, V., Dias, T.G., Falcão E Cunha, J.: Understanding commercial synergies between public transport and services located around public transport stations. Transp. Res. Procedia **27**, 125–132 (2017)
14. Páez, A., Trépanier, M., Morency, C.: Geodemographic analysis and the identification of potential business partnerships enabled by transit smart cards. Transp. Res. Part A Policy Pract. **45**(7), 640–652 (2011)
15. Transportes Intermodais do Porto. Relatório e Contas (2013)
16. TfL: Transport assessment best practice, guidance document (2010)

Intermodal Routing Model for Sustainable Transport Through Multi-objective Optimization

Cecília Vale$^{(\boxtimes)}$ (iD) and Isabel M. Ribeiro (iD)

Faculty of Engineering, Construct, University of Porto, Porto, Portugal
{cvale,iribeiro}@fe.up.pt

Abstract. To contribute to the sustainable development of transport and to the efficient mobility of people and goods, optimizing multimodal transport is a requirement. This paper presents a novel routing model for the optimization of intermodal one-way trips problems by considering multiple objective functions.

The main goal of the developed model is to optimize simultaneously two objectives for intermodal routing, by having available several transport modes between a pair of nodes of a transport network. In the problem in study, the functions to minimize are: (1) the travel time between two nodes of a network; (2) the CO_2 emissions, but additional objective functions may be considered. Furthermore, the model allows to have mandatory (or fixed) nodes and optional nodes, being the origin of the travel always a defined node. The destination may be a fixed node - defined destination, or any fixed node of the network - undefined destination. The mathematical formulation of the model leads to a multi-objective mixed binary linear program, and a classical scalarization method is performed to solve the problem. There is a lack of intermodal routing models in literature and specifically no multi-objective models on this matter were found. Therefore, as a sustainable transport both freight and passenger is a societal goal, the proposed model can be a valuable tool for transport managers.

In terms of outcome, the developed program allows the decision-maker to choose from a set of Pareto solutions (corresponding to different weights of the objective functions in minimization) a suitable solution from the point of view of transport engineering. The computational experience included in the paper reveals the efficiency of the proposed model.

Keywords: Sustainable transport · Intermodal routing ·
Multi-objective optimization · Transport modes

1 Introduction

Innovative transport policies must contribute to an environmentally sustainable transport system, which means the need to reduce pollution to control climate change is one of the main issues that the transport managers are facing.

According to Sheffi [1] and Bell and Iida [2], a traditional network optimization focuses exclusively on the treatment of traffic congestion, minimizing the total time of travel, which is an insufficient approach to the actual challenges for a green transport.

© ICST Institute for Computer Sciences, Social Informatics and Telecommunications Engineering 2019
Published by Springer Nature Switzerland AG 2019. All Rights Reserved
J. C. Ferreira et al. (Eds.): INTSYS 2018, LNICST 267, pp. 144–154, 2019.
https://doi.org/10.1007/978-3-030-14757-0_11

To contribute to the sustainable development of transport, ensuring not only an efficient mobility of people and goods, but also for a better environment, optimizing multimodal transport is a requirement. Multimodal transport involves two or more transport modes in a journey.

The importance of multimodal networks is huge as Nes and Bovy [3] show by looking at some of the implications of multimodality in urban trips and highlighting their importance in multimodal transportation systems. However, the consideration of multimodal networks in transportation problems adds complexity to algorithms and models, because the different transport modes should be optimized together for the same network and not separately. A large number of algorithms and models that can be found in the literature for optimizing transport in a network is not suitable for inter-modal transport because considers the optimization of each transport modes individually. Therefore innovated approaches need to be considered to solve intermodal transport problems with several objective functions. It must be also mentioned that the current multimodal applications only consider one-way journeys, but real journeys are often roundtrips and not simple one-way trips [4]. For many reasons, modelling intermodal transport is more complex than modelling unimodal systems and the consideration of multi-objective functions adds additional complexity to calculation and no actual literature was found on this subject. The present research aims to contribute positively for the modelling of optimal intermodal and sustainable transport through multiobjective optimization as extension of the initial work of Ribeiro and Vale [4]. This is an innovated research that aims to close some gaps on transportation modelling.

2 Model Formulation

The main goal of the developed model is to minimize simultaneously two objectives functions. The first function considers the travel time between two nodes of a network and the second one, the CO_2 emissions, which are two very important aspects that transport managers seeking to minimize. In addition, the proposed model considers a multimodal transportation system, which means that different transport modes are available. Therefore, the underlying optimization problem is able to identify which one is the mode of transport to be used in each pair of nodes in order to minimize simultaneously the objectives functions presented in Eqs. (1) and (2)

$$Minimize\ f_1(x) = \sum_{i \in V} \sum_{\substack{j \in V \\ j \neq i}} \sum_{k \in M} t_{ijk} x_{ijk} \quad \text{(travel time)} \tag{1}$$

$$Minimize\ f_2(x) = \sum_{i \in V} \sum_{\substack{j \in V \\ j \neq i}} \sum_{k \in M} co_{ijk} x_{ijk} \text{(CO_2 emissions)} \tag{2}$$

where:

- V is the set of nodes and $N = |V|$;
- M is the set of transport modes and $N_m = |M|$;

- t_{ijk} is a parameter that represents the travel time between nodes i and j by transport mode k;
- co_{ijk} is a parameter that represents the CO_2 emissions between nodes i and j by transport mode k;
- x_{ijk} is a binary variable associated with the trip from node i to node j with transport mode k, and takes the value 1 or 0 depending on whether or not this trip is held on the one-way trip.

The constraints considered in the proposed model are the same as those described in Ribeiro and Vale [4] for the intermodal one-way trips problem:

- network nodes may be mandatory (fixed) or optional visited;
- the origin node of the trip is always defined by the user and it is a fixed node;
- each fixed node, except for the origin node, is visited once during the trip by one transport mode only;
- each optional node may or may not be visited during the trip;
- the destination may be a defined fixed node (defined destination) or any fixed node of the network (undefined destination). Note that, in the latter case, if the user does not define the destination, the optimal trip ends at any of the fixed nodes.

In terms of mathematical formulation, the proposed model leads to a multi-objective mixed binary linear program and to solve it, a linear scalarization method is used [5]. The reduction of the multi-objective optimization problem to a single-objective one is carried out by a weighted-sum method as presented in Eq. (3):

$$Minimize\ F(x) = w_1 f_1(x) + w_2 f_2(x) \tag{3}$$

with $w_1 \geq 0, w_2 \geq 0$ are parameters and $w_1 + w_2 = 1$.

The parameters w_1 and w_2 represent the weights that the manager can choose to each objective function. For example, if w_1 assumes the value of 0.25, this means that, in the minimization of function (3), a weight of 25% was given to the travel time and 75% to the CO_2 emission. The algorithm, proposed in this paper, allows the decision-maker to choose any set of values for (w_1, w_2) in order to obtain several nondominated solutions. The present multi-objective model is applicable for on-way trips only but it can be easily extended for roundtrips.

If the optimal solution of the weighted-sum scalarizing function (3) exists and is unique, it corresponds to a nondominated solution (Pareto solution). This solution is always a vertex of the convex hull of the nondominated solution set in the objective function space of the multi-objective mixed binary linear program [6]. The proposed method obtain some of the Pareto solutions, which are the nondominated solutions that results from the convex combination of vertex solutions. This means that, the non-dominated solutions located in the interior of the convex hull and dominated by a convex combination of vertex solutions are not attained by the method. Despite this mathematical limitation, the solutions given by the method are enough and provide to the decision maker in a very short space of time a good set of optimal solutions from which the final decision can be made.

3   Computational Experiments

In this section, a computational experience is reported. These experiences have been performed on an Intel(R) Core(TM) i5 CPU 2.4 GHz with 4 GB of RAM. The commercial MIP solver Cplex of the GAMS collection has been used to process the mixed integer linear programming programs.

3.1   Data

The network in study (Fig. 1) comprises nine nodes and twelve possible links that are indicated in Table 1. In this table, the corresponding travel time by car, bus and bike and the CO_2 emission for each transport are shown. All the links between the nodes have two directions, except node 1 because it has been defined as origin of the transport for all the scenarios. Although the simplicity of the network, this system allows the validation of the developed routing model.

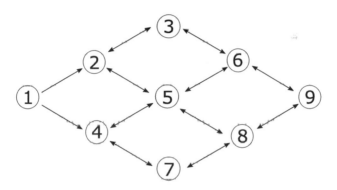

Fig. 1. Network

Table 1. Data of the network

Node	Node	Time (h)			CO_2 emission (g/km)		
		Car	Bus	Bike	Car	Bus	Bike
1	2	0.111	0.178	0.261	26191.53	13161.88	0
1	4	0.100	0.167	0.250	38763.47	18705.11	0
2	3	0.128	0.194	0.278	15141.98	8050.91	0
2	5	0.106	0.172	0.256	18284.65	9080.68	0
3	6	0.089	0.156	0.239	21777.23	10012.03	0
4	5	0.078	0.144	0.228	37272.56	16269.55	0
4	7	0.133	0.200	0.283	18215.91	9761.73	0
5	6	0.094	0.161	0.244	30928.30	14551.65	0
5	8	0.111	0.178	0.261	17461.02	8774.59	0
6	9	0.144	0.211	0.294	13459.54	7402.26	0
7	8	0.094	0.161	0.244	25773.58	12126.37	0
8	9	0.100	0.167	0.250	24227.17	11690.69	0

In the linear scalarization method, the combination of objective functions into a single objective function is not, in general, an easy task. As shown in Table 1, the parameters associated with the two objective functions (1) and (2) are expressed in different units and have different order of magnitude. Therefore, for the application of the scalarization method, the CO_2 emission values were scaled for their order of magnitude becomes similar to time travel.

To simulate different scenarios in terms of parameters weight, (w_1 and w_2) in this computational experience, w_1 varied from 0 to 1 with fixed λ increments of 0.25, 0.1 and 0.01.

3.2   Results and Discussion

To validate and test the model and its formulation, four scenarios have been defined:

- Scenario 1: Fixed destination (node 9) and the remain nodes optional;
- Scenario 2: Fixed destination (node 6) and node 8 mandatory visited;
- Scenario 3: Undefined destination and nodes 6 and 8 mandatory visited;
- Scenario 4: Undefined destination and all nodes mandatory visited.

The attained Pareto solutions of the four scenarios with $\lambda = 0.01$ are indicated in Figs. 2, 3, 4 and 5.

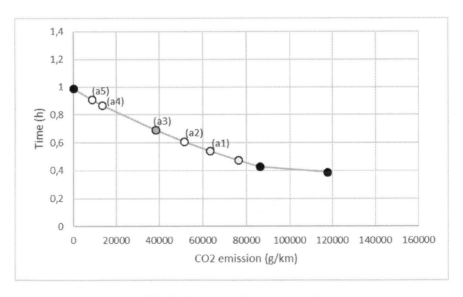

Fig. 2. Pareto solutions: scenario 1

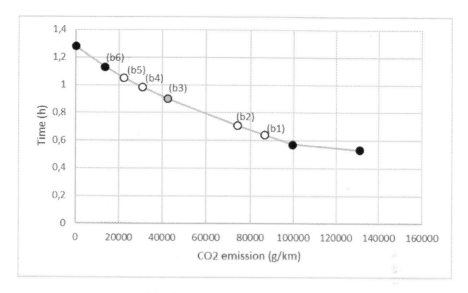

Fig. 3. Pareto solutions: scenario 2

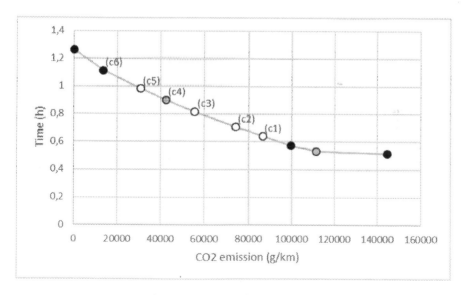

Fig. 4. Pareto solutions: scenario 3

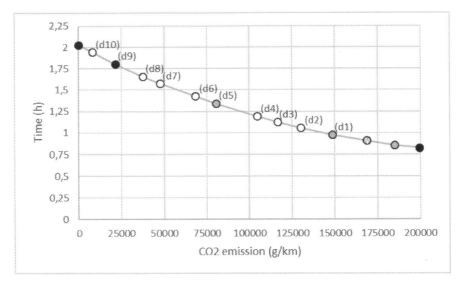

Fig. 5. Pareto solutions: scenario 4

In the Figures, there are four types of points represented by circles filled with the following colours:

- Black: represents nondominated solutions attained with the three values of λ: 0.25, 0.1 e 0.01.
- White: represents nondominated solutions attained only with $\lambda = 0.01$.
- Gray: represents nondominated solutions attained with $\lambda = 0.1$ and $\lambda = 0.01$.
- Little black points: represents nondominated solutions attained with $\lambda = 0.25$ and $\lambda = 0.01$.

In Figs. 2 and 3 (scenarios 1 and 2), nine different nondominated solutions for $\lambda = 0.01$ are found while in Fig. 4 (scenario 3), there are ten. In Fig. 5 (scenario 4), fourteen solutions were attained with $\lambda = 0.01$ but only four were obtained with $\lambda = 0.25$ (circles filled with black or little black points) and six for $\lambda = 0.1$ (circles filled with black or gray).

Taking into account scenarios 2 and 3, it would be expected that the nondominated solutions of scenario 2 could be solutions of scenario 3. However, as it can be seen in Fig. 6, the nondominated solutions S2_3 e S2_4 for scenario 2 are located in the interior of the convex hull of the Pareto solutions for Scenario 3 which means that those are dominated by a convex combination of vertex solutions. In addition, solutions S2_1 and S2_2 are dominated by S3_1 and S3_2, respectively.

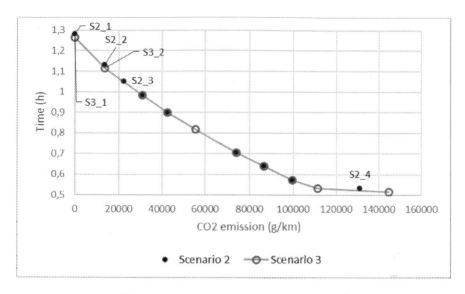

Fig. 6. Comparison between scenarios 2 and 3

The results attained at the four scenarios differ not only in terms of time and CO_2 emission but also on the number of transport mode changes.

In Table 2, only the trips with more than one transport mode involved (intermodal trips) are indicated for each scenario. In this table, each transport mode is represented by a letter: c for car; b for bus and bk for bike.

Table 2. Solutions with more than one transport mode involved

	Fig.	CO_2 emission (g/km)	Time (h)	N° change	Trip sequence
Scenario 1 (O: 1; D: 9)	(a1)	63540.63	0.539	1	**1**-b-**2**-c-**3**-c-**6**-c-**9**
	(a2)	51775.43	0.606	3	**1**-b-**2**-c-**3**-b-**6**-c-**9**
	(a3)	38613.55	0.689	3	**1**-bk-**2**-c-**3**-b-**6**-c-**9**
	(a4)	13459.54	0.866	1	**1**-bk-**4**-bk-**5**-bk-**6**-c-**9**
	(a5)	8774.59	0.906	2	**1**-bk-**4**-bk-**5**-b-**8**-bk-**9**
Scenario 2 (O: 1; D: 6; M: 8)	(b1)	86594.26	0.639	1	**1**-b-**2**-c-**5**-c-**8**-c-**9**-c-**6**
	(b2)	74057.78	0.706	3	**1**-b-**2**-c-**5**-c-**8**-b-**9**-c-**6**
	(b3)	42611.25	0.900	3	**1**-bk-**4**-bk-**5**-c-**8**-b-**9**-c-**6**
	(b4)	30920.56	0.983	3	**1**-bk-**4**-bk-**5**-c-**8**-bk-**9**-c-**6**
	(b5)	22234.13	1.050	3	**1**-bk-**4**-bk-**5**-b-**8**-bk-**9**-c-**6**
	(b6)	13459.54	1.133	1	**1**-bk-**4**-bk-**5**-bk-**8**-bk-**9**-c-**6**

(continued)

Table 2. (*continued*)

	Fig.	CO_2 emission (g/km)	Time (h)	N° change	Trip sequence
Scenario 3 (O: 1; M: 6 and 8)	(c1)	86594.26	0.639	1	**1**-*b*-2-*c*-5-*c*-8-*c*-9-*c*-**6**
	(c2)	74057.78	0.706	3	**1**-*b*-2-*c*-5-*c*-8-*b*-9-*c*-**6**
	(c3)	55776.91	0.817	4	**1**-*b*-2-*c*-3-*b*-6-*bk*-5-*c*-**8**
	(c4)	42611.25	0.900	3	**1**-*bk*-4-*bk*-5-*c*-8-*b*-9-*c*-**6**
	(c5)	30920.56	0.983	3	**1**-*bk*-4-*bk*-5-*c*-8-*bk*-9-*c*-**6**
	(c6)	13459.54	1.116	2	**1**-*bk*-4-*bk*-5-*bk*-6-*c*-9-*bk*-**8**
Scenario 4	(d1)	148819.02	0.972	1	**1**-*b*-4-*c*-7-*c*-8-*c*-5-*c*-2-*c*-3-*c*-6-*c*-**9**
	(d2)	130113.91	1.055	1	**1**-*bk*-4-*c*-7-*c*-8-*c*-5-*c*-2-*c*-3-*c*-6-*c*-**9**
	(d3)	116466.70	1.122	5	**1**-*bk*-4-*c*-7-*b*-8-*c*-5-*c*-2-*c*-3-*b*-6-*c*-**9**
	(d4)	104701.50	1.189	1	**1**-*bk*-4-*c*-7-*c*-8-*c*-5-*c*-2-*c*-3-*c*-6-*c*-**9**
	(d5)	80715.26	1.340	4	**1**-*bk*-4-*bk*-5-*c*-2-*c*-3-*b*-6-*c*-9-*b*-8-*b*-**7**
	(d6)	68588.89	1.423	5	**1**-*bk*-4-*bk*-5-*c*-2-*c*-3-*b*-6-*c*-9-*b*-8-*bk*-**7**
	(d7)	47694.23	1.572	5	**1**-*bk*-4-*bk*-5-*b*-2-*c*-3-*b*-6-*c*-9-*bk*-8-*bk*-**7**
	(d8)	37682.20	1.655	5	**1**-*bk*-4-*bk*-5-*b*-2-*c*-3-*bk*-6-*c*-9-*bk*-8-*bk*-**7**
	(d9)	21510.45	1.805	4	**1**-*bk*-4-*bk*-5-*bk*-2-*b*-3-*bk*-6-*c*-9-*bk*-8-*bk*-**7**
	(d10)	8050.91	1.943	2	**1**-*bk*-2-*b*-3-*bk*-6-*bk*-5-*bk*-4-*bk*-7-*bk*-8-*bk*-**9**

In *scenario 1*, the nodes sequence (1-2-3-6-9) appear three times, however the transport modes involved in each trip are different. For (a4) and (a5), the nodes sequence (1-4-5-8-9) is also the same and it can be said that the most ecological trip is the last one because by considering transport by bike and bus, the CO_2 emission is the lower one.

In *scenario 2*, only two solutions in terms of node sequence exist and one of them (1-4-5-8-9-6) coincides with one of the solutions in scenario 3. In scenario 2, all trips end at node 6 because this node was defined as the destination. From all the trips the one with the higher travel time (b6) is the most ecological trip because most of the route is done by bike.

In *scenario 3*, there is no fixed destination; all nodes of the network may be visited except nodes 6 and 8 that are mandatory visited. From Table 2, four solutions have node 6 as destination, and in the other two solutions, destination is node 8. In this scenario, the most ecological trip with more than a transport mode involved is, as expected, the case where the weight given to the CO_2 emission is higher. The faster optimal trip with more than a transport mode involved is (c1).

In *scenario 4*, where the destination is undefined and all nodes are mandatory, from the fourteen Pareto solutions obtained by this method, only in four nondominated solutions there was no change of transport mode. It should be noted that in one of these solutions, the last node to be visited is was node 3. This case is curious if we take into account the sequences presented in Table 2 for this scenario, where in the attained solutions, for more than one transport mode involved, the final destination of the trip is always the node 7 or 9. The faster optimal trip with more than a transport mode involved is (d1) and the most ecological one is (d10). Although in both solutions two modes of transport are used, in (d1) there is only one change of transport while in (d10) there are two.

Summary and Conclusions

There is a lack of transport models that can contribute for an ecologically sustainable transportation. Therefore innovation is needed in models definition and mathematical formulations. That novelty may come from multi-objective formulations and the consideration of transport constraints that best represents the reality in terms of transport goals.

This paper presents a new approach for intermodal transport by using a multi-objective methodology which can be applied for one-one trips or in roundtrips, after extending the present methodology. The model formulation is flexible because the nodes of the network may be optional or mandatorily visited and the destination may be fixed or undefined. Also the number of transport modes involved in the problem and the number of the parameters of the multi-objective function may be defined by the transport manager to best describe the transport problem to be solved.

In the computational experiment presented in the paper, a subset of the Pareto solutions of this problem is provided with a diversity of solutions, depending on the defined set of weights of the objective functions. From those solutions the transport managers can then select the most suitable one. The proposed method requires a very small computational effort to determine these subsets of the non-dominated solutions revealing that is a very promising tool. In the present calculations in the worst case, the computation effort was about 3 s.

Acknowledgments. This work was financially supported by: Project POCI-01-0145-FEDER-007457 - CONSTRUCT - Institute of R&D In Structures and Construction funded by FEDER funds through COMPETE2020 - Programa Operacional Competitividade e Internacionalização (POCI) – and by national funds through FCT - Fundação para a Ciência e a Tecnologia; Project Reference if applicable and Scholarship Reference if applicable.

References

1. Sheffi, Y.: Urban Transportation Networks: Equilibrium Analysis with Mathematical Programming Methods. Prentice-Hall, Englewood Cliffs (1985)
2. Bell, M.G.H., Iida, Y.: Transportation Network Analysis. Wiley, Chichester (1997)
3. Nes, R., Bovy, P.H.L.: Multimodal traveling and its impact on urban transit network design. J. Adv. Transp. **38**(3), 225–241 (2004)
4. Ribeiro, I.M., Vale, C.: Optimal one-way and roundtrip journeys design by mixed-integer programming. Eng. Optim. **49**(12), 2117–2132 (2017). https://doi.org/10.1080/0305215X.2017.1284831
5. Steuer, R.: Multiple Criteria Optimization: Theory, Computation and Application. Wiley, New York (1986)
6. Antunes, C., Martins, A., Brito, I.: A multiple objective mixed integer linear programming model for power generation expansion planning. Energy **29**, 613–627 (2004)

Future 5V

A Low Latency SCAN-Flip Polar Decoder for 5G Vehicular Communication

Yu Wang$^{(\boxtimes)}$ (iD), Lirui Chen, Shikai Qiu, Li Huang, and Zuocheng Xing

National University of Defense Technology, Changsha, China
{wangyu16,chenlirui14,qiushikai17,huangli16,zcxing}@nudt.edu.cn

Abstract. Polar codes are widely considered as one of the most promising channel codes for future wireless communication. However, at short or moderate block lengths, their error-correction performance under traditional successive cancellation (SC) decoding is inferior to other modern channel codes, while under list decoding outperforms at the cost of high complexity and long latency. Successive cancellation flip (SCF) decoding is shown having competitive performance compared to that of list decoding but suffers from a long decoding latency. In this work, we propose the SCAN-Flip decoding algorithm by introducing the flipping idea into soft cancellation (SCAN) decoding. The proposed algorithm improves the error-correction performance of soft cancellation decoding and accelerates the convergence of iterative calculation, leading to lower execution-time. Besides, we also propose a new path metric to improve the performance of our SCAN-Flip decoder further. Simulation results show that the proposed decoder has a much smaller average number of iterations than that of SCF at equivalent frame error rate. At equivalent max number of iterations, the error-correction performance of SCAN-Flip outperforms SC-Flip by up to 0.25 dB at bit error rate of 10^{-4}.

Keywords: Successive cancellation flip · Soft cancellation ·
Belief propagation · Low latency · Polar codes

1 Introduction

Recently vehicle-to-vehicle (V2V) communication is widely considered as one of the most promising technology for intelligent transportation systems (ITSs) to ensure traffic safety [2]. However, its requirements of ultra reliability and low latency pose significant challenges for physical layer design. As a key enabling technology, channel coding has significant influence on reliable transmission. In this domain, polar codes [4] are the first channel codes that provably achieve the capacity of various communication channels and have been recently selected for the control channel in the 5G enhanced Mobile BroadBand (eMBB) scenario [12] to provide low latency and reliable communication. However, for polar

Supported by the NSF of China (Grant No. 61170083) and Specialized Research Fund for the Doctoral Program of Higher Education (Grant No. 20114307110001).

J. C. Ferreira et al. (Eds.): INTSYS 2018, LNICST 267, pp. 157–170, 2019.
https://doi.org/10.1007/978-3-030-14757-0_12

codes at short to moderate block lengths, the error-correction performance under successive cancellation (SC) decoding is worse than the turbo or low-density parity-check (LDPC) codes. In order to improve the performance of the finite block length, many decoding methods, such as SC list (SCL) decoding [13] and SC stack (SCS) decoding [8], are introduced. Nonetheless, these methods suffer from higher computational complexity and longer decoding latency than that of the original SC decoding algorithm. On the other hand, in order to reduce the decoding latency, belief propagation (BP) decoding is proposed in [3], with parallel message propagating. However, its error-correction performance is worse than that of SC decoding.

As an alternative decoding method of SC, the soft-cancellation (SCAN) decoder proposed in [9] is a combination of SC decoder and BP decoder, based on a sequential message propagating schedule, which is similar to the SC decoding process. The SCAN decoder has better performance than SC and BP decoder. As another iterative decoder, the successive-cancellation flip (SCF) decoder proposed in [1] is shown to be capable of providing error-correction performance comparable to that of SCL decoder with a small list size, while keeps the complexity close to that of SCAN. The idea of SCF decoder is to allow a given number of new decoding attempts, where one or several positions are flipped in the sequential decoding. However, this decoding method suffers from a higher worst-case latency when choosing the wrong flipping position.

Contribution: In this work, we introduce the flipping idea of SCF decoder into SCAN decoder by initializing the β log-likelihood ratio (LLR) according to previous decoding pass. The simulation result shows that the new decoding algorithm has a better error-correction performance and lower decoding latency than that of the original SCF decoder. Besides, we propose a new path metric for our decoder to further improve the error-correction performance.

The remainder of this work is organized as follows: in Sect. 2, an overview of polar codes, SCAN decoding, and SCF decoding algorithms are presented. In Sect. 3, the SCAN-Flip decoding method is detailed, while Sect. 4 describes a modification on SCAN-Flip by introducing a new path metric to correct more erroneous bits. Section 5 reports the simulation results, and conclusions are drawn in Sect. 6.

2   Preliminary

2.1   Polar Codes

Polar codes characterized by $(N, K, \mathcal{I})$ belong to linear block codes, where $N = 2^n$ is the length of the polar code, K is the number of information bits, and a set $\mathcal{I}$ indicates the positions of the K information sub-channels. Polar codes can achieve channel capacity via the phenomenon of channel polarization [4]. The channel polarization theorem states that, as the code length N goes to infinity, a polarized subchannel becomes either a noiseless channel or a pure noise channel. By transmitting information bits over the reliable subchannels and transmitting frozen bits which are known by both transmitter and receiver over the unreliable subchannels, polar codes can achieve the capacity under an SC decoder. The encoding procedure of a polar code can be represented with a matrix multiplication like $\mathbf{x} = \mathbf{u}G_N$, where vector $\mathbf{u}$ means the source codeword containing information bits, while vector $\mathbf{x}$ means the encoded codeword and G_N is the generator matrix.

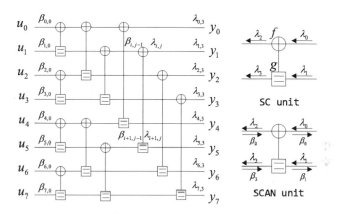

Fig. 1. Factor graph and message propagation mechanism for $N = 8$ polar code.

As for the decoding process, we denote by vector y_0^{N-1} the data received from the channel and use them as the decoder input. The output of decoder is denoted by vector $\hat{u}_0^{N-1}$, as shown in Fig. 1, where $\lambda_{i,3}$ denotes the LLR value of y_i. The decoding procedure of the SC decoding can be interpreted as an iterative procedure with a complexity of $\mathcal{O}(N\log N)$ for one decoding attempt. Let $\hat{u}_i$ denotes the estimate of the bit u_i at the final hard decision. Each estimate $\hat{u}_i$ is calculated according to the LLR value $\lambda_i = \log(\frac{\Pr(\mathbf{y},\hat{u}_0^{i-1}|u_i=0)}{\Pr(\mathbf{y},\hat{u}_0^{i-1}|u_i=1)})$ by using the hard decision function h:

$$\hat{u}_i = h(\lambda_i) = \begin{cases} u_i & \text{if } i \notin \mathcal{I} \\ \frac{1-\text{sign}(\lambda_i)}{2} & \text{if } i \in \mathcal{I} \end{cases} \tag{1}$$

where by convention $\text{sign}(\lambda_i) = \pm 1$. At the same time, the LLRs at different calculation stage l are computed iteratively as follows:

$$\lambda_{i,l} = \begin{cases} f(\lambda_{i,l+1}; \lambda_{i+2^l,l+1}) & \text{if } \frac{i}{2^l} \text{ is even} \\ g(\hat{s}_{i-2^l,l}; \lambda_{i-2^l,l+1}; \lambda_{i,l+1}) & \text{otherwise} \end{cases} \tag{2}$$

where $\hat{s}$ denotes the partial sum of $\hat{u}_0^{i-1}$, which are the previously decoded bits from 0 to $i - 1$. And in the LLR domain, the function f and g perform the following calculation for given inputs LLRs λ_a and λ_b.

$$f(\lambda_a, \lambda_b) = \log(\frac{e^{\lambda_a+\lambda_b}+1}{e^{\lambda_a}+e^{\lambda_b}}) \tag{3}$$

$$g(\lambda_a, \lambda_b, u_s) = (-1)^{u_s}\lambda_a + \lambda_b \tag{4}$$

2.2 Soft Cancellation Decoding

The SCAN decoding algorithm could be seen as a mixture of the SC and BP decoding algorithms [11]. Its operating schedule is similar to the SC decoder, while its message propagation is close to the BP decoder. The message propagation mechanism of SCAN decoding is illustrated in the factor graph Fig. 1. The left-propagating and right-propagating LLRs at row i and stage j is denoted by $\lambda_{i,j}$ and $\beta_{i,j}$, respectively. Compared with the original SC decoding, the introduction of $\beta_{i,j}$ propagating increases the efficiency of information dissemination in the decoding process.

In the factor graph, the LLR values $\lambda_{i,n}$ and $\beta_{i,0}$ do not update during the decoding process, since the $\lambda_{i,n}$ are the LLRs of received bits, while the $\beta_{i,0}$ are the LLR values initialized by the bit type such that:

$$\beta_{i,0} = \begin{cases} +\infty & \text{if } i \notin \mathcal{I} \\ 0 & \text{if } i \in \mathcal{I} \end{cases} \tag{5}$$

The message propagating of a unit factor graph is shown in the bottom right corner of Fig. 1. In the kth iteration, for a unit factor graph, the $\lambda_{i,j_0}^{(k)}$, $\lambda_{i,j_1}^{(k)}$, $\beta_{i+1,j_2}^{(k)}$ and $\beta_{i+1,j_3}^{(k)}$ are LLR values sent to the unit, while $\beta_{i,j_0}^{(k)}$, $\beta_{i,j_1}^{(k)}$, $\lambda_{i+1,j_2}^{(k)}$ and $\lambda_{i+1,j_3}^{(k)}$ are LLR values sent from the unit and can be computed as follows:

$$\lambda_{i+1,j_2}^{(k)} = f(\beta_{i+1,j_3}^{(k-1)} + \lambda_{i,j_1}^{(k)}, \lambda_{i,j_0}^{(k)}) \tag{6}$$

$$\lambda_{i+1,j_3}^{(k)} = f(\beta_{i+1,j_2}^{(k-1)}, \lambda_{i,j_0}^{(k)}) + \lambda_{i,j_1}^{(k)} \tag{7}$$

$$\beta_{i,j_0}^{(k)} = f(\beta_{i+1,j_2}^{(k)}, \beta_{i+1,j_3}^{(k)} + \lambda_{i,j_1}^{(k)}) \tag{8}$$

$$\beta_{i,j_1}^{(k)} = f(\beta_{i+1,j_2}^{(k)}, \lambda_{i,j_0}^{(k)}) + \beta_{i+1,j_3}^{(k)} \tag{9}$$

The function f in the above equations is the same as that in the SC decoder. After predetermined maximum T_{max} iterations, the estimation of $\hat{u}_i$ can be computed by Eq. 10, which is a little different from the hard decision function of SC decoder.

$$\hat{u}_i = h(L_i) = \begin{cases} u_i & \text{if } i \notin \mathcal{I} \\ \dfrac{1-\text{sign}(\lambda_{i,0}^T + \beta_{i,0}^T)}{2} & \text{if } i \in \mathcal{I} \end{cases} \tag{10}$$

2.3 Successive-Cancellation Flip Decoding

The SCF decoding algorithm is a slightly-modified SC decoding algorithm. The procedure of SCF decoding starts by going through a regular SC decoding pass. After the first decoding pass of SCF, the nested cyclic redundancy check (CRC) is verified and a flipping list of least reliable estimated bits is built. In case the CRC matches, the decoding procedure stops, and the estimated $\hat{u}_0^{N-1}$ is output. Otherwise, another SC-decoding pass is launched according to the flipping list. In this pass, once the location of the information bit that corresponds to the least reliable bit is reached, its estimated bit is flipped, and the subsequent positions are decoded by using the standard SC decoding. And when a decoding attempt finishes, the CRC is verified again. The nested CRC codes are concatenated with the information bits, and can be calculated on-the-fly. In this regard, the real coding rate for polar codes is $R = (K + L_{CRC})/N$, where L_{CRC} denotes the length of CRC codes.

The above procedure is repeated until the CRC check pass or a predetermined maximum number of decoding attempts is reached. Consequently, the SCF decoding keeps the computational complexity close to that of SC, while having error-correction performance close to that of SCL. It provides a tunable trade-off between the decoding performance and the decoding complexity. However, since the sequential nature of flipping list, the decoding throughput of SCF decoding is variable, and the average decoding latency depends on the channel condition.

3   SCAN-Flip Decoding

Different from the SC decoder, the SCAN decoder can use the information after $\hat{u}_i$ in the decoding procedure by $\beta_{i,j}$ propagating. Due to its efficient dissemination of information, the SCAN decoding algorithm has a lower bit error rate (BER) than SC decoding. However, considering the erroneous bit decisions caused by error propagation in SC decoder, the error propagation also affects SCAN decoder, which is caused by the calculation of $\beta_{i,j}$ LLRs in the message propagation. For these reasons, we introduce the flipping idea of SCF to SCAN decoding and propose the SCAN-Flip decoding algorithm.

3.1   SCAN-Flip Decoding Algorithm

The error propagation mechanism in SCAN decoder is different from that in SC decoder, whose previous erroneous estimated bits would affect subsequent estimation directly by partial sum $\hat{s}$ calculation. In SCAN decoder, the error information is propagated by the calculation of $\beta_{i,j}$ LLRs. Furthermore, the calculation of $\beta_{i,j}$ LLRs are affected by both initial value $\beta_{i,0}$ and $\lambda_{i,j}$ LLRs. Besides, it was proved in [9] that clipping the $\beta_{i,0}$ LLRs of already correct estimated bits to $+\infty, -\infty$ can accelerate the convergence of subsequent iterative calculation at the end of one iterative calculation.

Based on these points, we first propose SCAN-Flip decoding algorithm by introducing the flipping idea into SCAN decoder. It starts iterative decoding by performing a standard SCAN decoding. At the end of the first pass, we use the nested CRC code to check the result. If the CRC checking pass, the estimated codeword is assumed to be correct. If not, a second iteration is launched. In parallel with the first SCAN decoding pass, a set of low reliable estimated bits are stored and sorted. The second iteration starts from the least reliable one $\hat{u}_{i-least}$ in the set. In this iteration, the $\beta_{i,0}$ LLRs before the corresponding index i-least with the least reliable decision are initialized by $+\infty, -\infty$ according to the estimated bits got in the first pass, while the $\beta_{i-least,0}$ is set the opposite value. The remaining $\beta_{i,0}$ LLRs are set according to its bit type just like that in standard SCAN decoding.

$$
\beta_{i,0} = \begin{cases} \frac{1-\text{sign}(\hat{u}_i)}{2} * \infty & \text{if } i < i_{least} \\ -\frac{1-\text{sign}(\hat{u}_i)}{2} * \infty & \text{if } i = i_{least} \\ +\infty & \text{if } i > i_{least} \ \& \ i \notin \mathcal{I} \\ 0 & \text{if } i > i_{least} \ \& \ i \in \mathcal{I} \end{cases} \tag{11}
$$

The second SCAN iteration starts basing on this initialization and is followed by a CRC check. This procedure is repeated until either the CRC pass or a predetermined maximum number of iterations T_{max} is reached. The details of SCAN-Flip decoding process are described in Algorithm 1.

Algorithm 1. SCAN-Flip Decoding Algorithm

Input: the received vector y_1^N, maximum iteration T_{max}
Output: a decoded vector $\hat{u}_1^N$
1: Init$\beta_1(I)$
2: $(\hat{u}_1^N, \{\lambda_i^{(1)}\}_{i\in I}) \leftarrow \text{SCAN}(y_1^N, \beta_1)$
3: **if** $\text{CRC}(\hat{u}_1^N)$=success **then** return $\hat{u}_1^N$
4: **else** Init$\beta_2(\{\lambda_i^{(1)}\}_{i\in I})$
5: **end if**
6: **for** t = 2,...,T_{max} **do**
7:     $(\hat{u}_1^N, \{\lambda_i^{(t)}\}_{i\in I}) \leftarrow \text{SCAN}(y_1^N, \beta_t)$
8:     **if** $\text{CRC}(\hat{u}_1^N)$=success **then** return $\hat{u}_1^N$
9:     **else** Init$\beta_{t+1}(\{\lambda_i^{(1)}\}_{i\in I})$
10:     **end if**
11: **end for**
12: return $\hat{u}_1^N$

3.2 Oracle-Assisted SCAN Decoder

In order to examine the potential benefits of modified initialization of $\beta_{i,0}$ LLRs, we employ an order-ω oracle-assisted SCAN (OA-SCAN) decoder, which can get the accurate index of ω erroneous bits in the estimated codeword. The $\beta_{i,0}$ LLRs before these indexes are initialized correctly.

As shown in Fig. 2 we compare the performance of the standard SCAN decoder with that of the oracle-assisted order-ω SCAN decoder for a polar code with $N = 1024$ and $R = 0.5$ over an AWGN channel. In Fig. 2, the ideal OA-SCAN decoder means the initialization of $\beta_{i,0}$ LLRs is wholly set according to u_0^{N-1}. The performance of OA-SCAN decoder with order-1 could be seen as the lower bound of SCAN-Flip decoder. From Fig. 2, we observe that the ideal oracle decoder can significantly improve the performance of the SCAN decoder, while

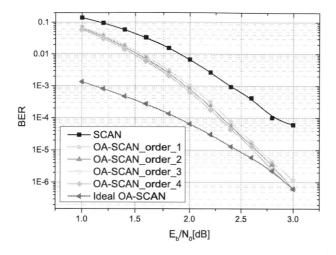

Fig. 2. BER performance of oracle-assisted SCAN decoders with different order compared to the SCAN decoder for $N = 1024$ and $R = 0.5$.

the OA-SCAN decoder with order-ω decoders perform inferior at low signal-to-noise ratio (SNR). Besides, the OA-SCAN decoders with different ω order have similar performance. Based on this, in the latter work, we focus on approaching the performance of order-1 OA-SCAN decoder.

3.3 Metric for SCAN-Flip Decoder

Based on above discussion, it is clear that, by identifying the flipping position of the erroneous bits and using this information to initialize the $\beta_{i,0}$ can improve the performance of the SCAN decoder significantly. However, we can not exactly locate the positions of erroneous bits by CRC checking. In order to identify the positions and correct the erroneous bits, in [10], a Viterbi-aided SC decoder is proposed to provide additional protection for the noisiest bits. To verify its effectiveness, we first analyze the distribution of erroneous bits decision in the decoded codeword via Monte Carlo simulations. In this analysis, we employ an ideal OA-SCAN decoder to identify the positions of erroneous bits, which are caused by channel noise, in decoding a polar code with $N = 1024$ and $R = 0.5$ over AWGN channel with various SNR.

From Fig. 3, we observe that the distribution of erroneous bits is irregular. In other words, we still need to identify the flipping positions in the decoding process. In order to identify the positions more accurately and rapidly, we need to use more efficient metric, since the metric affects the rank in the flipping list. In current researches, the absolute LLR values are used as the metric in the original SC-Flip decoder, while a new metric for determining the position of erroneous bits is proposed in [6,7]. This metric is designed to find the bits, which have more probability to correct the trajectory of the SC-Flip decoder by considering the sequential aspect of the SC decoder. In [14], a critical set containing the

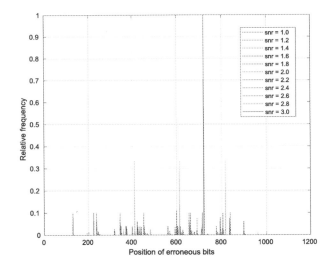

Fig. 3. Normalized distribution of error for polar code (1024,512) over AWGN channel with various SNR[dB], obtained simulating 2×10^7 frames.

first information bits of each rate-1 constituent codes is proposed to reduce the comparing scope. In order to compare the effectiveness of these metrics, we make a hit ratio comparison of these metrics via Monte-Carlo simulation, by running an order-1 OA-SCAN decoder to find the position of the first error, then declaring a hit if the position is in the list got by different metrics.

From Fig. 4, we can conclude that the metric M_α proposed in [6] has a much higher hit ratio than other metrics. Higher hit ratio means earlier to find the first erroneous bit position, which leads to lower decoding latency. Therefore, we choose the M_α as our metric in SCAN-Flip decoder. Furthermore, in order to improve the hit ratio of M_α, we make Monte-Carlo simulation to find the optimal parameter α of M_α as that do in [6]. In Fig. 5, the simulation result shows that different values of α have little effect on the BER performance, while the average rank of the first error bit in the set first degrades as α increasing and then upgrades when α adopting more higher values. Based on this result, we adopt $\alpha = 0.9$ to calculate the M_α value in our SCAN-Flip decoder.

4   Enhanced SCAN-Flip Decoding

In the above simulations of proposed SCAN-Flip decoder, we find that for many wrong estimated codewords the first error is already identified by the flipping list, while the CRC check fails. The reason for this phenomenon is that there are more than one error in the estimated codeword or that the decoding algorithm can not find out all of the errors in the limited decoding attempts. If we use the result got by wrong bit-flip decoding, we will miss the result with less errors. Therefore, we need to check the correctness of each bit-flip decoding attempt, in order to

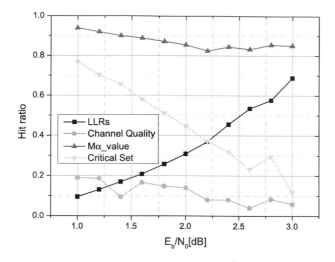

Fig. 4. Hit ratio curves of different flipping sets got by oracle-assisted SCAN decoders for decoding polar code (1024,512) with different metric over AWGN channels.

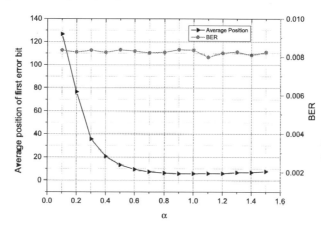

Fig. 5. BER performance and average position of first error bit in the flipping set got by oracle-assisted SCAN decoders for decoding polar code (1024,512) with different α over an AWGN channel with $E_b/N_0 = 2.5\,dB$.

find more than one erroneous bit in the subsequent iterative calculation. From the view of decoding attempts, the SC-Flip decoder could be seen as a variation of SCL by exploring different decoding paths in different decoding attempts. Inspired by this, we modify the decoding procedure of our proposed SCAN-Flip decoder, basing on the path metrics. By comparing the path metrics of different decoding attempts, we could affirm the correctness of current flipping.

Different from the path metric proposed in [5], we use the accumulation of M_α as the path metric $Path_{M_\alpha}^{(t)}$. After each decoding attempt, we compare its path metric with the previous one. If the new path metric is lower than the previous one, we use the new result to update the flipping set and initialize the $\beta_{i,0}$. If not, we still use the result of the previous one. The details of this Enhanced-SCAN-Flip (E-SCAN-Flip) decoding process are described in Algorithm 2.

Algorithm 2. Enhanced SCAN-Flip Decoding Algorithm

Input: the received vector y_1^N, maximum iteration T_{max}
Output: a decoded vector $\hat{u}_1^N$

1: Init$\beta_1(I)$
2: $(\hat{u}_1^N, \{\lambda_i^{(1)}\}_{i\in I}, Path_{M_\alpha}^{(1)}) \leftarrow \text{SCAN}(y_1^N, \beta_1)$
3: **if** $\text{CRC}(\hat{u}_1^N)=$success **then** return $\hat{u}_1^N$
4: **else** Flipping_set($\{\lambda_1^{(1)}\}_{i\in I}$) Init$\beta_2(Flipping\_set)$
5: **end if**
6: **for** t = 2,...,T_{max} **do**
7:     $(\hat{u}_1^N, \{\lambda_i^{(t)}\}_{i\in I}, Path_{M_\alpha}^{(t)}) \leftarrow \text{SCAN}(y_1^N, \beta_t)$
8:     **if** $\text{CRC}(\hat{u}_1^N)=$success **then** return $\hat{u}_1^N$
9:     **else**
10:         **if** $Path_{M_\alpha}^{(t)} < Path_{M_\alpha}^{(t-1)}$ **then**
11:             Flipping_set($\{\lambda_i^{(t)}\}_{i\in I}$)
12:             Init$\beta_{t+1}(Flipping\_set)$
13:             Update($\hat{u}_1^N$)
14:         **else**
15:             Init$\beta_{t+1}(Flipping\_set)$
16:         **end if**
17:     **end if**
18: **end for**
19: return $\hat{u}_1^N$

---

5   Simulation Results

In this section, the BER performance and the average number of iterations of the proposed SCAN-Flip decoding algorithm are investigated via Monte-Carlo simulation. Specifically, we focus on the transmissions with BPSK modulation over AWGN channel. In order to compare with other researches, the interest SNR regime is 1.0 dB to 3.0 dB. Polar codes are constructed targeting a SNR of 2.5 dB with parameters $N = 1024$ and $K = 512$ using Gaussian approximation construction method and concatenated with a CRC-8 with generator polynomial $g(D) = D^8 + D^7 + D^6 + D^4 + D^2 + 1$.

The BER performance of SCAN-Flip decoders with different predetermined maximum decoding attempts T_{max} are shown in Fig. 6. From the comparison, we observe that the maximum number of iteration has little effect on the performance since these decoders have the same correcting order. They can only

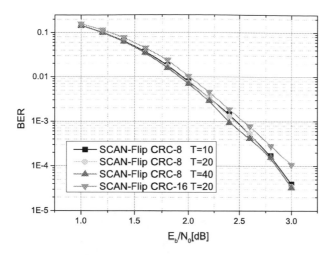

Fig. 6. BER performance of SCAN-Flip decoder with different predetermined maximum decoding attempts T_{max} and different CRC code lengths for polar code (1024,512). CRC-16 is the 16 bits CCITT CRC code.

correct one single error in a codeword. Then, we make a comparison of SCAN-Flip decoders with different length CRC code. The decoder with CRC-16 has a little inferior performance for its real code rate is little large than that of the decoder with CRC-8, which also reflects that the CRC-8 can provide enough checking capability for SCAN-Flip decoder as shown in Fig. 6.

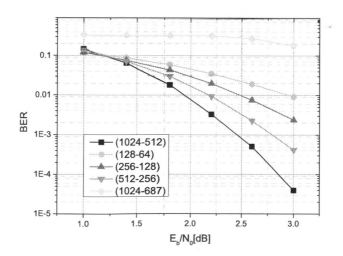

Fig. 7. BER performance of polar codes with different code rates and code lengths, concatenated with CRC-8, $T_{max} = 10$.

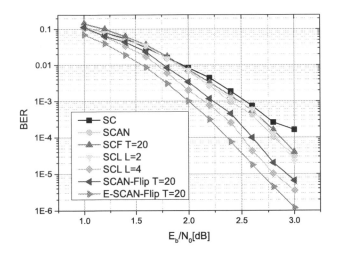

Fig. 8. BER performance for polar code (1024,512), CRC-8 with different decoding approaches.

In order to evaluate the BER performance of SCAN-Flip decoders with different code rates and different code lengths, we make comparison with the same condition above. In Fig. 8, these polar codes are all constructed targeting a SNR of 2.5 dB, concatenated with CRC-8, while the predetermined maximum decoding attempt is $T_{max} = 10$. We could conclude that as the code length increases, the BER performance of SCAN-Flip decoder improves, since the longer polar codes have better rate of polarization. And the error-correction performance of SCAN-Flip decoder degrades when the code rate increases. The reason for this is that the polarization is not complete at the code length $N = 1024$. Higher code rate means that more information bits will be transmitted through the subchannels with noise, which increases the probability to be estimated erroneously.

In Fig. 8, we compare the performance of SCAN-Flip with that of CRC-aided SCL with $L = \{2, 4\}$ and CRC-8, the SCF decoder with the maximum number of iterations $T_{max} = 20$ and CRC-8, SCAN decoder and SC decoder as the baseline decoding method. We observe that the performance of the SCAN-Flip decoder with $T_{max} = 20$ is a little weaker than that of SCL decoder with list size $L = 4$. At the bit error rate of 10^{-4}, SCAN-Flip outperforms SC-Flip by up to 0.25 dB. Moreover, we further plot the performance of our enhanced SCAN-Flip decoder. Its error-correction performance is even better than that of SCL ($L = 4$) decoder, at the cost of higher computational complexity.

In order to evaluate the computational complexity of SCAN-Flip decoder, we make simulations to calculate its average number of iterations, since it is directly proportional to the computational complexity. In Fig. 9, we compare the average number of iterations of SCAN decoder, SCF decoder, SC decoder, normalized SCL decoder, and our SCAN-Flip decoder. The comparisons are made at frame error rate (FER) of 10^{-4} with same parameters as above. At high SNR, the SCF

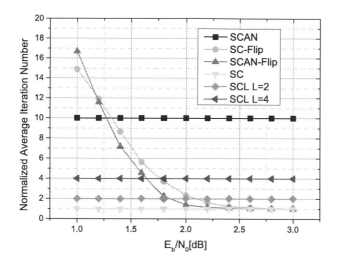

Fig. 9. Normalized average iteration number for polar code (1024,512), CRC-8, $T_{max} = 20$ with different decoding approaches.

decoder and SCAN-Flip decoder both have low iteration number. However, since the SCAN-Flip decoder has a more efficient message propagating mechanism, it has a lower iteration number than that of SCF decoder at low SNR.

6   Conclusion

In this paper, we propose the SCAN-Flip polar decoder by introducing the flipping idea into the SCAN decoder. It works by initializing the $\beta_{i,0}$ LLRs corresponding to the former iteration result and affecting the estimated result using message propagation. Furthermore, we propose a path metric designed for correcting more errors of our proposed SCAN-Flip decoder. The simulation results show that the performance is competitive with SCL decoding, while the computational complexity is almost as low as that of the SC decoder. Besides, at the equivalent FER, the SCAN-Flip decoder has less number of iterations than that of SC-Flip decoder, which leads to lower decoding latency.

References

1. Afisiadis, O., Balatsoukas-Stimming, A., Burg, A.: A low-complexity improved successive cancellation decoder for polar codes. In: 2014 Asilomar Conference on Signals, Systems and Computers, pp. 2116–2120 (2014)
2. Araniti, G., Campolo, C., Condoluci, M., Iera, A.: LTE for vehicular networking: a survey. Commun. Mag. IEEE **51**(5), 148–157 (2013)
3. Arikan, E.: A performance comparison of polar codes and Reed-Muller codes. Commun. Lett. IEEE **12**(6), 447–449 (2008)

4. Arikan, E.: Channel polarization: a method for constructing capacity-achieving codes for symmetric binary-input memoryless channels. IEEE Trans. Inf. Theory **55**(7), 3051–3073 (2008)
5. Balatsoukas-Stimming, A., Parizi, M.B., Burg, A.: LLR-based successive cancellation list decoding of polar codes. IEEE Trans. Signal Process. **63**(19), 5165–5179 (2014)
6. Chandesris, L., Savin, V., Declercq, D.: An improved SCFlip decoder for polar codes, pp. 1–6 (2017)
7. Chandesris, L., Savin, V., Declercq, D.: Dynamic-SCFlip decoding of polar codes. IEEE Trans. Commun. **66**(6), 2333–2345 (2018)
8. Chen, K., Niu, K., Lin, J.: Improved successive cancellation decoding of polar codes. IEEE Trans. Commun. **61**(8), 3100–3107 (2013)
9. Fayyaz, U.U., Barry, J.R.: Low-complexity soft-output decoding of polar codes. IEEE J. Sel. Areas Commun. **32**(5), 958–966 (2014)
10. Fazeli, A., Tian, K., Vardy, A.: Viterbi-aided successive-cancellation decoding of polar codes. In: GLOBECOM 2017–2017 IEEE Global Communications Conference, pp. 1–6 (2017)
11. Hussami, N., Korada, S.B., Urbanke, R.: Performance of polar codes for channel and source coding. In: IEEE International Symposium on Information Theory, pp. 1488–1492 (2009)
12. Support, M.: Final report of 3GPP TSG RAN WG1 #87 v1.0.0 Feburary 2017. http://www.3gpp.org/ftp/tsg_ran/WG1_RL1/TSGR1_88/Docs/R1-1701552.zip
13. Tal, I., Vardy, A.: List decoding of polar codes. IEEE Trans. Inf. Theory **61**(5), 2213–2226 (2012)
14. Zhang, Z., Qin, K., Zhang, L., Zhang, H., Chen, G.T.: Progressive bit-flipping decoding of polar codes over layered critical sets (2017)

Author Index

Ag Ibrahim, Ag Asri   81
Araújo, Paulo   66

Baras, Karolina   95
Borges, José Luís   113
Brito, Lina   95

Chen, Lirui   157
Costa, António   66
Costa, Vera   113

Dias, Bruno   66
Dias, Teresa Galvão   113, 133

e Cunha, João Falcão   133

Faria, Ricardo   95
Ferreira, João Carlos   3, 26, 41
Ferreira, Marta Campos   133
Fontes, Tânia   113

Gama, Oscar   66
Garrido, Nuno   15
Gonçalves, Fábio   66
Gonçalves, Frederica   3

Hapanchak, Vadym   66
Hasirlioglu, Sinan   53
Huang, Li   157

Leau, Yu-Beng   81

Macedo, Joaquim   66
Maia, Rui   3, 26
Martins, Ana Lúcia   3, 26, 41

Nicolau, M. João   66
Nisar, Kashif   81
Nunes, Ana Catarina   41

Park, Yong Jin   81
Pereira, Rita   41

Qiu, Shikai   157

Ribeiro, Bruno   66
Ribeiro, Isabel M.   144
Riener, Andreas   53

Santos, Alexandre   66
Serrão, Carlos   15
Silva, José   95

Vale, Cecília   144

Wang, Yu   157

Xian Wee, Low   81
Xing, Zuocheng   157

Yan, Zhiwei   81

Printed in the United States
By Bookmasters